MAKE MONEY DOING NOTHING

SIR PATRICK BIJOU

Other Books by Sir Patrick Bijou

- SECRET OF WEALTH CREATION
- TRADE DERIVATIVES AND CFDS TO MAKE MILLIONS
- CRYPTOCURRENCY MILLIONAIRE
- UNLOCKING THE SECRETS OF BITCOIN CRYPTOCURRENCY
- GUIDE TO PRIVATE PLACEMENT PROJECT FUNDING TRADE PROGRAMS

TABLE OF CONTENTS

INTRODUCTION

Passive income is highly sought after and often misunderstood.

Passive income streams require an upfront investment and a lot of nurturing in the beginning. After some time and hard work these income streams start to build and are able to maintain themselves, bringing you consistent revenue without much effort on your part.

Speaking from personal experience, adding passive income streams to your portfolio can help you increase your earnings and accelerate your financial goals in tremendous ways.

For example, you can use passive income streams to help you get out of debt or achieve financial independence sooner. Like Fundrise - you can start investing in real estate for just $500. It's one of our favorite ways to build passive income.

Are you interested in earning money without having to kill yourself working for it? Does the idea of having money coming in on a regular basis get you excited? Are you tired of being paid based on how many hours of work you've put in? If so, you should consider becoming involved with something that will earn you passive income.

Passive income is revenue that continues to come in over time, after you have done a minimal amount of work. Minimal means that the most work you will do, will be in the beginning of your venture. Once you are set up, there is little maintenance work that will need to be done. In most cases, weekly maintenance is enough to keep the money flowing. There are many passive income ideas to take into consideration.

They include;

CHAPTER 1
DIVIDEND STOCKS

"When reward is at its pinnacle, risk is near at hand."
- John Bogle, founder of Vanguard Group

Appreciating the fears many investors have, diversifying your portfolio is a good strategy to survive market instability. There are plenty of choices for diversification- stocks, bonds, mutual and exchange- traded funds, Canadian income trusts, and many others. For many investors, dividend stocks offer the best possible balance of risk and return.

Dividends are Attractive

Dividend stocks pay out distributions to shareholders. Through dividend payments, a company distributes a portion of its earnings to its shareholders on a regular basis and re-invests the remaining profit into company's operating activities to fuel its continuing growth. Consequently, investors benefit from both: share price appreciation and profit generation without selling shares.

Dividend stocks are a good investment choice in today's market climate. They provide a steady flow of passive income, which you can either spend or reinvest. Therefore, this type of stocks is particularly attractive to retirees aiming to earn some supplemental income.

Divide and Conquer!

Beware of over-concentration in your portfolio. Do not fill your investment basket with dividend stocks from only one company, sector, or industry. By diversifying your portfolio you are not only increasing your wealth accumulation opportunities, but also lower your profile risk.

On one hand, companies that pay dividends are considered to be more stable than those that do not. Startups usually do not make distributions among their shareholders, because they reinvest the entire profit in company's growth. Once the company has attained a sustainable level of growth and success, the board of directors can vote to pay dividends to shareholders. In this manner, the company maintains constant tight relationship with its shareholders.

On the other hand, companies are not legally required to pay dividends- they are optional. In most cases dividends are paid only when the company has sufficient money to cover its operating cost. If the management decides that the profit can be better utilized, dividend payments can be cut or held for a while.

Touchstones of Dividend Stocks

Looking for a promising dividend stock, the investor has to focus on the following three criteria: payout ratio, yield, and dividend growth. Payout ratio is the percentage of a company's profit that is paid out as a dividend to shareholders. A higher ratio is better. Payout percentage between 60% and 80% speaks highly for the company's financial health, but if it exceeds 100% it is a red flag. More than 100% payout ratio means that the money is not coming from profit. Most likely the company has financial difficulties and borrows money, which means is going into debt. The second factor that has to be considered is the percentage return on your investment- yield. High-yield dividend stock is a sign of a well- managed company that demonstrates consistent growth and the possibility dividend payments to be increased are relatively high. This brings us to the third criteria-dividend growth, which measures a company's ability to earn ever- increasing profits and shares ever- increasing dividends with shareholders.

Dividend Investing for Your Portfolio

All in all, dividend investing can be a great way to mitigate risk, as well as provide a steady stream of income from your investments. Investors simply need to remember the three basic touchstones above and invest wisely.

Reasons to Own Dividend Stocks

One mistake many beginner investor makes is ignoring dividends. Sure, it may seem dividends are only a small part of any stock portfolio - everyone wants to see the price go up, up and up! But smart investors (or those who want to be) listen up: When it comes to long-term investing, dividend stocks have their advantage - after all, when was the last time someone PAID you for owning something? When doing some stock market investing, it's best to look to the future, and what dividend stocks can do for you. Here are three reasons why you should buy into dividend stocks:

1. (Almost) Risk-Free Stock Market Investing

There's no such thing as 100% safe when you invest, but when a company has enough funds to pay out their investors, then it is most likely a strong company. Most dividend stocks are companies with solid backgrounds, and can withstand most economic situations. Because they are making good profits, and are able to pay their expenses and STILL have excess income to share with their investors, then you know this a great company. Between a company who pays out dividends and one with a stock price that fluctuates - which one do you think has a better chance of protecting your capital?

2. Increase Capital Gains

Some companies offer DRIPs or dividend reinvestment plans. Basically, instead of paying you the cash out, your share of the dividends gets reinvested to buy you MORE stock - that means you are essentially getting stock FOR FREE. And when that stock price goes up, then more capital gains for you. Eventually, this type of plan can benefit you when doing long-term investing.

3. Dividend stocks = passive income

Can you imagine, sitting on the beach, sipping a margarita and money keeps going into your bank account. Dividends are income which are handed to you on a silver platter - without you having to lift a finger! Aside from what you're reaping from increasing stock prices, you get a regular payment in form of dividends. Buy more of the dividend stock and you get even more income.

Do whatever you want with it - use it to pay debt, buy a fancy car or, if you were thinking of long-term investing, set up a system where you take your payments and invest in more dividend stocks. When you have enough shares, well then just keep sipping that margarita on the beach and enjoy your income!

Of course, when the economy is not doing so well, a company can cut back on its dividends. Still, a successful value investing strategy require smart investors know that dividend stocks which have a high yield is a way to collect income from a source which will be around for a long time.

Brian Tay White is a professional equity research analyst in one of Asia's largest investment banks. During his free time, he holds seminars and workshops on stock market investing based on value investing strategies so that they too can be financially free.

CHAPTER 2
PEER TO PEER LENDING

Income-seeking investors have been drawn to peer-to-peer lending on account of the attractive returns on offer. Here's everything you need to know about this growing sector

The Bank of England may have nudged the base rate up to 0.75% – its highest level in almost a decade – but this rise hasn't been passed on to most savers.

Three quarters of banks and building societies have failed to pass the rate rise on to customers, with the average easy-access savings account offering a pitiful interest rate of just 0.52%, according to MoneyFacts.

Almost a decade of low interest rates has caused many income-seekers to veer away from traditional savings accounts. With a number of peer-to-peer (P2P) platforms offering returns above 10%, savers have been abandoning their traditional cash savings accounts in favour of P2P.

P2P has gone from a quirky financial outsider to a billion-pound industry, winning approval from financial watchdog the Financial Conduct Authority

(FCA) and the government. What is more, Innovative Finance Isas (IF Isas) allow savers to enjoy tax-free returns on their P2P investments.

So what exactly is P2P and how can you get in on the action?

P2P: the basics

The idea is pretty straightforward: you lend your money to individuals or businesses using a P2P platform as the middleman. Interest rates on loans are still considerably higher than the returns available on savings accounts. For example, the recent base rate rise was swiftly passed on to borrowers, so you can enjoy a better interest rate as a lender.

Because you are cutting the banks out of the deal, P2P is good for both borrowers and lenders. The person borrowing money gets a lower interest rate than they would from a traditional lender and the person lending the money is offered a higher interest rate than they would receive from a traditional savings account.

Some of the best-known P2P platforms are Funding Circle, LendingCrowd, Lending Works, RateSetter and Zopa. Expect returns of between 3% and 7% a year, depending on which account you choose.

P2P platforms operate in different ways: some require you to spread your money across numerous loans, while others allow you to choose exactly which firms to lend money to.

Avoid the banks

The prospect of cutting out the banks attracted David Ivison, 55, a teacher from East Sussex, to P2P lending.

"Back in 2007 I required a loan, so approached my bank of 25 years and was given a loan offer with what I considered to be a very high interest rate. It seemed that loyal customers are just another group to be exploited, so dissatisfaction with the traditional financial institutions was a big factor in my interest in peer to peer," he explains.

David has been investing with Funding Circle since 2012 and has gradually built up his P2P loan portfolio.

"With Funding Circle, I like the thought that I am lending (almost) directly to small businesses which need the money and want to bypass the banks. It gives me a feeling that I am really involved in helping them. Most are very small and have maybe been refused by a bank.

"Of course, I have to trust that Funding Circle can correctly assess the loan, but, so far, I am happy to say that it has my trust," he explains.

Get tax-free returns

Back in April 2016, P2P got a boost when the IF Isa launched, allowing savers to generate returns on their P2P investments tax-free. Individuals can invest part or all of their £20,000 Isa allowance into an IF Isa during this tax year.

However, it has taken a while for the IF Isa to gain traction. This is because P2P platforms required FCA approval before they were able to launch these products, and this took a surprisingly long time – up to a year in some cases. In the end, some of the lesser-known names managed to get through the red tape first.

During the 2017/18 tax year, investors subscribed to 31,000 IF Isas, up from 5,000 the previous tax year. While this represents a significant increase, it pales in comparison to subscriptions of 7.8 million in Cash Isas and 2.8 million in Stocks and Shares Isas.

However, it is worth noting that individuals who subscribed to an IF Isa invested relatively large sums. The average IF Isa attracted £9,355 during the 2017/18 tax year, which compares to £5,114 for a Cash Isa and £10,124 for a Stocks and Shares Isa.

Today, close to 85 companies are authorised to offer IF Isas – including Zopa, RateSetter, Funding Circle and Lending Works – and the number of people opening accounts is expected to steadily increase.

The lure of attractive returns

The prospect of higher returns in comparison to traditional savings accounts attracted Hazel Johnson*, 60, a university professor from north London to P2P investing. She has invested with RateSetter for several years.

"I had received an inheritance and put this aside in 'protected accounts' [Isas and savings accounts] funds that were needed for my children's education and other essentials. So I only used P2P for funds that were at the very limit I could lose, but the aim was clearly to get a better return than was offered by typical lenders.

"I also read widely to get a sense of which P2P company seemed the most reliable and had self-regulated protections in place to deal with bad loans, so I went for a calculated risk."

Hazel also took steps herself to keep the risk to a minimum.

"I put funds in the rolling fund [easy withdrawals] to keep control and when there was some publicity in the press about a bad commercial loan that RateSetter had made, I removed some funds.

"I am not so flush that I could take more than calculated risks. However, when it became clear that this bad loan had resulted in no loss to individual investors, I reinvested funds into RateSetter," she says. Beware of the risks

When it comes to P2P, remember the first rule of investing: the prospect of higher returns may mean that you are taking on more risk. It is not the same as putting your money in a savings account at a bank.

Despite the fact that several comparison websites including GoCompare and LoveMoney list P2P alongside savings products on best-buy tables, your cash is at risk and you may get back less than you put in.

By lending your money out to individuals or businesses, you run the risk of a borrower defaulting on their repayments and leaving you out of pocket.

It's also worth noting that P2P platforms are not covered by the Financial Services Compensation Scheme. This means that if the platform goes bust, you could lose your money.

Understandably, you may presume that opting for a P2P platform that offers the highest interest rates means you are taking on the most risk. However, this isn't necessarily the case. Every platform assesses risk differently – so if a P2P lender offers a lower interest rate, it may not mean that you are taking on less risk.

The P2P market has been going strong for the past 10 years, which has been a period of relative stability for financial markets. The sector is yet to experience a downturn, in which a large number of borrowers default on their loans. A financial crash could also increase the amount of time it takes you to sell your loans on the secondary market if you want to get your money out.

"P2P has not yet been through a full normal market cycle, so we have not experienced the impact of high interest rates, high inflation and high default levels on the market," says Danny Cox, chartered financial planner at investment platform Hargreaves Lansdown.

"The interest cost of a P2P loan is actually quite small. It is the repayment of the capital that is the problem. This means the business lending P2P market will be sorely tested when businesses start to flounder or fail in a recession, and on the personal lending side when unemployment rises," he adds.

In the past, many P2P platforms tried to mitigate the risks associated with lending by having safeguard or provision funds in place. These acted as a safety net to cover losses in the event that one of your borrowers defaulted on their loan. However, it is not clear how these funds would cope in a financial crash, as they don't hold enough money to cover the platform's entire loan book.

What is more, several big P2P platforms don't have provision funds at all. For example, Zopa started phasing its out last year, while Funding Circle doesn't have one in place.

"We don't believe the provision fund model is the best way to provide investors with stable returns. Instead, diversification and transparency are the best way for investors to manage risk effectively," says Kendra Bruckner, a communications executive at Funding Circle.

It is essential to ensure diversification across your P2P portfolio.

Neil Faulkner, founder of 4thWay, a peer-to-peer lending ratings agency, notes that spreading your money across at least half a dozen P2P platforms and many hundreds of loans can "tremendously lower your risks".

"Lenders should not allow themselves to believe they can accurately select a small number of loans to outperform," he adds.

Moneywise verdict

P2P investing offers a lifeline to savers looking for a better return than those on offer from traditional savings accounts.

But be aware of the fact you are investing: this is higher risk than simply keeping your money in a savings account. Take steps to keep that risk down by diversifying your P2P portfolio, making sure only a fraction of your savings are in P2P and keeping some money in a traditional savings account for emergencies. Also, make sure you are comfortable with the fact your investments could go down in value.

Comparing P2P platforms can be complicated, so Moneywise recommends that beginners stick with a mainstream provider until they gain more experience in the sector. After some time, they may wish to invest via a specialist platform that provides control over where the loans are allocated.

Our top picks are highlighted above – Zopa, RateSetter, Lending Works and Funding Circle. They all scored highly at the Moneywise Customer Service Awards 2018, with Zopa named the Most Trusted P2P Provider and Lending Works taking the award for the Best P2P Platform for Investors, with Funding Circle, RateSetter and more property-focused Assetz Capital and Lendy also shortlisted.

CHAPTER 3
RENTAL PROPERTIES

Buy-to-let is much tougher than it once was. A tax crackdown on buying property investments and a tax raid on landlord's rental income has seen to that.

But for many Britons the idea of investing in property still appeals, as they trust bricks and mortar and may feel that they can add value to a home in a way they can't to an investment fund.

A world of low interest rates helps polish the attraction of buy-to-let. Returns on savings are low and mortgages are cheap.

But interest rates are forecast to rise and the 3 per cent stamp duty surcharge eats a large amount of your money, while the loss of full mortgage interest tax relief has eaten into returns.

Buy a £150,000 home and you will lose £5,000 in tax on stamp duty and your rental revenue will now be taxed not your profit.

Nonetheless, buy-to-let remains popular. So if you are considering it, or are an existing landlord looking to up your game, here are This is Money's top ten buy-to-let tips - in our long-running essential guide to property investing and being a good landlord.

Why invest in buy-to-let?

As an income investment for those with enough money to raise a big deposit buy to let looks attractive, especially compared to low savings rates and stock market swings.

Meanwhile, the property market bouncing back after its financial crisis lows has encouraged more investors to snap up property in the hope of its value rising.

House price rises have priced most people out of London property investment, but some areas of the UK are still to regain the ground lost after the financial crisis slump and investors are increasingly looking there for stronger returns.

Mortgage rates at record lows are helping buy-to-let investors make deals stack up.

But beware low rates. One day they must rise and you need to know your investment can stand that test.

There is also a tax rise being put in place, as buy-to-let mortgage interest relief is axed and replaced with a 20 per cent tax credit.

Additionally, since April 2016 landlords now have to pay an extra 3% stamp duty on property purchases.

It's also worth noting that the Bank of England has buy-to-let mortgages in its sights.

Yet despite the tax changes and potential for buy-to-let mortgage costs to rise, there are positives.

Greater demand from tenants, rents that should rise with inflation and the long horizon for interest rate rises, mean many investors are still tempted by buy-to-let.

If you are planning on investing, or just want to know more, we tell you the ten essential things to consider for a successful buy-to-let investment below.

Like any investment, buy-to-let comes with no guarantees, but for those who have more faith in bricks and mortar than stocks and shares below are This is Money's top ten tips.

1. Research the market on buy-to-let

If you are new to buy-to-let, what do you know about the market? Do you know the risks, as well as the benefits.

Make sure buy-to-let is the investment you want. Your money might be able to perform better elsewhere.

In recent years a high-rate savings account would beat most investments. Now rates are lower, but investing in buy-to-let means tying up capital in a property that may fall in value.

This compares to the possibility of a 5% annual return from an income-based investment fund, or 3 per cent on a fixed rate savings account.

Remember that the return from an investment in funds, shares or an investment trust through an Isa will see you escape tax on income and get capital growth tax free. You will also have the ability to sell up quickly if you want.

The flipside is that you cannot buy an unloved investment fund and set about renovating it and adding value yourself.

Investing in buy-to-let involves committing tens of thousands of pounds to a property and typically taking out a mortgage. When house prices rise, this means it is possible to make big leveraged gains above your mortgage debt, but when they fall your deposit gets hit and the mortgage stays the same.

Property investing has paid off handsomely for many people, both in terms of income and capital gains but it is essential that you go into it with your eyes wide open, acknowledging the potential advantages and disadvantages.

If you know someone who has invested in buy-to-let or let a property before, ask them about their experiences - warts and all.

The more knowledge you have and the more research you do, the better the chance of your investment paying off.

2. Choose a promising area to invest in property

Promising does not mean most expensive or cheapest. Promising means a place where people would like to live and this can be for a variety of reasons.

Where in your town has a special appeal? If you are in a commuter belt, where has good transport? Where are the good schools for young families? Where do the students want to live?

You need to match the kind of property you can afford and want to buy with locations that people who would want to live in those homes would choose.

These questions might sound overly simplistic, but they are probably the most important aspect of a successful buy-to-let investment

In most cases people tend to invest in property close to where they live. On the plus side, they are likely to know this market better than anywhere else and can spot the kind of property and location that will do well. They also have a much better chance of keeping tabs on the property.

Yet it is also worth bearing in mind that if you are a homeowner then you are already exposed to property where you live - and looking for a different type of home in a different area might be a good move.

3. Do the maths on buy-to-let

Before you think about looking around properties sit down with a pen and paper and write down the cost of houses you are looking at and the rent you are likely to get.

Buy-to-let lenders typically want rent to cover 125 per cent of the mortgage repayments - often now 150 per cent - and most now demand 25 per cent deposits, or even larger, for rates considerably above residential mortgage deals.

The best rate buy-to-let mortgages also come with large arrangement fees.

Once you have the mortgage rate and likely rent sorted then you must be clinical in deciding whether your investment work out?

Don't forget to factor in maintenance costs.

What will happen if the property sits empty for a month or two?

These are all things to consider. Make sure you know how much the mortgage repayments will be and if it is a tracker allow for rates to rise.

4. Shop around and get the best buy-to-let mortgage

Do not just walk into your bank and building society and ask for a mortgage. It sounds obvious, but people who do this when they need a financial product are one of the reasons why banks make billions in profit.

It pays to speak to a good independent broker when looking for a buy-to-let mortgage. They can not only talk you through what deals are available but they can also help you weigh up which one is right for you and whether to fix or track.

You should still do your own research though, so that you can go into the conversation armed with the knowledge of what sort of mortgages you should be offered.

This is Money's carefully chosen mortgage broker partner London & Country offers fee-free advice, you can find out more and use our comparison tool to find the best buy-to-let mortgage for you here.

5. Think about your target tenant

Instead of imagining whether you would like to live in your investment property, put yourself in the shoes of your target tenant.

Who are they and what do they want?If they are students, it needs to be easy to clean and comfortable but not luxurious.

If they are young professionals it should be modern and stylish but not overbearing.

If it is a family they will have plenty of their own belongings and need a blank canvas.

Remember that allowing tenants to make their mark on a property, such as by decorating, or adding pictures, or you taking out unwanted furniture makes it feel more like home.

These tenants will stay for longer, which is great news for a landlord.

It is also possible to take out an insurance policy against your tenant failing to pay the rent, usually known as rent guarantee insurance. This can cost as little as £50, and is available as a standalone product from a specialist provider, or as part of a wider landlord insurance policy.

6. Don't be greedy, go for rental yield and remember costs

We have all read the stories about buy-to-let millionaires and their huge portfolios.

But while you may expect long-term house price rises, experts say invest for income not short-term capital growth.

To compare different property's values use their yield: that is annual rent received as a percentage of the purchase price.

For example, a property delivering £10,000 worth of rent that costs £200,000 has a 5% yield.

Rent should be the key return for buy-to-let.

Most buy-to-let mortgages are done on an interest-only basis, so the amount borrowed will not be paid off over time.

This is tax efficient, as you can offset mortgage payments against your tax bill.

However, whereas once you could offset your entire mortgage cost against tax that is now being eaten into and by 2020 you will get a maximum 20 per cent tax credit on your mortgage payments.

If you can get a rental return substantially over the mortgage payments, then once you have built up a good emergency fund, you can start saving or investing any extra cash.

Remember though, people rarely buy a home outright and they come with running costs, so mortgage costs, maintenance and agents fees must be worked out and they will eat into your return.

You may want to consider whether buy-to-let still beats an investment fund or trust once these costs are taken into account.

Once mortgage, costs and tax are considered, you will want the rent to build up over time and then potentially be able to use it as a deposit for further investments, or to pay off the mortgage at the end of its term.

This means you will have benefited from the income from rent, paid off the mortgage and hold the property's full capital value.

7. Look further afield or doing a property up

Most buy-to-let investors look for properties near where they live. But your town may not be the best investment.

The advantage of a property close by is being able to keep an eye on it, but if you will be employing an agent anyway they should do that for you.

Cast your net wider and look at towns with good commuting links, that are popular with familes or have a sizeable university.

It is also worth looking at properties that need improvement as a way of boosting the value of your investment. Tired properties or those in need of renovation can be negotiated hard on to get at a better price and then spruced up to add value.

This is one way that it is still possible to see a solid and swift return on your capital invested. If you can add some value to a home straight away then it gives you a greater margin of safety on your investment

However, remember to ensure that the price is low enough to cover refurbishment and some profit and that you allow for the inevitable over-run on costs.

A good rule to follow is the property developers' rough calculation, whereby you want the final value of a refurbished property to be at least the purchase price, plus cost of work, plus 20 per cent.

8. Haggle over price when invest in property

As a buy-to-let investor you have the same advantage as a first-time buyer when it comes to negotiating a discount.

If you are not reliant on selling a property to buy another, then you are not part of a chain and represent less of a risk of a sale falling through.

This can be a major asset when negotiating a discount. Make low offers and do not get talked into overpaying.

It pays to know your market when negotiating. For example, if the market is softer and homes are taking longer to sell you will be better able to negotiate. It is also useful to find out why someone is selling and how long they have owned the property.

An existing landlord who has owned a property for a long time - and is cashing in their capital gains -may be more willing to accept a lower offer for a quick sale than a family that needs the best possible price in order to afford a move.

9. Know the pitfalls of buy-to-let

Before you make any investment you should always investigate the negative aspects as well as the positive.

House prices are on the up right now but growth has slowed and they could fall again. If property prices dip will you be able to continue holding your investment?

Meanwhile, rates are low at the moment and that is encouraging people to invest with rent comfortable covering the mortgage, but what will you do when rates rise?

Consider too the standard variable rate you may move to after a fixed rate period. What will happen if you can't remortgage?

Even in popular areas properties can sit empty. One rule of thumb many buy-to-let investors apply is to factor in the property sitting empty for two months of the year - this gives a substantial buffer.

Homes often need repairing and things can go wrong. If you do not have enough in the bank to cover a major repair to your property, such as a new boiler, do not invest yet.

It's also essential to read up on tax on buy-to-let. It now incurs an extra 3 per cent stamp duty surcharge and soon all mortgage interest will no longer be able to be set against rental income before income tax is calculated. Instead a 20 per cent tax credit will be phased in. Read about tax on buy-to-let here.

10. Consider how hands-on a landlord you want to be

Buying a property is only the first step. Will you rent it out yourself or get an agent to do so.

Agents will charge you a management fee, but will deal with any problems and have a good network of plumbers, electricians and other workers if things go wrong.

You can make more money by renting the property out yourself but be prepared to give up weekends and evenings on viewings, advertising and repairs.

If you choose an agent you do not have to go for a High Street presence, many independent agents offer an excellent and personal service.

Select a shortlist of agents big and small and ask them what they can offer you.

If you are considering going it alone look at where you will advertise your property and where you will get documents, such as tenancy agreements from.

It really pays to look after your tenants. Do this and they will look after you.

The biggest drag on many buy-to-let landlord's investment returns is the void period. A time when you don't have anyone in the property. Good tenants who want to stay help avoid this - and if they move on they may even recommend your property to someone they know.

Keep up with maintenance, make sure your property is a nice place to live and try and build a good personal relationship with your tenants.

CHAPTER 4
HIGH YIELD SAVINGS ACCOUNT
AND MONEY MARKET FUNDS

With near-zero interest rates have been the norm for some time, you have probably been conditioned to accept rates on your liquid cash that barely register on your account statements. According to bankrate.com, the average money market account (MMA) rate in the nation was 0.20%, when we checked on August 29, 2018, which would earn $20 on a $10,000 deposit after the first year. You can find better rates by shopping and comparing. If you're willing to do your banking in the Internet cloud, you can sometimes find MMA rates topping 2.0%.

However, there's another option that can have even better rates: high-interest checking accounts. These can pay in the 3% to 5% range and are usually found at smaller community banks, credit unions or online banks. It is easy to become captivated by the comparatively alluring rates they offer, but, with all the caveats involved, they are definitely not for everyone.

Money Market Account

Money market accounts are federally insured short-term interest-bearing instruments that generate a variable yield while preserving principal. They tend to deliver interest rates that are higher than those for savings accounts, but they also often call for a higher minimum deposit. Some require a minimum balance to receive the highest rate. The interest rates on MMAs are variable, which means they rise and fall with the interest rate market.

Most MMAs come with limited check writing and balance transfer privileges. However, federal regulations limit the number of transactions in MMAs to six a month.

High-Interest Checking Account

High-interest checking accounts have all the trappings that normally come with regular checking accounts. Many offer unlimited checks, a debit card, online account management and perks such as rewards points and free overdraft protection. Many will waive the monthly maintenance fee if you maintain a minimum daily balance.

The accounts are usually capped, meaning that the higher interest rate is paid only up to a certain level of money on deposit. Most accounts are capped at $25,000, but the caps can go as low as $1,000. Deposits that exceed the cap earn a much lower rate, as low as 0.1%.

Which Is Better?

Although high-interest checking accounts offer rates that are significantly higher than those available on savings accounts or MMAs, you have to meet a number of conditions to earn a higher rate. For instance, with many high-interest checking accounts, you must accept direct deposit and electronic statements. Many accounts require 10 transactions; if you only make nine, you lose the higher rate for the statement period. And these accounts sometimes require at least one bill pay or transfer from the account per statement period.

Though none of these requirements are insurmountable, meeting them means that you have to actively manage the account. Most people are used to a more passive approach to account management.

An MMA is generally a better option if you want to park some cash for a short period, or if you don't want to actively manage your savings. It gives you access to your money when you need it while requiring a minimum amount of effort on your part.

If you're willing to manage your account actively, a high-interest checking account can generate significantly higher interest earnings than a typical

MMA. If in the normal course of a month, you expect to make the required number of debit transactions and have at least one bill you can set up on automatic bill payment, a high-interest checking account shouldn't be much to manage.

The most difficult aspect is the cap. To optimize your interest rate earnings, you need to make sure that the amount on deposit doesn't exceed the cap. You will likely need to keep transferring from lower-yielding accounts to ensure you maximize the amount that can be earning the higher yield. For a $10,000 deposit in a high-interest checking account earning 2.5% interest, that is about $240 more in earnings than a typical MMA.

The Bottom Line

High-interest checking accounts and money market accounts can both earn you more in interest than a plain old savings account. The former takes more effort on your part but can result in the highest yields. The latter has the advantage of not needing constant oversight. They still give you access to your money when you need it, like a savings account, but earn a better, though variable, rate of interest. Each is a good reason not to leave all of your hard-earned money sitting in a savings account, where it can barely earn interest at all.

CHAPTER 5
CD LADDERS

A CD ladder is a strategy in which an investor divides the amount of money to be invested into equal amounts in certificates of deposit (CDs) with different maturity dates. This strategy decreases both interest rate and re-investment risks.

BREAKING DOWN CD Ladder

A Certificate of Deposit (CD) is an investment product that offers a fixed interest rate for a specified period of time. The invested funds, which are insured up to $250,000 by the Federal Deposit Insurance Corporation (FDIC), are locked in by the issuing bank until the maturity date of the CD. Maturity dates for these savings instruments are typically set at three months, six months, one year, or five years. The higher the term for which funds are committed, the higher the interest paid. To take advantage of the various interest rates offered for different periods, investors can follow a strategy known as the CD ladder.

A CD ladder strategy is followed by investors who value the safety of their principal and income. This strategy also provides investors with steady cash flow as the CDs will mature at different times. An investor that incorporates this strategy will allocate the same amount of funds across CDs with different maturities. This way, s/he benefits from the higher interest rates of longer-term CDs and does not have to repeatedly renew a short-term certificate of deposit that holds all his or her funds.

Investors that put all their funds in one CD may miss out on higher interest rates that may result while their funds are locked away. With a CD ladder, however, the investor can take advantage of short-term interest rates by reinvesting proceeds from maturing CDs into newer CDs with higher interest rates. On the other hand, if interest rates fall, CD holders still enjoy the benefits of the high interest rates that their existing long-term CDs provide. A CD ladder, thus, provides regular opportunities to reinvest cash as the CDs mature, while reducing interest rate risk.

In the event that an emergency ensues and an investor needs cash, the laddering strategy ensures that the investor consistently has a CD maturing, thereby, reducing liquidity risk.

For example, an investor has $40,000 to invest. Rather than putting the entire funds in one CD, he decides to put $10,000 in each of four certificates of deposit maturing in 6 months, 12 months, 18 months, and 24 months.

CHAPTER 6
ANNUITIES

An annuity is simply a way of providing a regular income. This is most typically to provide an individual with income once they have stopped working.

There are two basic types of annuity: Pension Annuities and Purchased Life Annuities

Pension annuities

Pension Annuities can only be bought with money/funds held within registered pension plans/ schemes.

In practice pension annuities fall into two types - lifetime annuities and scheme pensions. They are similar in that they provide an income for life but they have different rules. The differences are even more marked following the Taxation of Pensions Act 2014.

Although historically we use the term "pension annuity" where the rules apply equally to the scheme pension and the lifetime annuity, great care should be taken as scheme pensions do not enjoy much of the flexibility now available for lifetime annuities.

Scheme Pensions

A Scheme Pension is a pension income payable either from the scheme itself or from an insurance company selected by the scheme.

Defined Benefit schemes can only provide pension income via a scheme pension. If the member wishes to access the flexibilities now offered under lifetime annuities they must transfer their benefits prior to crystallisation.

It is possible for a money purchase/defined contribution pension scheme to provide a scheme pension, but a scheme pension may only be paid if the member had an opportunity to select a lifetime annuity instead.

Scheme pensions must:

- be paid at least annually, and
- not have a guaranteed period of more than 10 years
- not reduce unless in specified circumstances (changes to income), and
- be paid by the scheme administrator or an insurance company selected by them.

- The rules governing scheme pensions are generally more restrictive than those for lifetime annuities.

Lifetime Annuities

Lifetime Annuities are payable by an insurance company where the member had the right to choose the insurance company.

The member's right to choose the insurance company is a key difference compared to scheme pensions.

Prior to 6 April 2015 the basic rules applying to a lifetime annuity require that:

- it was paid by an insurance company
- the member could choose the insurance company
- it was payable at least annually and for life
- if it had a minimum guaranteed period, that period was not more than 10 years
- the amount of annuity either could not decrease or could change only in accordance with specific rules set out in regulations
- the potential survivor of a joint life annuity was usually limited to a formal dependant of the member

- it couldn't create a lump sum on death (other than capital protection)
- it couldn't be surrendered or assigned, although this was possible through the will for guaranteed periods or to comply with a pensions sharing order. This is also the current situation, but please see the post-6 April 2015 rules for important proposals.

After 6 April 2015, the basic rules applying to a lifetime annuity require that:

- it's paid by an insurance company
- the member could choose the insurance company
- it is payable at least annually and for life
- if it has a minimum guaranteed period, that period needn't be limited to 10 years

annuities now have a wider definition of allowed decreases the potential survivor of a joint life annuity needn't be a formal dependant of the member. Previous limitations on the term 'dependant', (spouse, civil partner, child under age 23 etc.) no longer apply to lifetime annuities. The annuitant can select anyone to become a joint annuitant. However, this will be subject to acceptance by the provider and may have an impact of the amount of annuity payable.

In addition to the survivor's joint life annuity, which can be paid to a dependant or nominee, if there are any unused pension funds available on the death of a member (they could be uncrystallised funds or unused drawdown funds that haven't been used in the provision of a dependant or nominee annuity) they can be used to provide a successor's annuity.

A lifetime annuity can't create a lump sum on death. A lifetime annuity can't be surrendered or assigned, although this is possible through the will for guaranteed periods or to comply with a pensions sharing order. See Finance Act 2004: Sch 28, Para 3 (as amended by the Taxation of Pensions Act 2014)

A section 32 buyout policy will provide a lifetime annuity because the member will be able to transfer it to another insurance company to pay the income – i.e. the member can choose the insurance company that ultimately pays the annuity.

How the law allows annuity income to vary

Scheme Pensions

The law is fairly restrictive on when it allows an amount of scheme pension to change. There is no room for variation (unlike with Lifetime Annuities) and the legislation states the circumstances where Scheme Pensions may be reduced or stopped.

There are currently 9 situations where a Scheme Pension may be reduced or stopped:

- the reduction of the pension if the member became entitled to it by reason of the ill-health condition being met
- all the members in the scheme are having their pensions reduced at the same time
- it was a bridging pension and state pension age has been reached
- on wind up where the scheme cannot support paying the pensions at their existing level
- subsequent to a pension sharing order being applied to the pension
- a court order has directed so
- on abatement. This applies to public sector schemes where the member returns to employment in the public sector and means their pension may be reduced
- reduction due to forfeiting benefits
- The reduction of the pension in any other circumstances prescribed by regulations made by the Board of Inland Revenue See Finance Act 2004: Sch 28, Para 2(4) (as amended by the Taxation of Pensions Act 2014)

Finance Act 2005: Para 11(6) and (7)

The Pension Schemes (Reduction in Pension rates) Regulations 2006 - SI 2006/138 as amended by SI 2009/1311

Lifetime Annuities

A lifetime annuity may increase or decrease in line with any one or a combination of the following:

- retail prices index/consumer prices index
- the value of 'freely marketable assets' (e.g. shares, OEICs, Unit Trusts, unit-linked pension funds)
- an index of 'freely marketable assets' (e.g. FTSE 100, Dow Jones Industrial Average)

With-Profits funds

After allowance for any contractual charges

Conventional lifetime annuities purchased prior to April 2015 are annuities which do not decrease, or any falls are determined by regulations made by the Board of Inland Revenue.

However, The Taxation of Pension Act 2014 details changes to annuities that are purchased post April 2015. From 6th April 2015, in addition to reductions determined by the Board of Inland Revenue, annuities can decrease by "allowed decreases", which widens the circumstances in which annuities can reduce. Exactly what annuity options will be made available by providers under the relaxed legislation is yet to be clarified.

Notwithstanding the annuity design possibilities of the change in the post April 2015 legislation, detailed above, different annuity contracts may currently use different methods. The following methodology will continue for annuities purchased pre April 2015.

They can:

- move fully in line with the change in the linked investments/index
- vary based on the anticipated growth of the linked investment / index
- have maximum and minimum income limits that are reviewed at regular intervals based on the value of the underlying investment / index (See Finance Act 2004: Sch 28, Para 3(1)(d) (as amended by the Taxation of Pensions Act 2014)

Finance Act 2005: Sch 10, Para 13(2) and (4)

The Registered Pension Schemes (Prescribed Manner of Determining Amount of Annuities) Regulations 2006 - SI 2006/568

1. Fully Linked

Fully linked annuities operate just as it says. The annuity income will rise and fall based on the increase or decrease in the underlying investment or index. An example is an inflation-linked annuity.

Inflation-Linked Annuities

As the name suggests, inflation-linked annuities vary according to the rate of inflation. This is usually the retail prices index (RPI) but could also be the consumer prices index (CPI).

This provides protection against the effects of inflation – an annuity linked to RPI will increase by 3.8% in a year if RPI is 3.8% for that year. The change will usually apply at each one year anniversary of the date the annuity started.

The starting level of an inflation-linked annuity will depend to some extent on the provider's view of future inflation. It may start higher or lower than a fixed escalating annuity depending on the rate of fixed escalation chosen. For example, an annuity increasing by 5% pa might have a lower starting level than an inflation-linked annuity, but one with a 2% pa fixed escalation may have a higher starting level.

POINT TO NOTE: the relative difference in the starting level of a fixed escalating annuity and an inflation-linked annuity will vary depending on economic outlook/circumstances and may change over time - it is important not to assume one will always start higher than the other.

In a period of deflation (i.e. negative inflation) an inflation-linked annuity may be expected to reduce. For example, if inflation is -2.4% in a year, the annuity would reduce by 2.4%. However, some inflation-linked annuities are written so that they will not reduce even where there is deflation - the annuity will remain at its previous level instead.

POINT TO NOTE: pensioner inflation (inflation for those who are older) tends to be higher than the general measure of RPI or CPI. This means that while an inflation-linked annuity may keep pace with inflation generally that does not mean it will keep pace with inflation for the individual.

2. Investment-Linked Annuities

Investment-linked annuities are those that can alter in accordance with:

the value of 'freely marketable assets' (e.g. shares, OEICs, Unit Trusts, unit-linked pension funds); or
an index of 'freely marketable assets' (e.g. FTSE 100, Dow Jones Industrial Average)
With-Profits funds
After allowance for any contractual charges
The most common are unit-linked annuities and with-profits annuities.

While investment-linked annuities can, and do, use different underlying investments to determine the amount of annuity payable, they all operate using the same general principles:

- a starting level of income is chosen, usually by the individual from a range set by the annuity provider
- the starting level will equate to a certain rate of growth each year – sometimes referred to as the anticipated growth rate
- the actual rate of growth each year is determined by the growth on the underlying investments chosen - e.g. with-profits fund, unit linked funds
- if the actual rate of growth each year is the same as the anticipated growth rate the annuity will remain level
- if the actual rate of growth each year is lower than the anticipated growth rate the annuity will reduce
- if the actual rate of growth each year is higher than the anticipated growth rate the annuity will increase POINT TO NOTE: the starting level of an investment-linked annuity will vary depending on the anticipated growth rate (AGR) chosen at the start. For a fund of £100,000 the starting annuity will be higher if an AGR of 6% is chosen as compared to an AGR of 2%. As a general rule, as the chosen AGR gets higher the starting annuity will become closer to the annuity provided through a fixed level annuity. It is usually

possible to select an AGR that will provide a starting annuity of the same amount as a fixed level annuity.

Investment-linked annuities do carry investment risk which neither fixed nor inflation-linked annuities have. This investment risk may help combat the effects of inflation, whilst also providing the opportunity for the individual's money to still be linked with investment performance. The client's income will vary in accordance with investment performance.

POINT TO NOTE: The difference in starting annuity, based on the anticipated growth rate (AGR) chosen, reflects the level of investment risk being taken. The higher the AGR, the higher the investment risk, the greater the chance of the annuity reducing in future, the lower the chance of it increasing in future. A balance has therefore to be struck between the level of risk a client is willing / able to accept, the AGR and the starting level of the annuity.

3. Variable Annuities

Variable annuities offer an alternative 'middle ground' between conventional (fixed/inflation-linked) annuities and income drawdown.

In a similar manner to investment-linked annuities they offer the ability for a continued link between the annuity income and investment performance.

However, they go one step further than investment-linked annuities in that they can provide wider income limits, have greater income variability and allow for income reviews to be undertaken, all of which are similar in nature to the old rules that were applicable to income drawdown.

Variable annuities are not, however, able to replicate all of the death benefits permitted under income drawdown; in particular, they are not able to return a lump sum on death as income drawdown can.

The income from a variable annuity can be chosen from within a set range which is 50% - 120% of the amount of level annuity the fund could purchase with the variable annuity provider

If the variable annuity provider does not offer level annuities itself the limits will be calculated based on the average of three current market annuity rates for a level annuity. The individual may choose an income at any point between these limits and can vary the amount of income at any time agreed with the annuity provider, as long as it stays within the above limits.

The minimum and maximum income range/limits must themselves be reviewed by the annuity provider at least once every 3 years. That review will set the minimum and maximum for the period until the next review date.

POINT TO NOTE: At the outset the fund used to calculate the income limits will be an actual pension fund but at future reviews it will be a notional fund. This is because an annuity contract does not have an actual fund value as such - if it did then it would not qualify as an annuity under tax law. The money has been used at the outset to buy the lifetime annuity but a notional fund value will be maintained and used when calculating the income limits at subsequent reviews.

When the amount of annuity has been chosen the same basic approach to investment returns, as that for investment-linked annuities, can be applied.

The notional fund is linked to underlying investments, such as a with-profits fund or unit-linked funds, and the value of that notional fund will go up or down in line with their investment performance. The annuity is paid from that notional fund and so will also impact its value.

If the value increases, the income limits at a review will also increase, thus increasing the maximum annuity that may be paid.

If the value reduces, the income limits at the next review will also decrease, thus decreasing the maximum annuity that may be paid

It is therefore possible for the notional fund under a variable annuity to increase or reduce significantly depending on the level of annuity and investment performance.

POINT TO NOTE: this means that the level of investment risk associated with a variable annuity is higher compared to an investment-linked annuity with an investment-linked annuity the amount of annuity previously paid out does not have any effect on the possible future annuity, but under a variable annuity it does.

POINT TO NOTE: variable annuities provide a solution to the lack of flexibility in being able to alter income, which is associated with other annuities. They provide a further step toward income drawdown although their inability to offer the same range of death benefits as income drawdown mean they will not be appropriate for those to whom the death benefit is the key factor.

4. Other Annuity Types

Conventional Annuities

As detailed above, prior to 6 April 2015, conventional annuities could not usually decrease. This limitation will continue to apply to conventional annuities purchased prior to 6th April 2015.

Although post 6 April 2015 annuities are allowed to reduce by "allowed decreases", at the time of writing (April 2015), it is still unclear what impact this will have on the shape of annuity products offered by providers.

In respect to conventional annuities issued prior to 6 April 2015, they fall into one of two basic varieties:

those that remain level throughout the time they are paid; or
those that increase by a fixed amount/rate at set intervals.

A level annuity will pay the same amount throughout the period it is paid.

A fixed increasing (also known as an escalating) annuity will normally increase by a set percentage each year, on a compound basis. For example, an annuity starting out at, say £10,000 per annum might increase by 3% each year, to £10,300 in year 2, to £10,609 in year 3 and so on.

POINT TO NOTE: a level annuity will generally provide the highest starting amount of annuity as compared to most other annuities (variable annuities being a notable exception). This is because if increasing annuity options are incorporated, the cost of providing those must be met and that is through the starting level of annuity. So, an increasing annuity will have a lower, possibly much lower, starting point than a level annuity.

The risk of the amount of a conventional annuity reducing is very low - that would only potentially happen if the provider paying the annuity became insolvent. Even in that scenario the protection afforded by the Financial Services Compensation Scheme is 90% of the annuity value.

POINT TO NOTE: This credit risk applies to all annuities, not just fixed annuities.

Guaranteed Pension Annuities do, however, carry an inflation risk. Inflation erodes the purchasing power of money over time - £100 in today's money will buy you less than £100 in, say, 5 years' time because of the effects of inflation on the cost of living.

So an annuity that is level will lose its value over time, where inflation is positive.

An increasing annuity provides some protection against this, although the level of that protection depends on the difference between the rate of fixed increases and the rate of inflation -- if the rate of

inflation is higher than the rate of escalation, the annuity will reduce in value over time and vice versa.
Protected Rights Annuities

Annuities paid from 'protected rights' pension funds are subject to some specific legislation.

If the member is married the annuity must include a survivor's annuity where a guaranteed period is included it cannot be more than 5 years.
The Personal and Occupational Pension Schemes (Protected Rights) Regulations 1996, SI 1996/1537

Historically there were greater restrictions on protected rights annuities, but these have been removed gradually over time. There are no longer any other legal restrictions regarding the form of protected rights annuities and so all of the other options described above are available.

Protected Rights were abolished from April 2012, at which time the above restrictions also disappeared. However, protected rights annuities already set up will continue to operate on the basis they were set up.

Enhanced and Impaired Life Annuities

Enhanced Annuities are annuities that provide higher amounts than a 'normal' annuity because of the individual having a lower than 'normal' life expectancy.

This reduced life expectancy could be due to long-standing lifestyle or health issues. For example, smokers, those with high blood pressure or relating to the specific health of the individual.

Enhanced annuities usually operate on the basis of a standard, higher, annuity rate being applied. For example, a smoker may get a set annuity rate, which is higher than for a non-smoker. There is no assessment of the individual's health as the enhanced rate is a 'standard' enhancement to the ordinary annuity rate.

Impaired life annuities are, however, specific to the individual. They involve an underwriting assessment of the individual in order to assess his or her life expectancy, based on his or her own health. A higher annuity rate might then be offered as a result of that assessment.

POINT TO NOTE: the terms 'enhanced' and 'impaired life' have tended to become mixed over time. The introduction of 'post code pricing' has not helped as these could potentially be regarded as 'enhanced' annuities. The terms are, perhaps, irrelevant, though as the most important point is if the individual will get a higher annuity because of his/her health.

Factors influencing the annuity amount

There are 3 main factors affecting the amount of annuity income payable from the annuity purchase price:

1. Life expectancy

This is linked to age, health and, until 1st December 2012, gender.

Age

Annuities are a guarantee of an income for life, therefore the rates they're based on change as life expectancy increases. The younger people are when they retire, the longer they are likely to have in retirement and the longer the annuity is likely to be payable. For this reason, a 60 year old will generally receive a lower income than a 70 year old.

Health

If the prospective annuitant, or one or both joint life annuitants or the dependant of an annuitant has a medical or lifestyle condition they may qualify for an increased income through 'enhanced' terms. This normally pays a higher income.

Gender

Until 21 December 2012 annuity rates could be based on gender. Generally, females received less income as they lived for longer. Since then annuity rates must be on a gender neutral basis by law.

2. Gilt Yields

Gilts are government bonds. The government issues gilts to raise money - in return they pay an amount of interest. In conventional Gilts this amount is fixed for the lifetime of the bond and is known as the coupon. For example, the government may issue Treasury 5% 2026.

This shows who issued the Gilt (Treasury), the interest rate to be paid (relative to the initial price) and when it is due to be repaid.

This means it has a coupon rate of 5% based on the initial nominal value of £100. £5 per annum will be paid out to the holder of the gilt until 2026 when the government will repay the £100 - a 5% yield.

After being issued by the Debt Management Office in the first instance, Gilts can then be traded on the secondary market where the demand for and supply of them will determine their value. If demand increases then prices rise so yields fall and vice versa. This means a good day for bond holders will see the asking price of their bonds go up but their running yield fall. Therefore a fall in bond yields is not necessarily bad news and may be good news depending on your objective.

In the example above, if demand caused prices to rise to £150 then the yield would fall to 3.33% (£5/£150). However, if the Gilt is held to maturity the government will repay the original £100 not the current market price (in this case, £150).

As well as those conventional Gilts discussed above there are index-linked gilts, double-dated gilts and undated gilts. Of these the index-linked is most common making up around 30% of the Gilt market. There are very few double-dated and undated Gilts remaining.

Annuity providers predominately buy gilts to match their annuity liabilities. Therefore, movement in yields will impact the annuity rates offered. Lower yields = lower rates and vice versa

3. Options chosen

There are many options available with annuities. They can be:

- single life or joint life (post 6th April the joint annuitant, subject to the provider's approval, may be anyone selected by the annuitant. The selected age etc. of the joint annuitant may have a significant impact on the initial annuity, for example if the annuitant selects a grandchild as a joint annuitant, the initial annuity will be considerably lower than if the joint annuitant was of a similar age to the member).

- guaranteed or not guaranteed (previous 10 year limit no longer applies to new annuities purchased post 6th April 2015)
- escalating or not escalating
- frequency of payments
- whether payment is in advance or in arrears
- with or without overlap

The more options added the lower the income will be. Likewise, the type of option taken has an impact. For example, a 15 year guaranteed annuity will pay less initial annuity than a 5 year guaranteed annuity and a joint life annuity where there is no reduction on death would pay less than one with a 50% reduction on death. (Please note that for annuities arranged after 6th April 2015 there is no limit on the guaranteed period that can be built into a Lifetime Annuity, subject to being offered by provider).

- Invest Automatically in the stock market

The lure of big money has always thrown investors into the lap of stock markets. However, making money in equities is not easy. It not only requires oodles of patience and discipline, but also a great deal of research and a sound understanding of the market, among others.

Added to this is the fact that stock market volatility in the last few years has left investors in a state of confusion. They are in a dilemma whether to invest, hold or sell in such a scenario.

1. Avoid the herd mentality

The typical buyer's decision is usually heavily influenced by the actions of his acquaintances, neighbours or relatives. Thus, if everybody around is investing in a particular stock, the tendency for potential investors is to do the same. But this strategy is bound to backfire in the long run.

No need to say that you should always avoid having the herd mentality if you don't want to lose your hard-earned money in stock markets. The world's greatest investor Warren Buffett was surely not wrong when he said, "Be fearful when others are greedy, and be greedy when others are fearful!"

2. Take informed decision

Proper research should always be undertaken before investing in stocks. But that is rarely done. Investors generally go by the name of a company or the industry they belong to. This is, however, not the right way of putting one's money into the stock market.

3. Invest in business you understand

Never invest in a stock. Invest in a business instead. And invest in a business you understand. In other words, before investing in a company, you should know what business the company is in.

4. Don't try to time the market

One thing that even Warren Buffett doesn't do is to try to time the stock market, although he does have a very strong view on the price levels appropriate to individual shares. A majority of investors, however, do just the opposite, something that financial planners have always been warning them to avoid, and thus lose their hard-earned money in the process.

"So, you should never try to time the market. In fact, nobody has ever done this successfully and consistently over multiple business or stock market cycles. Catching the tops and bottoms is a myth. It is so till today and will remain so in the future. In fact, in doing so, more people have lost far more money than people who have made money," says Anil Chopra, group CEO and director, Bajaj Capital.

5. Follow a disciplined investment approach

Historically it has been witnessed that even great bull runs have shown bouts of panic moments. The volatility witnessed in the markets has inevitably made investors lose money despite the great bull runs.

However, the investors who put in money systematically, in the right shares and held on to their investments patiently have been seen generating outstanding returns. Hence, it is prudent to have patience and follow a disciplined investment approach besides keeping a long-term broad picture in mind.

6. Do not let emotions cloud your judgement

Many investors have been losing money in stock markets due to their inability to control emotions, particularly fear and greed. In a bull market, the lure of quick wealth is difficult to resist. Greed augments when investors hear stories of fabulous returns being made in the stock market in a short period of time. "This leads them to speculate, buy shares of unknown companies or create heavy positions in the futures segment without really understanding the risks involved," says Kapur.

Instead of creating wealth, these investors thus burn their fingers very badly the moment the sentiment in the market reverses. In a bear market, on the other hand, investors panic and sell their shares at rock-bottom prices. Thus, fear and greed are the worst emotions to feel when investing, and it is better not to be guided by them.

7. Create a broad portfolio

Diversification of portfolio across asset classes and instruments is the key factor to earn optimum returns on investments with minimum risk. Level of diversification depends on each investor's risk taking capacity.

8. Have realistic expectations

There's nothing wrong with hoping for the 'best' from your investments, but you could be heading for trouble if your financial goals are based on unrealistic assumptions. For instance, lots of stocks have generated more than 50 per cent returns during the great bull run of recent years.

However, it doesn't mean that you should always expect the same kind of return from the stock markets. Therefore, when Warren Buffett says that earning more than 12 per cent in stock is pure dumb luck and you laugh at it, you're surely inviting trouble for yourself.

9. Invest only your surplus funds

If you want to take risk in a volatile market like this, then see whether you have surplus funds which you can afford to lose. It is not necessary that you will lose money in the present scenario. You investments can give you huge gains too in the months to come.

But no one can be hundred percent sure. That is why you will have to take risk. No need to say that invest only if you are flush with surplus funds.

10. Monitor rigorously

We are living in a global village. Any important event happening in any part of the world has an impact on our financial markets. Hence we need to constantly monitor our portfolio and keep affecting the desired changes in it.

If you can't review your portfolio due to time constraint or lack of knowledge, then you should take the help of a good financial planner or someone who is capable of doing that. "If you can't even do that, then stock investing is not for you. Better put your money in safe or less-risky instruments," advises Kapur.

CHAPTER 7
INVEST IN REAL ESTATE
INVESTMENT TRUST

Real estate investment trusts ("REITs") allow individuals to invest in large-scale, income-producing real estate. A REIT is a company that owns and typically operates income-producing real estate or related assets. These may include office buildings, shopping malls, apartments, hotels, resorts, self-storage facilities, warehouses, and mortgages or loans. Unlike other real estate companies, a REIT does not develop real estate properties to resell them. Instead, a REIT buys and develops properties primarily to operate them as part of its own investment portfolio.

Why Would Somebody Invest In REITs?

REITs provide a way for individual investors to earn a share of the income produced through commercial real estate ownership – without actually having to go out and buy commercial real estate.

What Types Of REITs Are There?

Many REITs are registered with the SEC and are publicly traded on a stock exchange. These are known as publicly traded REITs. Others may be registered with the SEC but are not publicly traded. These are known as non- traded REITs (also known as non-exchange traded REITs). This is one of the most important distinctions among the various kinds of REITs. Before investing in a REIT, you should understand whether or not it is publicly traded, and how this could affect the benefits and risks to you.

What Are The Benefits And Risks Of REITs?

REITs offer a way to include real estate in one's investment portfolio. Additionally, some REITs may offer higher dividend yields than some other investments.

But there are some risks, especially with non-exchange traded REITs. Because they do not trade on a stock exchange, non-traded REITs involve special risks:

Lack of Liquidity: Non-traded REITs are illiquid investments. They generally cannot be sold readily on the open market. If you need to sell an asset to raise money quickly, you may not be able to do so with shares of a non-traded REIT.

Share Value Transparency: While the market price of a publicly traded REIT is readily accessible, it can be difficult to determine the value of a share of a non-traded REIT. Non-traded REITs typically do not provide an estimate of their value per share until 18 months after their offering closes. This may be years after you have made your investment. As a result, for a significant time period you may be unable to assess the value of your non-traded REIT investment and its volatility.

Distributions May Be Paid from Offering Proceeds and Borrowings: Investors may be attracted to non-traded REITs by their relatively high dividend yields compared to those of publicly traded REITs. Unlike publicly traded REITs, however, non-traded REITs frequently pay distributions in excess of their funds from operations. To do so, they may use offering proceeds and borrowings. This practice, which is typically not used by publicly traded REITs, reduces the value of the shares and the cash available to the company to purchase additional assets.

Conflicts of Interest: Non-traded REITs typically have an external manager instead of their own employees. This can lead to potential conflicts of interests with shareholders. For example, the REIT may pay the external manager significant fees based on the amount of property acquisitions and assets under management. These fee incentives may not necessarily align with the interests of shareholders.

How To Buy And Sell REITs

You can invest in a publicly traded REIT, which is listed on a major stock exchange, by purchasing shares through a broker. You can purchase shares of a non-traded REIT through a broker that participates in the non-traded REIT's offering. You can also purchase shares in a REIT mutual fund or REIT exchange-traded fund.

Understanding Fees And Taxes

Publicly traded REITs can be purchased through a broker. Generally, you can purchase the common stock, preferred stock, or debt security of a publicly traded REIT. Brokerage fees will apply.

Non-traded REITs are typically sold by a broker or financial adviser. Non-traded REITs generally have high up-front fees. Sales commissions and upfront offering fees usually total approximately 9 to 10 percent of the investment. These costs lower the value of the investment by a significant amount.

Special Tax Considerations

Most REITS pay out at least 100 percent of their taxable income to their shareholders. The shareholders of a REIT are responsible for paying taxes on the dividends and any capital gains they receive in connection with their investment in the REIT. Dividends paid by REITs generally are treated as ordinary income and are not entitled to the reduced tax rates on other types of corporate dividends. Consider consulting your tax adviser before investing in REITs.

Avoiding Fraud

Be wary of any person who attempts to sell REITs that are not registered with the SEC.

You can verify the registration of both publicly traded and non-traded REITs through the SEC's EDGAR system. You can also use EDGAR to review a REIT's annual and quarterly reports as well as any offering prospectus. For more on how to use EDGAR, please visit Research Public Companies.

You should also check out the broker or investment adviser who recommends purchasing a REIT.

CHAPTER 8
REFINANCE YOUR MORTGAGE

You made it through one of the toughest challenges: buying a home. Now, perhaps just a few years later, you're ready to refinance your mortgage. How hard can it be? You may be surprised to find that it's not a couple-of-emails-and-a-phone-call-or-two process. In fact, there may be more paperwork involved this time around than when you first bought your home.

Let's consider some important initial steps of a mortgage refinance — and then run through the rest of the process step by step.

Why you might want to refinance

Before you begin, it's important to consider why you want to refinance your home loan in the first place. That guides the mortgage refinance process from the very beginning.

Lowering your payment is usually the goal. And it's tempting to refinance with another full 30-year term to really knock down that monthly payment. But that means you'll end up taking even longer to pay off your house and paying more interest.

Choosing a suitable loan term for your mortgage refinance is a balancing act between an affordable monthly payment and reducing your borrowing costs.

You'll want to take into account how much interest you've already paid on your old loan and how much you'll pay with the refinance. Loans are front-loaded with interest, so the longer you've been paying, the more each payment is going toward paying off the principal balance — and the more interest you've already paid. Comparing what you've paid in interest so far and what you will pay on your current loan versus the refi will give you a solid idea of your total loan costs for either option.

By resisting the urge to extend your loan term, you can instead refinance to reduce the term and to get a lower interest rate, which could significantly reduce the amount of interest you pay over the life of the loan.

Choosing a suitable loan term for your mortgage refinance is a balancing act between an affordable monthly payment and reducing your borrowing costs.

Use a mortgage refinance calculator.

Once you know you have a good reason and you've determined it's the right time to refinance, it's time to work the numbers. Using a mortgage refinance calculator can help you shop for the best mortgage.

You'll need to know (or make some educated guesses about) your new interest rate and your new loan amount.

After you input the data, the tool will calculate your monthly savings, new payment, and lifetime savings, taking into account the estimated costs of your refinance.

Working with a refinance calculator will give you a good idea of what to expect. Even better, when you have a few estimates from mortgage lenders you can enter the terms they offer you into the calculator to help determine which one offers the best deal.

It's also key to shop for the best refinance rates.

Now it's time for a little legwork — or more likely web work and phone calls. You want to shop for your best mortgage refinance rate and get a loan estimate from each lender. Each potential lender is required to issue the estimate within three days of receiving your basic information.

The estimate is a pretty simple three-page document that details the loan terms, projected payments, estimated closing costs and other fees.

Compare the loan details from each lender and decide which one is best for you. This is a good time to really work that mortgage refinance calculator.

Refinancing your home loan, step by step.

Ready to tackle the whole refinance process? Go!

Determine your goal. We've covered this: Refinance for the right reason. Aim to shorten — or at least maintain — your current loan term while lowering your interest rate.

Learn your current credit score. Check your credit history and get your credit score. The better your score, the better the mortgage refinance interest rates you'll be offered.

Research your home's current value. Check your neighborhood for recent sales of homes like yours. Estimate your home value with NerdWallet's free home value tool.

Shop for your best mortgage rate. Start by comparing refinance rates online. You can shop rates online all you want, but limit the window for submitting loan applications, or allowing your credit report to be pulled, to a two-week period to lessen the impact on your credit score.

Know your all-in costs. A home loan refinance can trigger a bunch of fees: application fees, the cost of an appraisal, origination fees, a document processing fee, an underwriting fee, a credit report charge, title research and insurance, recording fees, tax transfer fees and points, to name several. But remember, you'll get a clear estimate of mortgage loan fees from each lender you consider. And don't jump blindly for a "no-cost refinance" pitch. This means the lender is moving the upfront fees to your ongoing costs for the loan, in the form of a higher interest rate — or a greater loan balance.

Gather paperwork. This can be a bit harder these days because so many of us do our financial business online. But you'll have to gather, print or download statements, pay stubs, and whatever else the lender will need during the loan process.

Lock your rate. You'll have to decide whether or not, and when, to lock in your mortgage refinance rate with the lender, so the rate you're offered for your new loan can't change during a specified period prior to closing. For the logically minded, it's a hand-wringer — more art than science.

Have cash on hand. There are likely to be property taxes and insurance, closing costs and other expenses to pay at closing, so be sure to set aside enough to cover them. Again, it's listed in your loan estimate, so there should be no surprises. In some cases, these costs can be added to the mortgage balance, which, on the one hand, limits your upfront costs but, on the other, increases what you owe on your home.

Final tips.

If you owe more than your home is worth, you may want to consider whether a government-sponsored mortgage program can be a part of your refinance solution. These programs come and go — and change names from time to time — but they generally allow homeowners to refinance their mortgage no matter how little equity they have in their home.

And for any refinance, be sure to consider how long it will take for you to recoup the fees and expenses.

But refinancing — for the right reason, with a good rate and a suitable term — can enhance your financial position.

CHAPTER 9
PAY OFF OR REDUCE DEBT

A re you swimming in debt and don't know how you're ever going to pay it off? You're not alone. In fact, the average U.S. household has nearly $17,000 in credit card debt, according to a 2016 NerdWallet analysis.

1. Create a budget. "The first step to solving your debt problem is to establish a budget," writes former U.S. News contributor David Bakke. You can use personal finance tools like Mint.com, or make your own Excel spreadsheet that includes your monthly income and expenses. Then scrutinize those budget categories to see where you can cut costs. "If you don't scale back your spending, you'll dig yourself into a deeper hole," Bakke warns.

2. Pay off the most expensive debt first. Sort your credit card interest rates from highest to lowest, then tackle the card with the highest rate first. "By paying off the balance with the highest interest first, you increase your payment on the credit card with the highest annual percentage rate while continuing to make the minimum payment on the rest of your

credit cards," writes former My Money contributor Hitha Herzog.

3. Pay more than the minimum balance. To make a dent in your debt, you need to pay more than the minimum balance on your credit card statements each month. "Paying the minimum – usually 2 to 3 percent of the outstanding balance – only prolongs a debt payoff strategy," Herzog writes. "Strengthen your commitment to pay everything off by making weekly, instead of monthly, payments." Or if your minimum payment is $100, try doubling it and paying off $200 or more.

4. Take advantage of balance transfers. If you have a high-interest card with a balance that you're confident you can pay off in a few months, Trent Hamm, founder of TheSimpleDollar.com, recommends moving the debt to a card that offers a zero-interest balance transfer. "You'll need to pay off the debt before the balance transfer expires, or else you're often hit with a much higher interest rate," he warns. "If you do it carefully, you can save hundreds on interest this way."

5. Halt your credit card spending. Want to stop accumulating debt? Remove all credit cards from your wallet, and leave them at home when you go shopping, advises WiseBread contributor Sabah Karimi. "Even if you earn cash back or other rewards with credit card purchases, stop spending with your

credit cards until you have your finances under control," she writes.

6. Put work bonuses toward debt. If you receive a job bonus around the holidays or during the year, allocate that money toward your debt payoff plan. "Avoid the temptation to spend that bonus on a vacation or other luxury purchase," Karimi writes. It's more important to fix your financial situation than own the latest designer bag.

7. Delete credit card information from online stores. If you do a lot of online shopping at one retailer, you may have stored your credit card information on the site to make the checkout process easier. But that also makes it easier to charge items you don't need. So clear that information. "If you're paying for a recurring service, use a debit card issued from a major credit card service linked to your checking account," Hamm writes.

8. Sell unwanted gifts and household items. Have any birthday gifts or old wedding presents collecting dust in your closet? Search through your home, and look for items you can sell on eBay or Craigslist. "Do some research to make sure you list these items at a fair and reasonable price," Karimi writes. "Take quality photos, and write an attention-grabbing headline and description to sell the item as quickly as possible." Any profits from sales should go toward your debt.

9. Change your habits. "Your daily habits and routines are the reason you got into this mess," Hamm writes. "Spend some time thinking about how you spend money each day, each week and each month." Do you really need your daily latte? Can you bring your lunch to work instead of buying it four times a week? Ask yourself: What can I change without sacrificing my lifestyle too much?

Reward yourself when you reach milestones. You won't pay down your debt any faster if you view it as a form of punishment. So reward yourself when you reach debt payoff goals. "The only way to completely pay off your credit card debt is to keep at it, and to do that, you must keep yourself motivated," Bakke writes. Just make sure to reward yourself within reason. For example, instead of a weeklong vacation, plan a weekend camping trip. "If you aim to reduce your credit card debt from $10,000 to $5,000 in two months," Bakke writes, "give yourself more than a pat on the back when you do it."

CHAPTER 10
INVEST IN A BUSINESS

Why invest in businesses?

Beyond the potential profits that may come from investing in a portfolio of businesses, investors can enjoy a few additional benefits of buying into businesses they believe in.

First, it's a chance to be a part of the next big thing – to be like the dragons on Dragon's Den and pick exciting businesses, follow their progress as they grow and get credit and recognition for having been one of the first people to spot them.

Second, you get to contribute to the culture of innovation by supporting entrepreneurs when they need it most and giving them a chance to get great new businesses off the ground.

Third, it's a way to get involved with innovation in an area you're interested in or are passionate about, and share in the success of the business.

And, it is the opportunity to support your friends and family on their exciting new business endeavour.

What are you investing in?

Investing in businesses (equity crowdfunding) is about picking early-stage and growth-focused businesses that you think have the potential to grow. You invest money in them in exchange for a portion of their equity, meaning that you buy shares in their business. If a business that you've invested in succeeds, the shares that you own will become worth more than what you paid for them, and you may be able to sell them at a profit or receive dividend payments in the future. However, if the business fails – as many businesses do – you will lose some or all of your investment.

What are the main risks of investing in businesses?

There are three broad types of risks when investing in early-stage and growth-focused businesses. The first is that the business will simply fail – or even that it will tick along without ever really succeeding – and you won't get any of your money back.

The second is that even if the business succeeds, your investment is likely to be illiquid. Even a successful investment will be locked in for a long time – often several years – while the business grows. This means that you are unlikely to be able to sell the shares, and you will likely not receive dividends, in the early years of your investment no matter how successful it later turns out to be.

Finally, there is the risk of dilution. If the business raises more capital later on (which most successful startups need to do), the percentage of equity that you hold in it will decrease relative to what you originally had. Dilution in itself is not always a bad thing, and this blog post explains why it is often to be welcomed, but it is something of which you should be aware.

Read our Risk Warning for additional information about the risks associated with investing in early-stage and growth-focused businesses.

The importance of diversification

The key to investing in early-stage and growth-focused businesses successfully – and mitigating the risks described above – is diversification. Most businesses fail, but the few that do succeed can do so to such a degree that they more than make up for losses. This means that in order to achieve strong returns, you need to have invested in a few of the big winners. Your chances of doing so are much greater if you build a diversified portfolio by investing small amounts in many businesses rather than large amounts in just a few. And when we say many, we mean many. We believe that an effective portfolio should include at least 50 early-stage and growth-focused businesses and potentially 100 or more (there is even data out there to suggest that investing in as many as 800 companies may greatly increase your performance).

One of the main reasons we developed Seedrs was to make it easy to create a diversified portfolio of investments you choose. By setting the investment minimum very low, we make it possible to invest in many businesses – no matter how much money you are prepared to invest.

Earning returns

The main way you can make money from your investments is by selling your shares in the businesses for more than you paid for them. There is no active secondary market for shares in private businesses, meaning that you won't be able to sell them immediately. However, if the company grows to the point where it floats on a stock exchange, is bought by another company or conducts a share buyback, you are likely to be able to sell your shares – often at a significant profit – at that stage.

Alternatively, some businesses may begin paying dividends. This can occur if the business has achieved profitability but does not expect to continue growing significantly; it can also happen in cases such as theatre productions or films, where the company has a limited duration and distributes any profits at the end.

CHAPTER 11
SELL AN EBOOK ONLINE

Do you like the idea of selling ebooks online? Many people do, and it's the ideal lifestyle for a business online. Just imagine... no inventory to store, unlimited supply, instant downloading (no shipping anything off), and high profit margins. With all of these benefits, it's no wonder why people are jumping on the ebook train to make money online.

But you should know that selling ebooks online isn't a cake walk. You have to invest in advertising, do a lot of free advertising, and be willing to invest hours into marketing your ebook around the web. Now obviously if you have a large advertising budget, you can pretty much let your website run itself.

With paid advertising, you can get tons of qualified hits to your website, and hopefully get them to buy from you. But after you get the traffic to your site, it's your job to convert them into customers. There are many ways to do this, and depending on your price, you will want to test different approaches.

To create an ebook, it's very easy. You can write up a 50-page book in Microsoft Word, convert it into

"PDF" format online (pdfonline), price it at around $7 to $19, and upload it to your website for sale. Now you will have to create a sales description page to promote your product, and this takes a bit of copywriting skills. But it's nothing you should be worried about. As long as you have a "swipe file", you're good to go.

Selling ebooks online can be a big money-maker. You can earn money on the frontend, and earn tons of cash on the backend sales that you get from your existing and recurring customers. This is where 80% of your total business profits will come from. So backend marketing is a big reason why you should sell ebooks of your own.

If you sell affiliate products from a site like Clickbank, you can earn money on the frontend, but if you don't get the customer name, how will you get sales from the customer on the backend? The only way around this (to my knowledge) is to sign up to one of those web hosting affiliate programs (for example), and earn money month after month - for the duration that the customer is enrolled in the web hosting services.

Affiliate marketing and selling affiliate products is a different story, but let me continue on with selling ebooks and digital products of your own. It's a great lifestyle. You can be out on the beach all while you make money online. You could be sleeping all while you make money with your product. You could take a vacation and just sit back and watch how your sales and profits increase automatically without your intervention.

It's an amazing business to enter into, but you will have to know a bit about internet marketing to make it successful. The phrase "Build it and they will come" is non-negotiable online. You have to drive people to your site everyday, and be proactive with your approach.

Take these tips and use them to earn money with selling your own ebook today. It's incredibly easy, and once you learn the ropes, you'll b earning money with your ebook in no time at all.

So, you have successfully created ebooks that contain compelling and useful content. The next thing that you need to do to convert your creations to dollars is to sell them online. Here's how you can do that:

1. Pay per Click advertising. Create ads around keywords where your eBook content was based on. Make your ads easy to understand, powerful, and enticing. Use words that target human emotions and those terms that can evoke action. Bid higher compare to your competitors so your ads will show on top of the search page results each time your targeted keywords are used by online users. You will be billed by the search engines each time your ads are clicked. Charge will be based on your bid.

2. Article marketing. This is by far the best methods to use when selling your ebooks. Obviously, your potential clients would like to know if you have what it takes to offer them the kind of information that they are looking for. There is no better way to do that than sharing a slice of your expertise through your articles.

3. Affiliate marketing. Contact affiliate marketers to help you sell your ebooks online. As these people are equipped with the most effective and newest marketing tools, you can be assured that they can help you boost your sales by up to a hundredfold. You will share with them a fraction of your revenue each time they make a sale.

4. Forum posting. Connect with your target market by building an ongoing communication with them on forums. Offer answers to their questions and help them solve their pressing issues. Once you have earned their trust, you can go ahead and pitch in your ebooks.

By the way, would you like to get the newbie-friendly insider's secrets to building a stable, thriving business online... year after year.

CHAPTER 12
CREATE A COURSE ON UDEMY

Step 1: Plan Your Course

- Planning your course is the first step on your course creation journey and it's very important to provide yourself with a solid foundation for building the rest of your course.

- Decide what you want to teach. You probably have an idea of what you want to teach, and now it's time to get really specific.

- Identify what you want your users to learn from your course. Determining this now will go a long way in helping you create a great course structure.

- Scope the content of your course to ensure that there is enough content for users to engage with and achieve their objectives. This is also where you think through how you want to organize your content. Be sure to conclude each section with either a quiz or a summary to sum up what users have learned.

- Break down your course into smaller, bite-sized lectures and describe what they each need to accomplish. This step is to help you get more detailed about your content, and break it down into individual sections and lectures. Write a lecture description for each lecture, summarizing what users will learn.

Step 2: Produce Your Course

This is the most important part of your course creation process.

- As you're creating your lectures, consider different types of learners. Video lectures should alternate between the different lecture types and also between presentation styles such as "talking head", slides, screencasts and drawing boards. Upload your promotional video so that users can preview your course.

- Include practice activities throughout the course to keep learners engaged--at least one per section. These can take many different forms depending on the content, but may include quizzes, case studies or projects.

- Use the bulk uploader to upload your videos into your course. You can also use the uploader to upload any other resources you're including (supplemental resources, PDF, audio, or presentation lectures). Once your videos are uploaded, go through your outline and associate the videos with the correct lecture.

Step 3: Polish Your Course

This step involves making your course ready for publishing.

- Craft a compelling course summary
- Take another look at your course title, and add in a subtitle.
- Create a course image that meets our guidelines.

Step 4: Publish Your Course

- Admins: You are ready to publish your course!
- Non-admins: you will need to submit the course for review and an admin will need to approve it for publishing.

CHAPTER 13
CREATE AN APP

Like so many before you, you have a great app idea burring in your brain, and you have no idea how to bring it and all of its profit potential to fruition. And like those who have paved the way for app entrepreneurs, you need to learn the ropes. While some will advise you to hire a developer and invest a fortune in your idea, realists will tell you the risk is too big. There are tons of app building programs out there that can help you make your vision a reality, but the simple truth is with some planning and methodical work on your part, the process is fairly simple.

We've come up with a three-part guide that will walk you through the steps of profiting from your big idea. Let's start at the very beginning of how to create an app...

- Set a Goal.

Step away from any form of technology and get out a pen and paper and define what it is you want to accomplish. The starting line in the app development word is a pen and paper, not complex coding and designing. Ask and answer the following questions:

What exactly do you want your app to do?
How are you going to make it appeal to users?
What problem is it going to solve?
How will it simplify life for people?
How will you market your app?

You will not survive in any business if you don't have well defined, clearly set goals! A lack of vision will frustrate you and anyone who you employ to work for you. Before you do anything, create a clear picture of what you want done!

- Sketch your Ideas.

No! You still cannot turn on your computer. Now you need to use the pen and paper that has the answers to the questions about your apps purpose to develop a sketch of what it will look like. Here you move your clearly worded ideas into visual representations of your thoughts. Decide if you are going to give your app away and offer ads to generate money, or are you going to offer it as a paid download. You can also choose the option to offer in app purchases. If that is something you are going to do, make sure you sketch out those ideas as well.

- Research, research, and then research some more.

Now you can turn your computer on, but not to start blindly designing your app. The leg work is nowhere near done. You have to dig deep and research the competition of your app idea. I know you think you have one of a kind idea, but the numbers are not in your favor—odds are someone has already tried it. You can look at this in two different ways. One you can become deflated and give up, or two, you can examine the competition and make your app better. I prefer the latter. Read the competition's reviews. What did people like/dislike about the app? Then, use that information to your advantage. Refer back to your pen and paper from steps one and two, and modify and adjust your idea accordingly.

After reading and modifying, your research needs to shift focus a bit. It's time to harness the power of the Internet. Is your app a truly feasible idea? Here's where you will examine copyright restrictions and possible technical holds ups. This step is crucial because it will save you money in the long run. You can't move forward and spend time on an idea that won't work. Figure out any glitches, and find ways around them, (notice I didn't say give up—"an ounce of prevention..") so you don't have to back track.

Next, shift your research focus to sales and marketing. Reflect back to your sketch about how you are going to make money with your app. Are you going to stick with your original idea, or are you going to change it? What is your niche? Are you marketing to teens, parents, children, teachers, travelers, gamers? Determine that target audience right away. It will help you narrow down design ideas.

After you've exhausted your foresight skills, you can begin the fun stuff. Start to look for design ideas. 99design is a great showcase for examining new and innovative design ideas. Browse through and see what fits your fancy. Keep your target audience in mind when examining designs. A visual appeal is crucial to your final product.

- Wireframe

In the technology world, a wireframe is a glorified story board. Here is where you take your sketch and your design idea, and you give your idea a little more clarity and functionality. This will become the foundation for your apps development, so it really is a crucial step. There are stacks of wireframing websites that you can use to help you bring your sketches to digital life with functionality like click through and icons. The trick is finding one that you like and that is easy for you to use.

- Start Defining the Back End of Your App

We left off with your wireframe, so at this point in your app development, you have a storyboard of how you want your app to function. Now it's time to use that storyboard to start examine functionality.

Using your wireframe, you need to delineate your servers, APIs, and data diagrams. There are some great do-it-yourself app builders that can provide you with the tools to easily do this. Some of them even do if for you. If you are unclear of what this technical jargon means, you should probably use a service that provides hosting and a means of collecting data about your app usage.

Regardless of what method you choose to use to develop your app, it is imperative that clear diagrams are created as they will serve as the directions for everyone working on your project. Should you run across any technical difficulties, you should revise your wireframe to reflect any changes.

- Check Your Model

Here's where you need to call in the troops. Show your demo to friends, family, and anyone else who is willing to give you constructive criticism. Don't waste your time with people who will tell you, "Wow, that's neat." Seek out those cynics and critics. Brutal honesty is crucial at this phase.

Don't be afraid to look over their shoulder as they are checking out your demo to watch how they navigate things. If you need to revise any of the layouts or navigation paths, do so. Keep your users in mind, and try to follow their thinking, not your own.

Your end goal with this step is to finalize your apps structure and foundation. You need to have the brains of your app working before you start adding design to avoid frustration later in the process.

- Get Building

With the foundation in place, you can start to put the puzzle together to building your app. First, your developer will set up your servers, databases, and APIs. If you are using a quality do-it-yourself app builder, this will be done for you. Do not forget to reflect on the feedback you got from your testers. Modify the apps functionality to reflect any changes you made based on your first phase of testing.

At this point, it's time to sign up for the stores. You need to create an account with Google Play and Apple so that you can get your app on the market. It may take a few days to go through the process, so don't procrastinate this step.

- Design the Look

Now its time to employ the designers to create your UI, user interface. The user interface is a very important part of your app because people are attracted to how things look and how easy they are to navigate. Through the design process, you need to keep the feedback you got from your testers in mind, and you need to make sure the design and the navigation reflect the feedback you got. How to design your app?

If you've hired a graphic designer for your app, you will need to get high resolution skins, or visually appealing screens based on your wireframe, for your app.

If you are using a WYSIWYG editor, you need to pick your template and layout for your screens yourself. I'll stress again, keep that testing feedback in mind when developing the look of your app. You are building for users, not for you!

- Test Your App, AGAIN.

A second round of testing is imperative. In this round, you will have both a functioning app as well as a user interface to test. All the screens of your app should properly work at this point, and your app should be visually appealing as well.

You need to run a battery of tests on your app in its completed form to assure that both the look and the feel of the app meet your expectations. Proto.io and Pixate are great platforms for testing your app. Both of these programs will allow you to add clickable links to navigate your app. They will help you examine the final layers, interactions, and design of your app as well. You can use the information you get from this testing phase to help you move forward.

You may be scratching your head and asking, "Didn't I do this with my wireframe?" The answer is, "Well, kind of." While this may seem similar to your wireframe, it's a lot more detailed. Your wireframe was just the skeleton of your app. At this point, your app should be both aesthetically pleasing as well as functioning.

- Modify and Adjust

You've taken your prototype for a spin, and you've learned that there are still a few tweaks you need to make. Now that you've seen your app in it's fully functioning form, you need to call the troops back and ask they to do the same.

Ask the same people who viewed your app in it's development phase to examine it in it's testing phase as well. Again, open yourself up to constructive criticism, and use the feedback accordingly. Lastly, ask your developer and your designer to make any changes that you feel would be valuable to your app.

- Beta Testing

You've looked at your app through several different lenses, and you think you've managed to develop a smoothly functioning, aesthetically pleasing, problem solving app. Now, you need to examine how your app is going to function in a live environment.

Android makes this process simple, while iOS likes to keep things in a controlled environment. There's pros and cons to both approaches, but the bottom line is you need to jump through one last hoop. You can simply upload your app file on any android device and test it in a live environment. From here on out in your Android app development process, you can monitor your apps progress from your device.

iOS requires you use a platform called TestFlight to beta test your app. Apple is pretty thorough with its directions and instructions for using its beta test platform. A great feature to this beta testing option is that you can invite testers to review your app before taking it live. It's yet another user lens through which you can view your app.

- Release Your App

You've made it to the finish line. You've brought your idea to fruition, and the last step is to share it with the world. Hopefully, you've gone on to solve a major problem. If not, with any luck your app has some features that can simplify or bring enjoyment to someone's life. Regardless, you've accomplished something big. Now it's time to distribute it!

Android and iOS, again are very different with regard to marketing apps. If you stick with this business, you will see a pattern emerge—Android is a little less strict. Again, there are pros and cons to both approaches, but as an app entrepreneur, you will need to learn the rules for both.

You can simply add your app to the android store. It will not be reviewed right away. You will instantly be selling your app in the Google Play store. iOS, on the other hand, will review your app before it can go live. While there is no set time frame for the Apple team to review your app and push it on the shelves, you can guestimate about a week of waiting.

APP STORE

If you are anxious about getting your app onto the devices of users, you can also publish it in Pre-Apps. This is a great opportunity to have your app viewed by people who like to have a first look at new ideas. Keep in mind, these people are always reviewing up and coming ideas, so their feedback could be great for you. They are familiar with #trendingapps, so I'd advise taking this extra step—if for nothing more than to learn more about the app world.

CHAPTER 14
AFFILIATE MARKETING

The lure of affiliate marketing is undeniable; who can resist passive income?

But to make that passive income happen, you have got to put in some work first.

To succeed in affiliate marketing, there are a number of crucial steps you must take before you earn that first affiliate profits. And these steps are, well ... not passive.

The good news is that if you're determined to make this work and are willing to put in the time and effort, you're already well on your way to affiliate marketing success.

All the work you put in is to help you make your first affiliate marketing sale. There is nothing like a first sale to motivate you and make you keep at it.

So, what do you need to do to get started?

Steps to Earning Your First Affiliate Commission

We've broken down the process into seven steps for affiliate marketing beginners. Following this guide will set you on the right course and have you earning your first commission in no time.

1. Choose a Niche

Before you even begin building your first site, you'll need to decide which niche you're going to target.

Obviously, if you don't know what your site is about or who you're going to target with it, you can't really build a site around it...can you?

If you've already figured this one out, way to go! This is undoubtedly one of the most difficult and overwhelming steps.

If you don't quite know what your niche is yet, here's some advice that you might find useful.

Some key questions to ask yourself when determining your niche are:

What topics am I already passionate about?

It's much easier to work on something if you're passionate about it. Plus, when you have a passion, you're usually quite knowledgeable about it too, so that definitely helps. For example if you have a passion about about makeup, your niche of choice might be makeup related, too.

Is there money in this niche?

While following your passion is definitely the recommended option, sometimes the possibility of making money in a profitable niche trumps passion. So, you might not necessarily know much about your niche, but if it's likely to make you money, you can always learn more about it, right?

For example, KitchenFaucetDivas is clearly a site that was built for profit, not passion. Unless of course there is someone out there with a serious passion for kitchen faucets! ;-)

What topic could I see myself easily writing 25, 50, or 100 blog posts about?

The topic you choose must have enough depth that you can create a lot of content for it. This is important for building an authoritative site, for search engine optimization, and most importantly, for the end user. If you don't have enough content about a topic, you're not going to be taken very seriously as an authority on the topic and it's unlikely you can convince someone to make a purchase from you.

MoneySavingExpert is a great example of a site with a topic for which you would have a never ending supply of content ideas.

Is there room in this niche for another affiliate marketer?

There are several profitable niches that are also very popular among affiliate markets (e.g., weight loss). Before jumping on board with a hugely popular niche, make sure there's enough room for you. That is — will you be able to make money and compete with already established marketers? If not, keep looking.

Is there enough interest in/demand for products in this niche?

The niche you choose might draw enough interest from your audience when it comes to reading and acquiring knowledge, but are they willing to buy relevant products too? Without consumer interest in products, your niche isn't going to make you much money.

Are there affiliate programs available in this niche?

This is obviously a crucial factor to consider. You might come up with an idea for a niche you know a lot about, but are there affiliate programs for the niche? No affiliate program = no sales. Time to look for a different niche.

2. Research Affiliate Programs

Once you've decided on a niche, it's time to find out what's out there in terms of programs and products to promote. You've probably already done a bit of research for this while researching your niche — now you need to dig deeper.

Choosing an affiliate program will take some work, but don't be afraid to invest a significant amount of time into it because this is, of course, where your income will come from. Choosing the right program will make it well worth your while!

When choosing an affiliate program, keep these key points in mind:

What type of merchants use the program/ affiliate network?

You want to make sure other similar sellers are also using the network, as this can help you gauge your likelihood of success with the particular program.

How much commission are you likely to make from the products?

Make sure you sign up for programs that are profitable and generate a sufficient return in on investment. Some tips:

If using ClickBank, products should have over a 50% commission (preferably 60%), and have a high gravity rating (meaning they're in demand).

For CPA (cost-per-action) programs, commissions should be over $1, and products shouldn't be overly restrictive in how you can promote them.

For physical products, look for commissions over $40.

Do you want to be associated with the products and services?

The products and services you will be promoting to your audience must be relevant and good quality. Make sure you believe in them and know everything about them, because this will be crucial to you delivering the sales pitch to your audience. You need to build trust with your audience so make sure the products and services you choose to promote are trustworthy enough.

Ads like the one below often lead to sketchy products — do you want to be associated with a product that promises results that may or may not be true?

What kind of support does the program provide?

Be sure to check what kind of customer support you can expect from your affiliate program once you have signed up. Do your research online and if possible, speak to other sellers using the program to get their thoughts. Can you speak to someone via phone or Skype or do you have to wait 72 hours for email responses? Be clear on this because trust me, you will need support at one point or another.

3. Build a Site

Steps 1 and 2 are all about research and figuring out what's possible and profitable. Now, it's time to start putting your research into action.

Assuming you don't already have a website built, this will be the next step. Fortunately, building a site isn't as complicated or labor-intensive as it was in the past.

If you're a newbie to building sites, the easiest way to set up a site is by using WordPress. The WordPress CMS is very easy to use and while coding skills can come in handy, for the most part you will not require any tech knowledge to set up your site.

You need to follow a few steps to have your site up and running:

- Buy a domain.

Your domain is the address for your website (e.g., www.affilorama.com) so this is the first thing you will need to do when setting up your site. Considering there are millions of websites on the internet, it's possible that the domain name you want may already be taken by someone else. So make sure you have several options in mind. Be sure to read our advice on how to choose a good domain name.

- Purchase and set up hosting.

If your domain is your address, hosting is like the actual house within which your site will live. It's your own little slice of the internet — the place where all your website files live. Hosting is very affordable these days, so don't unnecessarily scrimp on costs. Go with a reputable, reliable provider because your affiliate marketing business depends on it.

- Install WordPress.

Once your hosting is set up, you need to install a content management system (CMS) for your site. We recommend WordPress because it is easy to use and a beginner (like you!) can quite quickly figure out how it works. Most good hosting providers will have a one-click install option for WordPress, which means it will only take you a couple of minutes and you will have WordPress installed on your site.

- Install your theme.

A WordPress theme provides all the styling of a site that you (and your audience) see on the front end. There are thousands of themes available, so choosing one might seem daunting at start. Our advice: go with something simple and easy to customize. You can always change it later.

The AffiloTheme is a great option. Completely customizable, and built specifically for affiliate marketers, you can use this WordPress theme to bypass much of the initial learning curve other affiliate marketers will experience. You can also search for themes on a site like Theme Forest.

Create content.

Finally, once your site is ready, it's time to create content for it. The content you create must be relevant to your niche but also interesting and engaging enough to keep your audience coming back. You should also ensure the site content is search engine-friendly. More details about content creation in Step 4.

4. Produce Excellent Content

Now that your site is set up and you've joined an affiliate program, you're ready to begin perhaps the most time-consuming (but potentially rewarding) part of the affiliate business: Producing content.

This is where the overused but truer-than-ever phrase "content is king" comes into play.

Your goal for your site will be to establish it as an authority site in your niche, and the main way to do this is to consistently produce unique, high-quality content.

This could consist of:

- Product reviews.

Your affiliate site model could be based off writing reviews about different products or services. This is a common model and if done well, can prove very useful in generating affiliate income.

For example, The Wire Cutter is focused on writing reviews of several different kinds of products and helping their readers make the best decision about the product they want to buy. After reading a review on their site, if the user clicks through to the product/service using the affiliate link, The Wire Cutter will earn a commission from.

Blog posts that address common problems, questions or issues relevant to your target market.

Creating blog content is a very useful and effective way of consistently building content on a site. When creating blog posts, it's a good idea to do some keyword research to figure out what it is that your audience is interested in and searching for online. Also, be sure to research competitors, forums and social media to narrow down on topics for your blog.

For example, Security Guard Training HQ has a very extensive blog on a variety of topics relevant for anyone interested in security guard training, jobs and more.

- Evergreen content.

If you are building a site that has the potential for information that will never age and remain useful for your audience, you have the opportunity to create what is known as evergreen content. It's important to carry out extensive keyword research before planning any evergreen content for a site like this, as your site could hugely benefit from the proper usage of keywords within such content.

For example, the content on Super Weddings is useful whether you're organizing a wedding today or next year. All the content on the site is created accordingly. To make things easier for the audience, it is separated into categories to make it very convenient for the reader to find what they're looking for. This, of course, is also very good for SEO.

- Informational products.

Giving away a free informational product such as an e-book, an email series or a mini-course is a popular tactic many affiliate marketers use. Usually, your readers will have to provide their email addresses to receive the product from you. You can then use this to sell to them via email marketing. Additionally, an informational product can generate interest in the actual product you're trying to sell. If your product is popular enough and brings enough traffic to your site, you could also monetize the traffic in other ways, such as AdSense.

A good example is DatingMetrics, where you're tempted with a Free Texting Crash Course in exchange for your email. The real marketing will begin once the user has downloaded this course.

The type of content you create for your website will largely depend on your niche, as certain types of content perform better in some niches than others.

Remember: Purchasing generic content is NOT an effective method to build your site. While it may be tempting to populate your site this way, in the long run it won't help you to position yourself as an expert in your niche (and ultimately means less traffic and fewer sales).

5. Build an Audience

Building an audience for your site will, in some ways, follow naturally once you start producing excellent content. An interested audience will not only bring you consistent traffic, but also result in consistent sales for you.

So how do you start building an audience for a completely new site? Here are some ideas:

- Promote your content via social media.

The easiest and most common way to start building an audience for a website is via social media. Depending on your niche and industry, you can choose from Facebook, Twitter, Instagram, Pinterest and several other niche and location-specific networks. Building up an engaged and interested following on social media is a great opportunity to build relationships and once you have their trust, promote your products and services to them.

I'll use MoneySavingExpert.com as an example again. The site has over 154,000 likes on its Facebook page and it connects with the audience by sharing links to content but also asking money-saving/budgeting related questions. The highly engaged readers then visit the website, where they read content and no doubt make purchases.

- Guest post on high-traffic blogs.

While your site is still new, it's a good idea to start capitalizing on someone else's audience. Continue focusing on building your own content, but also considering writing content for a few big, high-traffic blogs that are relevant for your niche. By writing content for a bigger site, you are able to get in front of another audience and showcase your expertise on a particular topic. This will eventually lead to more traffic to your site, as well.

- Build an email list.

Let no one tell you that email marketing is dead. An email list is crucial for every affiliate marketer. You can start building up your email list with a lead magnet (like the information products mentioned previously) or even just by encouraging your audience to sign up for your updates. You can then push your content to this audience via email and also direct them to your affiliate offers. Don't be sleazy about the sales, but if you build up enough trust with your email audience; when the time comes, they will not mind purchasing a product from you.

- Use basic SEO techniques to increase search engine traffic to your site.

Organic search remains an important source of traffic for any website, so it's important that you optimize your website for search engines as well. When creating your content, you must always do so keeping the reader in mind first, but don't forget to follow a few basic SEO principles as well.

Learn SEO yourself or hire a good SEO marketer to help you maximize on-page and off-page SEO opportunities for your site. If your site starts to appear in search results for terms relevant to your niche, it will be a huge boost towards building your audience (and your sales)!

- Invest in paid advertising.

Many affiliate marketers use paid advertising to generate additional traffic to their site and drive more sales. Paid advertising on social media is often a good place to start, as these networks tend to be more affordable.You may also want to consider taking out inexpensive banner ads on small niche sites. Depending on your niche, Google AdWords could also be a good option to drive some paid traffic to your site.

6. Promote Affiliate Offers

Finally, the part we've all been waiting for!

This, my friends, is where things really kick into high gear. Many fly-by-night affiliates will jump right to this step and bypass steps 1–5 completely. And this is what will set you apart.

Once you've shown that you can offer something of value in your niche, it's time to continue adding value by promoting products that will be useful and helpful for your audience.

You can promote your offers in a number of ways. It will depend on the type of site you've built and also what you're selling. Some ideas include:

- Product reviews.

Write honest, real reviews about products. Build up trust with your audience, and remember that they rely on your opinion. Don't just point out all the positives of a product and gloss over the negatives. An honest opinion will be valued. Add compelling images and make mention of useful features, specifications and other details.

Your product review can then link to the page (with your affiliate ID attached), where your audience can make a purchase if they're interested. If do, hooray! You've made your first sale.

- Banner ads.

You can put up banners on your site, to promote your affiliate offers. Most affiliate programs will usually provide their own creatives when you sign up for their offers. All you have to do is insert the banner on a highly trafficked page (your affiliate tracking is usually embedded within the code). Banner ads in the right locations can do a great job of driving sales.

Below are some examples of banners that Templatic provides to its affiliates.

In-text content links.

This is a very common way to promote offers. For example, you will often see a blog post with links to certain products or services. If the reader clicks through and makes a purchase, the blog owner will make a commission. These in-text links blend in with other content on your site and are a great way of promoting an offer within your content, without being over-the-top salesy with banners.

- Email promotions.

If you have built up an email list, you could also promote your affiliate offers via email promotions. Just make sure you build up a relationship with your audience first instead of going for the hard sell straightaway. The emails you send out must contain your affiliate links to products so when your audience click through. the sale is attributed to you.

- Discounts and giveaways.

Many affiliate programs will often run promotions with good discounts or giveaways that might be attractive to your audience. For example, if you're an Amazon Associate and the site have a big Holiday Sale, it would be the perfect opportunity for you to promote discounts to your website visitors. This is a great way to promote your offers while also providing good value to your audience.

When promoting affiliate offers, just make sure you are fully aware of all the terms and conditions attached to your affiliate program. Some programs can be strict about how they allow you to promote their products. For example, some may limit you to banner ads and links only, while others will allow you to use paid advertising, but won't allow email marketing.

Also, make sure you have a disclaimer on your website that advises your audience that you may have links that promote affiliate offers. This is necessary for several affiliate programs and also a basic courtesy to your website visitors. In the U.S., the FTC mandates disclosure for affiliate marketers (and anyone issuing endorsements), as well.

7. Rinse, Lather, and Repeat

Now that you're done with Steps 1 - 6, Step 7 is simply to keep doing what you're doing. Yes, seriously!

Your ongoing work as an affiliate marketer will be to repeat steps 4 - 6 on a continual basis. Building a site up to a point where it can make you consistent income takes a bit of work and you must be willing to constantly create, promote, market, innovate and of course, sell.

CHAPTER 15
NETWORK MARKETING

Many people are scared away from network marketing, also known as multi-level marketing (MLM), because of all the myths and misunderstanding about this type of business. Part of negativity comes from reported low MLM success rates. However, a multi-level marketing business isn't destined to fail any more than any other business. Regardless of the home business you start, success comes from doing the work to build it.

For some reason, many people don't view their MLM business as a business, like they would if they opened a franchise or started a business from scratch. One of the most important things you can do to insure your success is to treat your MLM venture as the business it is. Here are a few other tips to help you improve your multi-level marketing (MLM) and recruiting efforts within the world of direct selling:

1) Brush Up on the Realities of MLMs

To stay safe from pyramid schemes and MLM scams, arm yourself with knowledge. Learn about the direct sales industry as a whole, research MLM companies carefully, and determine if you're a good match with your sponsor. The truth is, while you can get rich in MLM, statistics show that less than one out of 100 MLM representatives actually achieve MLM success or make any money. However, that's not necessarily the MLM business' fault. Most athletes never make it to the Olympics, but that's not sport's or the Olympics' fault.

Any great feat requires knowledge and action.

2) Find a Company With A Product You Love

Too many people get caught up in the hype of potential big income from MLM, that they don't pay enough attention to what the company is asking you to sell. You can't sell something or share your business if you don't genuinely have pride in what you are representing. Do your MLM research and partner with a company that has a product you can get excited about. Don't forget to look into the company's compensation plan before you join and make sure it is favorable to you.

3) Be Genuine and Ethical

One reason that direct selling gets a bad rap is that many representatives use hype and sometimes deception to lure in new recruits. This leads many to believe that the MLM companies themselves encourage this behavior, when in truth, they don't.

Legitimate MLM companies want you to be honest in your dealings with customers and potential recruits. If you love your product, your enthusiasm is enough to promote it. Just make sure you're not over-the-top or making exaggerated or false claims.

Good business conduct will ensure that your customers and recruits don't feel duped, and as a result, will stick with you.

4) Don't Barrage Your Friends and Family

Nothing will annoy your family and cost you friends more than constantly pestering them about your business. There's nothing wrong with letting them know what you're doing and seeing if they have an interest, but if the answer is "no," let it go.

Many companies suggest making a list of 100 people you know, and while that's not wrong, you should consider that most successful MLMers have very few people from their original list of 100 people in their business. In most cases, friends and family who are in the business often come AFTER seeing the MLMer's success. Success in MLM comes from treating it like any other business in which you focus on the people who want what you have to offer. That means deciding who the target market is for your products/services, as well as the business opportunity.

5) Identify Your Target Market

One of the biggest mistakes new MLMers make is looking at everyone (including friends and family #4) as a potential customer or recruit. This is one area where the MLM industry gets it wrong. Like any other business, you're going to have greater success and efficiency if you identify your target market and focus your marketing efforts at them.

Someone who doesn't care about vitamins or health and wellness isn't a good person to pester about your business.

6) Make an Effort to Share Your Product//Business Plan Everyday

Many MLM sponsors will have you focus on recruiting new business builders; however, your income, in legitimate MLM, comes from the sales of products or services (whether through you or your recruits). Further, customers who love the products or services can more easily be converted into new business builders.

Just like any other business (home-based or otherwise), getting the word out about your product or service can benefit your target market is the key to generating new customers and recruits. Some ideas include sharing a product sample, inviting a neighbor to host a product party, or starting a website or social media account.

7) Sponsor, Don't Recruit

One of the benefits of MLM is the ability to bring in new business builders and profit from the sales they make in their business. While some see this as "using" others, the reality is that you're being rewarded for helping others succeed. But for them to succeed, you need to see your role not as racking up as many recruits as possible, but in being a leader and trainer. The focus then is on the success of those you help in the business, not on you.

That means you need to take time to train them, answer questions, celebrate their successes, and be a support when things are tough.

8) Set a Goal for Parties or Presentations

MLM is a person-to-person to business. While many people don't like that aspect, especially in the digital age, the reality is that it's the personal touch that sells the products and business, and retains customers and business builders.

Based on your compensation plan and goals, determine how many people you need to show your products or business to reach your goals in the time you want. Doing so will ensure you grow your business rather than just sustain it.

7) Listen and Sell the Solution

Many companies provide scripts to help you sell the product or service. While these can be helpful in teaching you about your product and dealing with objections, sales is all about being a solution to what a customer needs. By qualifying your contact first, and then listening to their needs, you can tailor your pitch so that you're the solution to their problem.

8) Learn How to Market

MLMers often stick to the three-foot rule (everyone within 3-feet of you is a prospect) and other traditional marketing tactics. But direct sales is like any other business. It can and should be marketed in a variety of ways that takes into consideration your target market, what it needs, how you can help it, and where it can be found. To that end, you can use a variety of marketing tools including a website (check your companies policies about websites), email, and social media to increase product sales and interest in your business.

9) Stand Out from Other Distributors

One of the challenges of MLM is convincing prospects to buy or join with you as opposed to the other reps that live in the neighborhood or they know online. You're selling the same stuff as thousands of others, meaning consumers have a choice. You need to do something that makes you unique compared to everyone else. Give people a reason to choose you over other reps. Some options include more personalized service, starting your own rewards program, or something that offers greater value.

10) Develop a System for Following Up

While you don't want to pester and annoy people, in many cases, with good follow up, you can make the sale or recruit at a future time. Sales is often about timing, and 'no' in sales doesn't always mean 'never.'

If someone tells you no, but there was something in the dialogue that suggested they might be interested in the future, ask if you can put them on your mailing or email list, or if you can call in six months to follow up. Many will give you their email or phone number just because they want to be nice. Even so, use your calendar or contact system to remind you when to call.

CHAPTER 16
DESIGN T-SHIRTS

Designing your own t-shirt can be a fun, creative activity, and may even bring you some money if you decide to sell your designs. Whether you intend to print the shirt yourself or send it off to a professional printer, you can still come up with the design for your shirt right at home.

Part 1 Planning Your Design

1.Think about what your design is going to represent. Maybe you are advertising your cleaning company, your rock band, or your favorite sports team. Maybe you're using a personal illustration. The purpose of the design will determine the design.

If you are advertising a company, band, sporting team, or brand, you will likely need to focus on logo. The Nike swoosh logo, for example, is a very simple but effective design. A design for a sporting team might feature the team colors or the team's mascot. A design for your band might focus on an image of the band or a graphic that represents the band's style or sound.

If you are making a t-shirt to showcase a personal illustration or drawing, you will need to focus on how it will look on a t-shirt. Think about how original the illustration is and how the colors are working in the illustration.

Consider using a photo in your design. Use your own photo. You may use a picture made by someone else, but only if you have acquired the legal rights to use that image. You can also buy a stock image.

2.Pick a color scheme. When designing a t-shirt, its important to think about color contrast. This means how certain ink colors in the design will appear against a lighter colored shirt or a darker colored shirt. Certain ink colors look more vibrant on a lighter or darker shirt on the computer screen than they actually do when printed.

17. When using lighter shirts, avoid pastel colors like yellow, light blue, or light pink. These colors will be visible on the shirts but may not be legible at a distance. And if you are designing a shirt with a logo, you want to make sure that logo is legible from far away!

18. If you decide to use pastel colors, add an outline of a darker color to the lighter color to highlight the text and make it easier to read.

19. Darker colored shirts look good with lighter ink colors, such as pastels. But be careful when using darker ink colors on darker colored shirts like cardinal (dark blue), maroon, or forest green. These colors may look great on the computer or in a drawing, but when they print, the shirt color sometimes distorts the ink color. As a result, they can appear more brown or dull.

20. If you decide to use Adobe Illustrator to create your design, the Global Colours settings can help immensely with color schemes.

3.Add dimension to the design. Once you've added your colors to the design, it may look good but still a bit flat or one dimensional. To create more depth to a certain area of the design, add a color that is the shade of the color beneath it. This will brighten up the design and give it some dimension.

- If you plan to use software with a high capacity for manipulation (such as Adobe Photoshop, InDesign, Gimp, Adobe Illustrator, or Paint Shop Pro), you can use a standard image and radically transform it to fit your needs.
- Creating a vector outline on Inkscape is an especially effective way to resize a photo if necessary.

4. Balance your design. This means combining all the parts or elements to form a whole. How you do this depends on the composition of your design. Maybe your design has a lot of smaller elements, like stars, plants or animals. Or may it is one large design with one main figure or image.

Think about how you can make the design look cohesive, so that all the parts or elements fit well together. A balanced image will immediately draw the eye in rather than away from an image.

5. Determine the placement of the design on the t-shirt. Would your design work better as a centered image, an image on the top left of the t-shirt or as a wraparound image?

If you are designing a t shirt for a brand or company, a simple design in the center of the shirt may be the most effective.

Don't forget you can also use the back of the t-shirt to include a branding slogan ("Just Do It"). Or a song lyric from a song by the band you are designing the shirt for.

6. Complete a final mock up of the design. It's best to sketch your ideas out before putting them on your t-shirt. Try out several different designs and color combinations. Keep in mind color contrast and

dimension. Make sure the image is balanced and cohesive.

When in doubt, get a second opinion. Ask friends, family, or coworkers what design and color scheme they like best.

Part 2. Making a Digital Image of the Design

1.Use Adobe Photoshop to touch up your paper sketches. If your paper sketches are not high quality or drawn with clear lines, this option may not work. If your sketch is high quality:

- Scan the sketches to your computer. Then, retouch them in Photoshop.
- Clean up the lines. Play with the filters, colors, brightness, contrast, saturation, or any other effects at your disposal.
- Add lines, flourishes, splatter effects, and other embellishments that might make the design more dynamic and balanced (where appropriate).
- Make sure that the entire layout is internally consistent by keeping proportions reasonable, styles consistent, and colors cohesive.

2. Use computer software to create the design. If you aren't happy with the quality of your paper sketches, use computer software to draw line art on Photoshop.

If you have a computer drawing tablet, you can color and draw straight onto Photoshop or a similar program.

3. Add text to the design, if desire. Look for a font that complements your overall design, rather than overwhelm it. The font should work with the image(s) in your design to create a balanced design.

- Think about the fonts on some of the more well known logos or designs. The font should relate back to the company or brand's overall style. Nike's Just Do It's slogan, for example, is in a bold and simple font, just like their bold and simple swoosh logo. In contrast, the font used for a sports team or a garage rock band may be more elaborate or ornate.
- Make sure any filters you are using on the design are also applied to the font. If you are working with layers on Photoshop, you will need to drag your font layers below the photo effects layers.
- Use free fonts from an online site like defont.com. You can also access free brush designs from brusheezy.com.
- Look at how to add fonts to your PC, Illustrator, or Photoshop if necessary.

- If you're feeling adventurous with design, you can make your own.

4. Create a prototype. The easiest way to do this is to print the design and iron it onto a plain shirt. However, if you want to test the quality of your design, you can hire a printing company to create a professional prototype.

5. Produce the shirt(s). For a small-scale operation, you can continue ironing on the design.
If you'd like to make shirts at a larger scale, however, you can pay a printing company to make them for you.

Part 3. Screen-Printing Your Design

1.Gather your supplies. To screen-print your design at home, you will need:

- A plain t-shirt
- 50 ml bottle of degreaser (available at your local art store)
- 1 liter cold water
- A large brush
- 500 ml of emulsion
- A small bottle of sensitizer
- A bottle of screen printing ink
- A squeegee or a coating tray
- A small wooden stick

- A hair dryer
- A transparency
- A printing screen

You can purchase a printing screen at your local art store. Or make your own by buying a mesh screen and a canvas stretcher frame. Stretch the mesh across the frame and staple the edges down so that the mesh is taut. For standard designs on a light shirt, a 110-195 mesh works best. For fine designs with multiple colors, use a 156-230 mesh.

2. Prepare the printing screen. Mix the degreaser and the cold water together. Place the brush in the mixture and then brush the mixture on to the screen.

Make sure you brush both sides of the screen. You just want to give the screen a light brush so don't worry about putting too much of the mixture on the screen.

Let the screen dry.

3. Mix the emulsion and the sensitizer together. Take 20 ml of water and pour it into the bottle of sensitizer. Mix the sensitizer well by shaking for an about a minute.

- Add the sensitizer into the emulsion.
- Use the small wooden stick to mix the sensitizer and the emulsion together.

- The color of the emulsion should change from blue to green. There should also be small bubbles forming in the emulsion.
- Place the lid loosely back on the emulsion and place it in a dark area or room for an hour. After an hour, check that all the small bubbles in the emulsion have disappeared.
- If they do not disappear after an hour, leave the emulsion to sit for another hour until the bubbles are gone.

4. Apply the emulsion on the screen. In a very dim room or with a low red light, drip a line of photo emulsion across the screen and use a squeegee to spread it around.

The emulsion will leak through the screen, so be sure to squeegee both sides of the screen.

You can also use a coating tray to apply the emulsion to the screen. Do this by placing the screen on a clean towel and tilting it away from you slightly. Place the coating tray at the bottom of the screen and carefully pour the emulsion on the screen as you move the tray up the screen.

Leave the emulsion to dry in a completely black room for about twenty minutes. Use a fan to help the screen dry.

5. Place the transparency down backward on the screen. Now you're ready to burn your image into the emulsion. Do this by placing the screen flat, placing the transparency down backward, and placing a piece of glass over the transparency to ensure that it doesn't move.

6. Burn the design into the emulsion. A 500-watt lightbulb will burn the transparency image into the emulsion in roughly fifteen minutes.

The exact times for this process depend on the light and emulsion you use.

Specific directions for the light needed should be on the packaging of the purchased emulsion.

7. Rinse the screen. Let the screen soak in a thin layer of water for about two minutes. Then rinse any excess emulsion off with a hose or in the shower.

8. Place waterproof tape around the edges of the underside of the screen. The flat side of the screen will go facedown on the shirt, and the side with the frame is where you will use the ink.

To make sure no ink ends up leaking around the frame, use waterproof tape to secure around the edges where the screen stretches over the frame.

9. Lay your t-shirt on a flat surface. Make sure there are no wrinkles. Place the screen on top of the t-shirt, where you would like your design to be. Place the screen on top, making sure that the screen and design are aligned.

Clip your shirt down to a firm piece of cardboard. Doing this will ensure your t-shirt remains flat and unwrinkled. It will also make it easier to move your t-shirt to a safe spot later to dry.

If possible, have a friend hold the screen down tight while you spread the ink.

10. Spread a tablespoon of screen printing ink on the top of the screen. Using your squeegee, coat the screen by spreading the line of ink from top to bottom.

The mesh is actually quite thick, so this step is more of a primer.

Use very light pressure so you don't push any ink through the screen.

11. Squeegee the screen. With the screen flooded, you're ready to transfer the design to the shirt.

Use the squeegee at a 45° angle in both hands to evenly distribute the pressure. If possible, ask a friend to hold the screen in place.

Drag the ink back up across the flooded screen over the design.

12. Cure the ink. Using a hairdryer, apply even heat to the design for several minutes.

Cure the ink before using the next screen to add additional layers of the graphic in different colors.
If you use the proper screen-printing technique and cure it, your t-shirt will be washing machine safe.

13. Wash your screen once you are done making your shirts. Use cold water and scrub it with a sponge to get the ink out. Let the screen air dry.

Part 4. Stenciling Your Design

1.Gather your materials. To stencil your design onto a t-shirt, you will need:

- A black and white print out of your design. Its important to use a black and white printout of your design so it will be easy to trace.
- A piece of contact paper, or a transparency
- A craft knife, or exacto knife
- A plain t-shirt
- A piece of cardboard big enough to cover the front area of the shirt

2. Tape the design to a piece of contact paper. Contact paper is clear paper used for covering books. It has a normal side and a sticky side that peels off. You want to tape your paper to the peeling side so that the design is visible through the front of the contact paper—the non-sticky side.

You can also use a piece of transparency or clear paper. Attach it to the printout of your design with tape.

3. Use a sharp craft knife to cut out the black parts of the design. Lay the attached papers on a flat surface, like a table.

Trace the lines with the craft knife or an exacto knife. Keep in mind the black parts you cut out are the parts of the design that will be filled with paint.

4. Peel the sticky side off the contact paper. Remove the normal paper with the design from the contact paper as well. Place the sticky stencil onto the t-shirt, making sure it is straight and not wrinkled.

If you are using a transparency or clear paper instead of contact paper, attach the transparency to the shirt with tape.

5. Place a piece of cardboard inside the t-shirt. Doing this separates the front and back so the ink doesn't bleed through to the other side.

6. Use a sponge brush to paint on the fabric paint. Only put paint on the spots that have been cut out of the contact paper—the spots that will be painted in dark on the t-shirt.

Let the paint dry. Test the paint by gently touching the painted spots. If paint comes away on your finger, it is not fully dry.

7. Peel the contact paper off of the t-shirt when the paint is dry. You will now have a stenciled on t-shirt. You can use the stencil to make another shirt if you want more than one stenciled t-shirt.

Part 5. Bleach Painting Your Design

1.Use bleach safely. Bleach painting is a fun, easy, and inexpensive way to create a design on a t-shirt, especially text based designs. But, remember bleach is toxic, so keep it out of reach of children.

Always protect your eyes, clothing, and any open cuts from coming into contact with bleach.

If you have sensitive skin, you should wear thin kitchen gloves while bleach painting.

2. Gather your supplies.

You will need:

- Fabric safe household bleach
- A synthetic bristle paint brush (go for an inexpensive one, as you'll just be bleaching it anyway!)
- A glass or ceramic bowl
- A white towel or rag
- White chalk
- A piece of cardboard
- A dark colored cotton blend shirt

You can try this method on a lighter colored shirt, but the bleach painting will show up better on darker colors.

3. Place your shirt on a flat surface. Then, slide the piece of cardboard inside your shirt. It will act as an even surface as you write your design. It will also stop the bleach from bleeding through the back of your shirt.

4. Use the white chalk to sketch out your design on the shirt. This could be your favorite saying ("Bazinga!" "Reach for the Stars"), the name of your band, or the logo of your brand.

Don't worry if you need the smudge out the chalk lines and re-sketch the design. The chalk lines will wash out once you've completed the bleach painting.

5. Fold the sides of the shirt under the cardboard. Secure the shirt to the cardboard with elastics or small clips. This will keep the cardboard from slipping while you bleach paint.

6. Prepare the bleach. Pour a few cups of the bleach into the glass or ceramic bowl. Use a towel to wipe up any drips. You don't want any drops of bleach to end up on your clothing.

7. Dip your brush into the bleach. Drag it on the edge of the bowl to eliminate any dripping.

8. Use steady strokes to trace the chalk lines of your design. For an even bleach line, reload your brush every two inches. The fabric will quickly soak up the liquid so work quickly, but with a steady hand.

9. Finish tracing your design. Then, take a break to allow the bleach to react with the fabric of the shirt. Look over the shirt. Are there any uneven spots or light areas? If so, go back in with your bleach filled brush and even out the design.

10. Let the shirt sit in the sun for at least an hour. This will allow the bleach to process and lighten. Depending on the cotton content of your shirt, the color of your design will range from dark red, to orange, to pink, or even white.

11. Rinse and hand wash your shirt. Hang it to dry. Admire your new permanent bleach design.
Wash the shirt with like colors. The chalk lines should wash out, leaving only the bleach design.

CHAPTER 17
SELL DIGITAL FILES ON ETSY

When Jenny Kun's daughter was born, Jenny designed a few prints to hang in the new nursery. One night, while browsing Pinterest, she discovered a digital download for sale on Etsy and inspiration struck. 'I uploaded a few products and I was shocked — I got a sale on my first night', Jenny says. Since opening her Etsy shop, The Crown Prints, in August 2015, Jenny has sold close to 5000 digital downloads of her original art. Jenny loves that digital downloads let shoppers make a purchase and have new art hanging in their home in minutes. 'As a consumer, I really enjoy that instant gratification', she says. Jenny also loves that selling digital downloads allows her to run a business without dealing with headaches like shipping. Shop owners across Etsy who offer digital downloads in their shop are selling everything from sewing patterns to party printables to beautifully designed resumé templates. Offering digital downloads is one way you can add more listings to your shop and exercise your creativity.

Selling digital downloads can also be a low-maintenance way to stay in touch with your creative and entrepreneurial passions. Claudine Hellmuth sells printable gift box templates that she illustrates and designs. When she first started selling digital downloads on Etsy in 2011, Claudine was self-employed and had more time to devote to creating new digital designs and marketing her shop. She recently went back to a full-time job as a graphic designer, but her Etsy shop remains a source of income on the side. 'It's such a great way to create passive income!' Claudine says. 'You don't have to store or ship your product and you can sell the same item multiple times.'

Whether you're thinking about starting a new shop or just want to try something new, these tips will help you get started selling digital items.

Jenny created these animal silhouette prints for her daughter's nursery and they inspired her to try selling digital downloads on Etsy. She's not currently selling these designs, but they'll be added to her shop soon.

Getting Started

Listing a digital download on Etsy is just like creating a listing for a physical product, except you'll upload the file your customers will receive when they make a purchase. After buyers purchase a digital file on Etsy, it's immediately available on their downloads page. You can upload audio, image or text files to your listing. See all the steps of listing a digital item.

Although no special skills are required to list a digital download on Etsy, a good working knowledge of design programs like Adobe Illustrator will make creating files easier, says Jenny. 'I use Adobe Illustrator because it's a vector-based programme that gives me the flexibility to resize my designs', she says. 'Once you get the hang of it, it's a great tool to have in your toolset.'

Remember that a big part of running a business on Etsy is learning and adapting your shop over time. Claudine recommends experimenting with selling digital downloads by starting with a few designs. 'You don't have to wait to have hundreds of designs to open your shop', she says. 'List a few designs, see what your customers respond to and then make more of whatever category is selling well.'

Tips for Success

If you're already familiar with the process of listing and selling on Etsy, listing your first digital item should feel familiar. But, there are some nuances to know about when photographing and pricing digital items, and shoppers might have different customer service expectations.

Photographing

In addition to stylized photos of a completed project, Sarah includes a fifth photo to explicitly state that the listing is for a downloadable sewing pattern.

Great photography is essential for any listing on Etsy, but photographing digital items and ensuring that shoppers understand exactly what they're buying poses certain challenges. Sarah Norwood sells hand-sewn lingerie and digital download lingerie patterns in her shops Ohhh Lulu and Ohhh Lulu Sews. Sarah includes photos in her listings that communicate the aesthetic of her brand and show shoppers what they can create with her patterns. 'I always try to create a mood with my photos', Sarah says. 'So even if it's just a picture of the pattern itself, I try to give it a romantic feeling or style it in such a way that people can really picture themselves using it.'

Adding a stylized photo of the pattern itself has dramatically cut down on the number of confused customers Sarah encounters who think they're purchasing the finished item and not a pattern. Emphasizing in your titles and tags that the item is a digital download can also help.

Simple props like a vase of flowers and clean marble and wood surfaces are essential to Jenny's home photo setup.

Jenny has also tailored her photography to best capture her downloadable art prints. When she first started selling her prints, she used standard mock-ups, many of which are sold on Etsy, that placed her art into a frame and setting photographed and designed as a separate image. 'I wasn't sure it was showing my products in their best light because a lot of sellers are using the same mock-ups', she says. Now, she sets up her own frames and props at home and photographs them herself. 'I like doing that because I feel like I have complete control over my branding and my look', she says.

Customer Service

A subtle banner across the bottom on her listing images lets shoppers know that Claudine's product is a printable kit.

Digital products will save you storage space and trips to the post office, but they can sometimes require extra customer service effort. As a pattern seller, Sarah has found that her communication with pattern customers is much more in-depth than the questions she gets from shoppers who purchase lingerie from her. 'Sometimes customers need more step-by-step instruction, especially if they're new to sewing', she says. 'So I might not spend a lot of time with order management, but I spend a lot of time helping people remotely.' Sarah uses her blog to share more in-depth details and how-to's with her customers. Creating these resources allows her to reply with a link for more info instead of repeatedly answering the same questions via Convo.

Claudine has also found that shoppers sometimes need some additional resources to make the most of their digital downloads purchase. On her YouTube channel, she shares videos that show exactly how to put together her printable, 3D gift boxes.

The questions and comments you receive from customers are a great opportunity to think about how you can improve your pattern or download to make things clearer for future customers — saving you time and improving your customers' overall experience.

When you start selling digital downloads, you might also find yourself answering customer's technical questions. 'You'd be surprised how many people do not know how to download and open a PDF or are unsure how to change their printer settings from portrait to landscape', Claudine says. She includes step-by-step directions in the email buyers receive with their files.

Jenny also recommends becoming familiar with the printing process and colour modes your customers might be using. 'Send your designs to various printers so you can see how they turn out and anticipate what your customers will experience', Jenny says.

Pricing

How do you place a value on a digital item? That question can be difficult to answer if you're just getting started selling downloads. Jenny started by thinking about how much she would have charged for the art if she had printed it, packaged it and mailed it. She also considered how much time she puts into each design and what she would consider a reasonable profit to reach her prices of $5.40 USD for single prints and $10.80 USD for sets. Then, she added on expenses like Etsy fees to settle on a final price. 'I feel like my customers have been pleased with the price they're paying', Jenny says. 'Many have come back and said it was so efficient and it cost them less than if they had purchased a print and had to wait for it to arrive in the mail.'

Another concern is that selling digital downloads might take away from sale of your other products on Etsy, but Sarah says it's unwarranted. 'I was nervous to start selling sewing patterns because I didn't want to take away from my lingerie sales, but I found that it's two different markets', she says. 'The people who want to make their own lingerie are not the same people who are going to buy made-to-order lingerie.'

Offering digital downloads can help you add more listings to your shop, reach different audiences and explore new sales channels. It might also save you some time, so you can focus on creating new products and designs. 'It frees you up to focus on the creative stuff', Jenny says. 'I'm having so much fun with it and I'm growing as an artist and a designer.'

CHAPTER 18
LIST PLACE ON AIRBNB

A new Airbnb or short-term rental venture will yield social capital and, of course, financial capital – both without necessarily requiring any investments on your end. There are a number of roads you can go down to maximize the benefits of property management that await, and any road leading to Airbnb success begins with publishing your first listing.

Of course, you can always optimize and recruit additional help along the way, but don't run to this solution before doing everything you can by yourself.

With that, I present you with this step-by-step guide to take you through the process of perfecting your first listing from its very inception. There's no reason to get overwhelmed: the work you need to put into creating your listing is the only work necessary. Once the listing is completed and published, you can hand us the keys to drive your Airbnb listing towards more bookings, with hands-off account management. Now, onto the slight collaboration needed on your end.

1. Getting Started

First things first: head to airbnb.com and select the 'list your space' option in the top right corner of the homepage. You'll be directed to a form prompting you to fill in the most general criteria of your place. Take note that you can only complete this first form prior to creating an account, so it may be more efficient to sign up (or log in) before you begin.

If you have not yet signed up or logged in, you'll be prompted to input your information at this point.

Home Type: These options are pretty straightforward. To avoid any confusion, Airbnb added a brief description of each home type that appears when your mouse hovers over. Select the option that best describes the property you are managing. Keep in mind that the drop-down menu to the right expands your list of choices pretty significantly, including everything from loft to castles, tents, and so forth.

Room Type: This distinction is one of the most important, as both you and your guests may be particular about maintaining a certain level of privacy. So, make sure that you're accurately building your listing as to attract the most apt guests for your property. Like with the home type, Airbnb provides short definitions of their room terminology to help guide you through selecting the option that best describes your accommodation.

Before choosing "Entire home/apartment," consider the fact that granting guests exclusive access to your place might include access to other amenities on the property, such as a pool house or a garage. Similarly, the "Private room" option includes more home sharing than you might typically expect, such as that of any connecting rooms, bathrooms, or kitchens. In addition, you will not be able to edit the number of beds offered in this listing unless you select 'Entire home/apt'; the other options will automatically register your property with 1 bed.

Accommodates: This menu allows you to select the maximum number of people that can comfortably fit in your listing. For now, calculate how many people you can accommodate if each has his or her own bed, sofa bed, or inflatable mattress, provided that the sleeping arrangement is as comfortable as you would expect if you were the guest yourself. Finally, select the appropriate number from the drop-down list given.

City: Once you begin typing the name of the city where your place resides, Airbnb will automatically suggest all relevant matches. Choose one, press 'Continue', and move on to the next step.

Now you've arrived at the hub of your listing's more specific details. Airbnb has split this next step into sections, so it will be easiest to cover all information if you take it from the top and fill out the sections in the order that they appear on the list.

If an inaccurate listing secures a booking, you will not be able to change the faulty criteria of that listing without first sending an alteration request to the guest in question. This could cost you a booking and waste your time. So, be diligent with your listing details, because a small error can have a big impact.

Keep in mind that at any point you can go back to edit the previous descriptions provided. Or, Make use of the 'Preview' button in the top corner of your screen to see how your potential guests will view your published content.

2. Calendar

Airbnb provides three options for specifying the availability of this particular listing. Currently, these options reflect how long you want your property to stay listed on the Airbnb market, rather than specifying actual dates for rental. . You can choose for it to remain listed indefinitely ('Always'), only for specific dates or a fixed periods of time ('Sometimes'), or limited to a single fixed period of time ('One Time'). The specific dates available for rental should be inputted as soon as you publish your listing and should be updated regularly.

3. Pricing

Airbnb will suggest a price for you to charge based on the information that you've provided thus far as well as on trends currently shaping the local rental market, such as holidays, increased tourism, and more.

You have the option to play around with the pricing generator yourself, but for first-timers who are new to the site like you, Airbnb recommends starting below the suggested rate, which can help you get a foot in the door before you've had a chance to build up your profile reviews and other credentials. However, it's important to remain relevant and competitive, so take this step further by comparing prices of similar Airbnb listings in your area on your own.

On top of general listing qualities and market activity, there are a few other factors you should consider when calculating a price. For one, you may want to exercise your option to tailor your listing's going rates by creating weekly or monthly packages to encourage longer rentals. You should also factor in the cost of utilities, taxes, or cleaning ahead of time – Airbnb even gives you the option to add an additional cleaning fee to the price.

It's important to note that while you cannot include these in a base rate, penalties for late check-ins or other situational variables that you plan on charging guests should be communicated before a booking is secured.

4. The Overview

Title: Think of the title as your first impression. You want to make those 35 characters engaging enough to capture attention and unique enough to accurately depict your place. Try using descriptive and pleasant adjectives to cushion your title.

Summary: A great summary covers the major features of your listing in 250 characters or less. People like a bit of personality, so let yours shine through while explaining exactly what it is that makes your place unique. Bullet points and short sentences can go a long way: too much writing looks daunting, so try to break it up.

Title: Think of the title as your first impression. You want to make those 35 characters engaging enough to capture attention and unique enough to accurately depict your place. Try using descriptive and pleasant adjectives to cushion your title.

Summary: A great summary covers the major features of your listing in 250 characters or less.

People like a bit of personality, so let yours shine through while explaining exactly what it is that makes your place unique. Bullet points and short sentences can go a long way: too much writing looks daunting, so try to break it up.

5. Photos

While you have the ability to add many photos, it's best to add only around 10 as to not overwhelm the potential guests. Regardless of how many you decide to upload, the first 3 are the most important as they frame the window into your listing before users make the decision to click into the post or not. This is all the more reason to offer standout and high-quality pictures. Try to take this opportunity to show off amenities, quirky rooms, or other features unique to your property. Airbnb recommends using bigger photos for better resolution (1024 x 683px) and even offers free professional photography sessions to help you best capture your place.

6. Amenities

This section has a lengthy list of features that ranges from common or extra rooms, to home safety measures. At this stage of the listing, you are only given the option to select from the available list of amenities,, but once the listing is created you will be able to edit this section and add additional or further descriptions and details. Make sure to include every appropriate feature as some guests can be swayed by certain extras, or uninterested due to a lack thereof.

If you're totally lost here, refer to this resource for the essentials that every host should include in order to maximize an Airbnb experience.

7. The Listing

Most of these listing details should already be filled in for you if the first steps are done properly. You can edit every item unless you're listing only a single room (either private or shared), in which case the number of bedrooms will be pre-registered as and unchangeable as 1.

8. Location

Simply input the location of your listing and voilà, you've completed the Airbnb listing process. Once you begin typing your address, Airbnb will suggest the remaining details to autofill for convenience and accuracy. After your location is filled in, Airbnb will prompt you with a box to add directions and generate a section below with a notice of your local property laws for reference. As noted on the sidebar, the indicated location will not be viewable to the public, so you don't have to be concerned with any private information circulating around the web. Instead, on your listing, a circle will appear on a map at the bottom of your listing to give an idea of your area and neighborhood.

When you've finished all this and are happy with your listing, you're ready to be published on Airbnb. One thing to keep in mind is to always be honest in your description: it won't take long for the truth to come out once your guests arrive. However, it will be helpful for you to try and spin the not-so-good features of your place in a positive light whenever possible.

Here's the best news: at this point, you have the option to wash your hands of managing your listing. Guesty can take care of everything for you from here, providing one inclusive and intuitive platform for listing optimization, guest & staff communication, booking management and more. What would it mean for you? It would mean that the only work you have to do as an Airbnb host is already behind you. Go ahead – sign up for a demo with Guesty and see for yourself!

CHAPTER 19
CAR WASH

Opening a car wash business can be a fun, interesting, and profitable business for somebody with business smarts and perseverance. With the right location, good marketing, and top-notch service, you can draw in numerous customers who need their cars washed quickly, efficiently, and at a good price. However, opening a car wash business also requires a significant investment, good planning, and attention to detail in order to make your business profitable.

Part 1.Planning Your Car Wash

1. Research the car wash business. Even if you've worked at a car wash business, you'll need to be up to date on all the latest trends and technologies to have a good understanding of the industry. Visit other car washes and figure out the type of car wash you would like to open (e.g. self-service, automatic, waterless, full detailing, etc.)

For example, people use car washes more when the economy is doing well and when motor vehicle sales are up. When people have more money to spend, they are more willing to pay for a car wash. Knowing the car sales statistics in your area could help you predict success for your business.

- Talk to car wash owners, car wash suppliers, and car wash equipment manufacturers. You want to understand the car wash business from all sides so you know what you are getting into.
- The International Carwash Association is a good resource to learn about the industry and the current trends.
- Read Internet trend reports and business periodicals. Find out what the demographics are in your area and read up on how car wash businesses are doing in areas with similar demographics.
- Read business publications to find out what the newest materials and equipment are. The car wash industry is developing more energy efficient and environmentally friendly materials, so it's important to stay abreast of new developments.

2. Investigate the competition in your area. In order for your business to be competitive, you need to thoroughly research the other car washes in your area. If you have already chosen a location for your car wash, scope out all the competition within a 5 mile radius. What services do they offer? What are their

prices? How do they market their business? How often are customers using the services?

- Take notes as you investigate the car washes. You can go back and review them as you make plans for your car wash.
- Also pay attention to the other businesses around the car washes. If a car wash has a high volume of customers, what are some of the factors that are contributing to this? Is it located in a busy shopping center or right off the highway?

3. Draw up a detailed business plan. A business plan will help you get financing to start your car wash and think through the details of your business. Make your plan as detailed as possible. The business plan should include an introduction (3-5 pages), market analysis (9-22 pages), company description (1-2 pages), organization and management (3-5 pages), marketing and sales strategies (4-6 pages), product/service (4-10 pages), equity investment and funding request (2-4 pages), financial information (12-25 pages).

- The introduction should include your Executive Summary, table of contents, and a cover page.
- Your market analysis demonstrates your knowledge of the car wash industry and the results of any market research and analysis that you have done. Who are your customers

and what are their purchasing habits? What are the risks, strengths, and weaknesses involved with opening a car wash? What is your projected revenue based on the current market and future market trends?

- Your company description should include information about your car wash business and why you think it will be successful.

- The organization and management section should detail the structure of your company, the board of directors, and the qualifications of your management team.

- The marketing and sales portion should clearly outline your marketing strategy. How will you get customers? What avenues will you use to reach them? What is your overall sales strategy?

- The product or service section outlines exactly what you will be selling. How does your car wash business fill a void in the market? Why would people want to use your car wash as opposed to other car washes?

- The equity and funding section details exactly how much money you will need to start your business and what financial resources you already have to invest in the business.

- The financial information is the most important part of your business plan and should be reviewed by an accountant or financial planner. Include your personal financial information, any existing businesses you have, a list of debts, projected income for 5 years, and certification that your information was reviewed by a 3rd party financial adviser.

4. Find the investment capital to open a car wash. You can finance your new car wash through bank financing, a Small Business Association (SBA) loan, or through private investors. You will also need to have some cash of your own saved up to secure financing from others.The best way to do this is by presenting your business plan to your potential investor and show how your idea can be a viable business.

- A bank loan requires a loan-to-value ratio of 75%. You will need to come up with 25% of the fair market value and the bank will fund the other 75%. It will be harder for you to secure bank financing if you have never owned a business before.
- An SBA loan will either be a 7a or a 504. If you get a 7a loan, the SBA will partner with a local investor. Your actual loan will be financed by the local lender. A 504 loan is actually financed by the SBA and has job creation criteria.
- The start up costs for a car wash range from $100,000 - $400,000.

5. Choose the location for your car wash business. Having the right location can make or break your business. A successful location should be near a shopping center, in a high traffic, residential area, be easily and visible accessible from the road, allow for expansions and business growth, and have enough space for cars to line up.

- Your sign is visible to drivers for at least 40 seconds. Ideally, traffic should travel past at no more than 40 miles per hour (64 km/hr) so drivers have time to see your signage and make that split-second decision to have their cars washed.
- Choose a venue large enough to accommodate the bays, pump rooms, vacuum and drying areas, and the office.
- Check your city's zoning regulations to be sure you are allowed to open a car wash at your chosen location. If you need a special permit, obtain it before you buy or lease your venue.
- It is helpful to work with a real estate agent, city planner, lawyer, and/or an accountant to get the best deal on a location.

Part 2. Opening Your Car Wash

1. Get the necessary permits and licenses. You will definitely need a permit or a license to open your business. However, the requirements will differ

depending on what state you live in. The SBA website maintains a list of business license offices to help you find the information. In addition to a business license, you will need a federal tax identification number and possibly a sales tax license, income tax withholding, and unemployment insurance tax.

- Ask your state business office about the insurance requirements for your car wash business.
- Once you get all of the necessary permits and licenses, keep track of your renewal dates and make a copy for your business records. You will also need to display your license in your car wash so that customers can see it.

2. Buy equipment. The equipment you buy will depend on the type of car wash you have decided to open and the services you offer. Full service car wash, self-service car wash, and an automated car wash will all have different needs. You will typically need to buy a washing system (e.g. pressure washer, conveyor, self-service equipment, mobile wash systems), chemicals (e.g. cleaning solutions, wax, spot free rinses, protectants, presoaks, etc.), dryers, blowers, vacuums, brushes, towels, compressors, pumps, and a water system (e.g. boilers, water heater, water filtration, extractor, etc.), and billing system.

- The International Carwash Association has a supplier guide to help you find reputable manufacturers.
- Look in trade magazines like Auto Laundry News and Modern Car Care to buy your chemicals. It is best to buy from big manufacturers.
- Popular equipment manufactures include Ryko, Hannah Industries, Belanger, Karcher, and WashTec.
- Make sure the distributor of your equipment is available to service your equipment when needed. Find out how they handle equipment servicing before you buy from them.
- Equipment typically lasts for 10 years.

3. Market your business. Use a multifaceted approach to advertise your business that includes flyers, posters, and an online presence. The signage for your car wash should be colorful with clear messaging. Make sure that people can easily see it from the road. A popular way to get new customers is by distributing coupons or discounts for car washes. Also, develop relationships with other small businesses located near your car wash.

- Social media is an important aspect of marketing these days. Set up a website and establish a presence on Twitter and Facebook. Make sure any of the paper items that you have include links to your website and social media accounts.

- Use your website to share information about taking care of your car and other relevant tips.
- Schedule a visit to your local radio station to discuss your new business.
- Consider starting a loyalty program. This will encourage repeat customers instead of people who use the coupon one time and never return.

4. Hire employees. A car wash business is very customer-focused. Your employees should be punctual, efficient, skilled, and have excellent communication skills. As you conduct interviews, pay attention to body language and communication skills to get an idea of how the person will interact with customers and coworkers. Always check the references of potential employees as well.

5. Open your car wash. Have a soft opening of your car wash before you have a big grand opening. Wait at least 30 days before you have the big event. You want to work out some of the kinks and feel comfortable with the car wash before you make a big deal. Think of a grand opening as a party and social event to generate publicity.

- Invite friends, neighboring businesses, your supplies, and the media

- Give away free car washes and promotional items.

Part 3. Running A Profitable Business

1. Add services. Many car washes have combined other services and businesses with their car wash to increase revenue. Additional services will make your car wash more attractive to customers and help your car wash stand out from the crowd. A convenience store restaurant, barber shop, or even an enhanced waiting area (e.g. television, free coffee, comfortable place to sit, etc.) are possible additions. Ask yourself some questions before you invest in an add on service.

- Do I have enough space or will I need additional space?
- How much will it cost?
- What will be the return on my investment?
- Will people buy this service?

2. Offer express detailing services. Express detailing services are services (e.g. wax, sealant, carpet shampoo) that can be done in 30 minutes or less and are done to maintain the appearance of your customer's vehicle. Because you already have the space and equipment, you can offer these services at a lower price than a free-standing detail shop. It is also more convenient for your customers to have their car washed and detailed at one location.

- It is important that you complete the detailing portion of your services is completed quickly. The speed and low cost of the service make it attractive to your customers.
- Make sure that you advertise your detailing services to your customers.
- Check the prices of similar services at a free-standing detail shop to help you determine your prices. Also, check the prices of other car washes in your area that offer these services so that you can be competitive.

3. Use text messages to contact customers. Text marketing is a low cost, effective way to market your business to your customers. Your customers will redeem mobile coupons at a much higher rate than printed coupons. Even if a customer does not use a coupon, you are still building your brand and making your business known.

- Choose a keyword (e.g. water, wash, clean) and advertise by saying, "Text water to 12345 to get special discounts, specials, or coupons." You could also say "Text 12345 to get $3 off your next car wash."
- It only costs one or two pennies to send a text message.
- Text your customers once a month with a special.

4. Offer monthly or unlimited passes. Monthly and unlimited passes offer steady revenue even when customers are not actually coming in for a car wash. This is also a method you can use to build a steady customer base. Carefully price these passes. The price should be low enough so customers feel they are getting a good deal, and high enough for you to make a profit.

Consider pricing your passes to cost of 2 or 3 times the price of a single wash. If you find that customers are not interested, you may need to adjust your price.

You can offer different price points based on the type of car washes you offer. For example, a monthly pass for basic car washes would be less expensive than a monthly pass for premium car washes.

CHAPTER 20
RENT OUT CAR

Think of it as 'Airbnb' for cars, with companies like Car & Away, hiyacar or Drivy all in the market of matching up people who need wheels with those who've got them to hire.

As a vehicle owner, setting out your pitch using one of the online rental companies is easy.

You list your vehicle details plus rental price, availability and location and wait for potential borrowers to get in touch.

Some companies offer 'keyless' technology so you don't even need to be around to hand over the keys.

And when it comes to insurance, your car's covered by the rental company insurance, (instead of your own), while it's hired out, and the usual deal is that cars should come back in the same condition and with the same level of fuel in the tank.

Heading abroad? Make sure you avoid rip-off fees when shopping with one of these cards

Your rental options & how much each will pay/charge

Car & Away

If you're flying from Gatwick and happy to hire out your car, you'll save on airport parking, get a free car wash and even make money too.

Vehicles must be under 9 years old, with under 100,000 miles on the clock along with a current MOT, tax and comprehensive insurance, even though the company insurance kicks in while it's being hired.

Choose the 'Rent & Earn' option when booking airport parking.

This saves around £40 a week compared with standard parking, and on the day, you drive up and leave your car plus keys with the concierge and you're within a two-minute walk from the terminal.

Pick up your car on your return and if it's been borrowed, you'll have money in your bank account too.

You can typically earn from £80 a week up to £160 a week. However, you'll need to factor in commission at a whopping 40%.

Drivy

Billed as hiring a car from locals, Drivy says the most popular cars for hire are a Volkswagen Polo and Skoda Fabian, which would typically earn you £45-£50 a day.

Payment is made direct to your bank account minus a 30% commission.

Vehicles must be under 6 years old with less than 60,000 mileage.

You can hand over the keys yourself or use Drivy's 'Open Rental' system, which means borrowers can book, unlock and complete the rental from their phone without any need for you to be around.

To do this, you'll need Drivy to fit its system into your car, but this is free and takes two hours.

However, if you use this system, you'll need to be happy to leave a spare key inside, which is something you might want to check with your insurer first.

Cars must be under 8 years old but there's no mileage limit.

No need to hang around and hand over your keys here either.

'QuickStart' technology means your spare key fob is used to create a smart box along with a 'virtual' key in the hiyacar app so enables borrowers can unlock your car.

Rental fees range from £18 a day for a Toyota Aygo to £127 a day for an Audi A5 and all fees incur a 30% commission charge, unless you're hiring an electric vehicle, in which case it's zero commission for the first three months.

easyCar Club

You can get away with older vehicles here providing they're under 15 years old with less than 120,000 mileage and a maximum value of £40,000.

Go online, pop your vehicle details on and when you get rental requests, just fix up a time to hand over the keys.

Or if you don't want to hang around, you can ask for a 'Keysafe' to be sent out.

One of the lowest commissions here as you'll only lose 10%.

How much you earn varies according to where you live and the car you've got, but as a rough guide, you can make from around £30 a day with a Vauxhall

Corsa in Bournemouth or just over £100 with an Audi A5 in London.

How to pick the right car insurance policy

Car insurance considerations before you sign up

Is this a hazard for your own insurer?

"If you're thinking of renting your car through these services, you should tell your insurer", says Direct Line's Chloe French.

"What one insurer will be happy with, another may not be".

And even if your vehicle comes back looking clean with fuel in the tank, you need to consider the 'wear and tear' on your vehicle along with any increased mileage warns Aviva's John Franklin.

"Vehicle mileage is one of many factors affecting insurance premiums and a higher mileage can potentially impact your future insurance risk".

Check you're protected

All the companies listed provide their own insurance cover, through the likes of Axa, Admiral and Allianz.

This works in place of your own policy and covers the cost of any damage while your car's hired out.

"Do check the precise level of cover and any limitations", warns Aviva's John Franklin, "as you may be disadvantaged in the event of an accident, if a courtesy car is not available while yours is being repaired".

Most companies do offer a 'courtesy car' as standard, but with Drivy, courtesy cars are only available if owners opt for 'Collision Damage Waiver' which increases the borrower's bill.

And even with companies using 'keyless' technology, if you're being asked to leave a spare key in the car, your own insurer may not be happy.

Nick Ansley, head of motor at Co-op Insurance warns that "leaving keys in cars tends to be one of the main exclusions under insurance policies, in the event of the car being stolen".

And that's about it. Head this way for more ways to make money from your car.

CHAPTER 21
VENDING MACHINE

The ads are alluring: "Make $500 an Hour in the Vending Business!" "Earn Money While You Sleep in a Vending Machine Business!" But they sound way too good to be true. Can vending machines really be a viable way to earn cash?

The National Automatic Merchandising Association reports that 18 percent of vending-machine operators make between $1 million and $5 million a year. But proceed with caution: The Better Business Bureau warns of scams, and a search of "vending machines" on the Federal Trade Commission's website unearths dozens of fines and lawsuits.

Here are a half dozen tips for getting into the vending-machine business safely and profitably.

1. Decide on the vending machine type.

Many vending machines are filled with a selection of drinks and snack foods. Others focus more narrowly on a particular category, such as ice cream, popcorn, cigarettes, videos (think Redbox), or personal hygiene. Some machines dispense individual units;

others offer items in bulk, such as hard candy and gumballs.

2. Get the proper licenses.

In some states you'll need a seller's permit to operate vending machines, and many states require you to charge sales tax on the items in the machines. The tax varies by state, as does the minimum price that launches the requirement to collect the tax. Be sure to check with your local licensing office to find about the requirements in your area.

3. Buy the machines.

Decide whether you want to buy new or used machines. Prices can vary wildly: A new machine often runs a few thousand dollars, while used ones go for a few hundred or less on Craigslist, eBay, or Amazon. Keep in mind that all machines eventually break down, so you'll need to either hire someone to repair them or learn to do so yourself. (Tip: You can buy parts from a manufacturer such as Vendors Exchange International.)

4. Buy or lease a truck.

Depending on how large your operation is, you'll need a van — or, perhaps, a specialized beverage truck — to carry products from machine to machine. A used truck starts at about $5,500 at places like

Specialty Trux, or you can lease a basic truck for about $500 a month.

5. Find a supplier.

You can buy products in bulk at a local big-box store or go online. Check out sites like Candymachines.com for bulk candy, or SmartVending for a full line of supplies. Markups will vary, depending on the product. Bulk items, such as candy and gumballs can be marked up 200 to 300 percent, while single items can typically be marked up between 60 and 100 percent. Of course, the more products you buy, the better price you'll get, so you may have to settle for lower markups when just starting out in order to be competitive, and then increase them as you add machines.

6. Secure a location or two.

Where you place your vending machines will determine how successful you are. Check out each site before you approach its owner. Look for a place that gets a lot of foot traffic, such as an airport, a parking lot, a shopping mall, a large office building, or a busy waiting room. Once you select a location, approach the owner and work out a deal. Some vending machine operators offer the owner a small percentage of their profits; others donate a portion of sales to charity. NAMA, in its publication Vending

101, suggests that you sign a written contract whenever you place a machine.

7. Service your machines.

Once your machines are placed, it will be up to you to keep them clean, well-stocked, and in working order. You may be able to do this by visiting once a week, but if the machine is popular, you may need to turn up more often.

Of course, all of this isn't quite as easy as earning money while you sleep. But with careful planning, hard work, and a little luck, you can run a successful vending-machine business.

CHAPTER 22
STORAGE RENTALS

There is a ton of bad information out there on the self-storage or mini-storage industry. Contrary to what you may read, there is virtually no money in building new facilities or buying them at a 7% cap rate. If you really want to make money in self-storage, you have to put in significantly more work, and follow a different game plan entirely. Buying an established facility with good occupancy at market rents will not lead to great riches ' only endless concern over making the note payment. The way to success is much more basic.

Buy low and sell high

Few people make a fortune owning self-storage facilities. They make their money selling them. To make money buying and selling self-storage facilities, you have to understand how to buy at the cheapest possible price and how to sell at the highest possible one. And it's not a whole lot different than other forms of commercial real estate. But it's shrouded in more bad information than most.

A lot of people got spoiled

During the 1970s and 1980s and even 1990s, you could not build a self-storage facility and go wrong. The industry was in its infancy, and the demand outstripped the supply in almost every market in the U.S. As a result, the 'build it and they will come' approach seemed to be 100% accurate at all times. Financing to build was easy to attain, and the facilities just started popping up everywhere ' in big cities and rural markets alike.

The reality of today

Supply and demand have now met, although in some markets supply still overshadows demand. Gone are the days of success being rewarded on poor strategy or execution. Some markets have significant vacancy and rents are stagnant. The good news is that the buildings are easy to maintain and the business model is simple and easy to understand. Plus, the typical customer is relatively stable and seems happy with the relationship.

How to buy them cheap

You need to buy self-storage facilities that are either poorly managed or in distress, such as foreclosure. A stabilized property that is professionally managed has no upside. You want a property where you can increase revenue through higher rents and increased occupancy, and decrease costs through renegotiating all the bills and proactively finding ways to cut costs.

The good news is that there has never been a better time to buy these facilities, as the current economic depression, coupled with the collapse of real estate financing has made these opportunites more abundant.

How to sell them high

Selling a self-storage facility at a good price is made possible today through the internet. Sites such as selfstorages.com and Loopnet.com have opened up the sea of investors to this asset class in a big way. You can reach one hundred times more buyers through internet postings in one month than in an entire career before. Sales is a volume business, and the volume is on your side.

Of course, to get a property sold, it must be reasonably priced. That's why it's essential that you buy them really, really cheap on the front end.

Conclusion

You can make big money in self-storage, but only it you are a very smart buyer and seller. People who pursue average deals will only, best case, achieve average returns, which are less than spectacular. You must seek out deals that are dramatically underpriced and turn them around if you want to really take advantage of this niche.

CHAPTER 23
LAUNDROMAT

Laundromats make it easier to get laundry done when customers either don't have a washing machine at home or need to wash more clothing than their machines can handle at home. Laundromats also sell detergents and soaps, dryer sheets, and other related items to help customers get their laundry done.

Who is this business right for?

This business is good for people who are looking for a full-time business but who also want something they can start in their spare time. Running a laundromat can either be a very hands-on or more passive business, allowing the entrepreneur to have flexible hours and scheduling.

However, as this business grows, it requires a great deal of management. Unless you can afford to hire a manager, this is a time-consuming business to own long-term.

What happens during a typical day at a laundromat?

Running a laundromat can be simple or more involved. It all depends on the type of laundromat you want to run. A simple business model for this type of business is an unmanned laundromat service.

A more involved version of this business would include daily monitoring of the laundromat, collecting money from customers, folding clothes for those who paid for full service, and managing the books.

What is the target market?

Preferred clients are businesses with long-term service contracts. However, a laundromat can also service the general public and bring in a consistent stream of revenue. Ideal customers are those living in apartments where there are no onsite laundry services or washers and dryers for self-service. This might mean placing the laundromat near low-rent or poor neighborhoods.

How does a laundromat make money?

A laundromat makes money by charging customers to wash and dry their clothes. A laundromat may choose to operate as a self-serve operation, where customers insert quarters into machines to operate the washers and dryers, or it may be run as a full-service business in which customers pay to have staff do their laundry for them.

This business usually handles transactions in cash. However, some laundromats do offer the use of credit cards, checks, and even laundromat-specific cards. Cash-based transactions help to keep costs down for the customers and owner because there are no credit card fees. However, accepting credit cards increases convenience, potentially leading to more customers.

What is the growth potential for a laundromat?

Growth potential for this type of business is almost unlimited. Laundromats can be operated at a small scale, with a single building servicing many customers with a handful of machines. You can even start a small business out of your home, offering full-service laundry and folding services.

It can also be operated at scale with multiple locations across a town or city. Some laundromats operate near colleges and dorms where college students can easily access the building to wash their clothes.

What are some skills and experiences that will help you build a successful laundromat?

Aside from having good business sense, good negotiation skills, and being mechanically-inclined, there are no special skills or education needed to start a laundromat.

What are the costs involved in opening a laundromat?

Costs for starting a laundromat are significant. Depending on the location, it can cost you between $100,000 and $200,000 to buy an existing business or it can cost up to $1 million or more.

Businesses you buy in larger cities tend to cost more. Also, some states are inherently more expensive than others. For example, buying a laundromat in California, Florida, or New York may be much more expensive than buying one in Idaho or Alabama.

If you're starting out of your home, you can start with little to no money upfront.

Expect total startup expenses for a small business outside the home to be between $100,000 and $250,000.

A big part of the startup cost is the machines. Get "like new" machines that have been well-serviced and you can save yourself some money and lower your startup costs. However, be aware that used machines may not come with reliable or accurate service records. New machines may initially cost more, but you will also know the entire service history.

If you finance the business, rather than pay cash, you may only need to put down 10% to 30% of the total cost. Utility costs are a big expense. While the machines themselves can cost you $500 to $700 each for top loader and $3,500 and $20,000 for front loaders, utilities to run them (water, heating, etc.) can run between $200 and $2,000 per month, each.

What are the steps to start a laundromat?

Once you're ready to start your laundromat, follow these steps to ensure that your business is legally compliant and avoid wasting time and money as your business grows:

- Plan your business. A clear plan is essential for success as an entrepreneur. A few important topics to consider are your initial costs, your target market, and how long it will take you to break even.
- Form a legal entity. Establishing a legal business entity prevents you from being personally liable if your laundromat is sued.
- Register for taxes. You will need to register for a variety of state and federal taxes before you can open for business.
- Open a business bank account. A dedicated checking account for your laundromat keeps your finances organized and makes your

business appear more professional to your customers.

- Set up business accounting. Recording your various expenses and sources of income is critical to understanding the financial performance of your business. Keeping accurate and detailed accounts also greatly simplifies your annual tax filing.

- Obtain necessary permits and licenses. Failure to acquire necessary permits and licenses can result in hefty fines, or even cause your business to be shut down.

- Get business insurance. Insurance is highly recommended for all business owners. If you hire employees, workers compensation insurance may be a legal requirement in your state.

- Define your brand. Your brand is what your company stands for, as well as how your business is perceived by the public. A strong brand will help your business stand out from competitors.

- Establish a web presence. A business website allows customers to learn more about your company and the products or services you offer. You can also use social media to attract new clients or customers.

- Should you consider joining a franchise?

Joining a laundromat franchise can be a good option for entrepreneurs who prefer to use a proven model rather than start from scratch. While joining one can mean slightly higher initial costs and less control, a quality franchise offers great benefits such as initial and ongoing support, marketing assistance, and brand recognition.

Opening a laundromat franchise typically requires $230,000-$600,000.

What are some insider tips for jump starting a laundromat?

These businesses sink or swim based on location. Try to get good real estate for your laundromat. Usually, this means setting up shop in neighborhoods where local residents don't have easy access to laundry services and machines.

Another tip is to focus on securing a few small corporate clients, like janitorial businesses and restaurants, as clients. This will give you a strong base of income to work off from.

How to promote & market a laundromat

Promoting a laundromat is pretty straightforward. Advertise in local neighborhoods and spread your marketing to areas in your town or city where there is limited access to machines and other laundry services.

How to keep customers coming back

The best laundromats are ones that maintain a clean and friendly environment. When the inside of the building is clean and well-maintained, and when all machines are functioning normally, then customers are more likely to clean up after themselves and treat the machines as their own.

How and when to build a team

A coin laundromat doesn't need a large staff and might be able to be non-staffed. However, you should consider hiring at least one to two employees to watch over the place, encourage customers to pick up after themselves, and to keep the place clean.

Each location can be minimally staffed, however.

How much can you charge customers?

Costs for laundry services are driven almost entirely by the location. In bigger cities, you can charge more. In smaller towns, less. On average, you can charge customers $3 per load of laundry, washed and dried.

What are the ongoing expenses for a laundromat?

The biggest ongoing expenses are the utilities. Expect to pay between $200 and $2,000 per machine just for the water and heating. You should also set aside money for maintenance. Maintenance costs can range from $50 to $150 per machine for simple maintenance and repairs.

How much profit can a laundromat make?

The average annual income of a laundromat in the U.S. ranges from $30,000 to $1 million, according to Brian Wallace of the Coin Laundry Association. Average profit margin is between 20% and 30%. Some laundromats make significantly less, however. An owner-operated laundromat may be able to sustain a high profit margin by doing his own maintenance, and working in the business instead of paying an employee.

A larger business, with multiple locations, may only net a 10% to 20% margin after operating costs.

How can you make your business more profitable?

One of the best ways to make your business more profitable is to offer additional services. For example, you could offer self-serve dry clean machines, sell detergent, snacks, and coat hangers, dry cleaning bags, and laundry bags. Offer free or discounted wifi

Internet services for customers to help them pass the time while they wait for their laundry.

Another way to dramatically reduce costs is to operate your business in an area where taxes and utilities are lower. Check county taxes and water utility rates. These can vary significantly from one location to the next.

Do your own maintenance. Maintenance on washing machines and dryers isn't too difficult for someone with basic handyman skills. If you purchase washers and dryers that are easily serviceable, you can save yourself several thousand dollars per year.

CHAPTER 24
CASHBACK REWARDS CARD

What is cashback?

When you buy something, you get a percentage of the amount it cost paid back to you. This means cashback is a way of getting money off things you buy – think of it like a reward or incentive. It's normally a feature of credit cards, but some current accounts also have cashback.

Often cashback is offered on specific purchases, like fuel or for bills. But many providers now offer cashback on anything that you buy.

How does cashback work

Each time you use the card, you earn a percentage of your spend back in the form of cashback.

For example if your card pays 2% cashback and you spend £100 in a shop, you will earn £2.

This cashback is generally paid annually, though some cards will pay cashback on a monthly basis.

Most cashback cards credit the amount you earned onto your statement, reducing your credit card bill. Some cards send the cashback to a bank account so you can spend it, or let you convert it to points or vouchers.

Reward points can normally be exchanged at any point once you have enough to qualify for a 'reward'.

Cashback cards come in various forms:

some will simply pay a flat rate of cashback, no matter how much you spend or where you spend it
others pay tiered rates of cashback depending on how much you spend. For example, 0.5% if you spend less than £6,000 annually, 1% if you spend more than that. Be careful this doesn't tempt you to spend more than you can afford to repay comfortably
some cards offer different rates of cashback depending on where you spend your money. For example, 1% on money spent in supermarkets, 2% on money spent in department stores and 3% on money spent on fuel.

When cashback cards are a good idea

If you pay your credit card bill off in full every month then cashback credit cards can be a great idea as you're getting rewarded for spending money that you would have spent anyway.

If you don't always pay off your credit card bill in full, then cashback credit cards are not such a good choice.

While you'll earn cashback on your spending, this will usually be less than the interest charged on your outstanding debt.

Don't get taken advantage of

Card providers might attempt to convince you to take out a cashback credit card by coming up with all sorts of scenarios where you'll earn a small fortune in cashback.

For example, they might use your spending on fuel or lunch at work to boost your total spend, and therefore the cashback you could earn, from the card.

However, if you normally pay for these things by debit card or cash, and don't intend to change that behaviour, you won't see the benefit in cashback.

If you're not comfortable paying by credit card for these things or you worry about getting into debt, you should avoid taking out a card.

If you have a cashback card, don't be tempted to spend more just to earn cashback or reward points.

Fees

Another thing to bear in mind before taking out a cashback credit card is that you might have to pay an annual or monthly fee for the card.

These usually range from a few pounds a month up to £25 a year paid annually for some cards.

Factor this fee in. If you only do a little spending on your card each month and don't want to increase that spending, then it might be that any cashback you would have earned will be wiped out by the fee.

Your spending habits

If you want to earn the most cashback possible, it can make sense to put all of the spending you usually do each month onto your credit card.

However, you shouldn't see this as an excuse to spend more than you usually would, simply to earn more cashback.

That extra cashback can be irrelevant if you're unable to pay off the credit card bill each month as it could easily be outweighed by interest charges.

The golden rule of cashback credit cards

MAKE MONEY DOING NOTHING

Always aim to pay off your credit card each month on time, and in full, otherwise any money earned in cashback will be taken away by interest owed or fees.

CHAPTER 25
CASHBACK SITES

How do cashback sites work?

If you want to buy something online or sign up to a finance product, rather than going direct, click to the company via a cashback site and you get paid for it. The amounts range from pennies for retail items to – at the top end – more than £100 for some mobile or broadband contracts.

You'll have to sign up to the cashback site, which should be free. If it's not, avoid it. Then simply log in and search for the online retailer you want to buy from, such as Argos or Tesco Direct. If it's listed, click the cashback site's link to visit that company.

Your visit is then tracked. If you buy something, an amount is put into your cashback site account once the transaction's processed. You can withdraw this once it arrives, which can take a few weeks, or even months. For some cashback sites, you need to reach a set threshold before you can withdraw.

Why do they pay out?

Cashback sites take advantage of the way commercial payments from one website to another work. They use affiliate links, which allow the retailer to track where the traffic is coming from and then pay the cashback sites for the lead.

This is a common system, used by sites that send people through from comparison results, unique content (MSE does this – see the foot of the page for more details) or using links on advertising promotions. Cashback sites simply drive traffic by giving their users some of the money they're paid.

The amount of money depends on what's spent on what as well as the commercial deal, so can vary widely. The cashback site may earn its money per click, transaction, application, or accepted applicant.

The technology's simple. Ready-made paying links are available from 'links warehouses'. Big cashback sites also have direct relationships with companies, which means they can offer a wider range of providers, earn more and negotiate their own exclusive deals.

The 5 MAJOR cashback safety rules

While cashback sites can generate some users £100s a year, it's very important you understand there can be substantial pitfalls in using these sites – and you need to understand them BEFORE you begin.

1. Think of cashback as a bonus only – it's not guaranteed

Tracking problems occur for many people using cashback sites. There are times when you'll expect to be paid but won't be.

If you do have problems getting paid, remember you need to contact the cashback site directly, not MSE..

However, problems don't only arise with cashback sites. They get the money from the retailers and product providers. Disputes in this area are common, so sometimes the cashback site doesn't receive the cash either.

Plus, unlike when you get cashback from a retailer, which is part of the product T&Cs, here you've fewer rights. The best way to approach this is to consider cashback as a bonus if you get it, but not to let it drive your purchasing decisions.

2. The cashback isn't yours until it's in your bank account

Never count on the cashback as being yours until it's in your bank account. This isn't just because of tracking and processing issues. Cashback sites are easy to set up and many are small companies which can go bust (and some have done just that).

If it happens, you've little protection. You may count as a creditor to the company but in all likelihood, your money will be gone.

3. Never store cash in a cashback site – withdraw it ASAP

Most cashback sites set a threshold which you must reach before you can withdraw cash. The best practice is to withdraw as soon as you hit that level.

Never leave cash building up in a cashback site account when you can take it out. Not only are you missing out on interest, but if the company goes kaput or changes its payout policy, your money could be lost.

4. Focus on the cheapest deal, not the biggest cashback

It's easy to be seduced by £50 cashback for buying an insurance policy or a 7% discount when shopping for clothes. Yet never let the cashback tail wag the dog. Not because of the warnings above, but simply because it may not actually be the cheapest option.

Regardless of the cashback, you want to get the best deal possible. If you've chosen something purely because of the cashback on offer, and the cashback doesn't happen, you could find you've dug yourself a hole.

Example 1: You want a new telly. A cashback site brings up Korma Electricals, offering 5% cashback, which means a £20 discount on a £399 TV. Yet two minutes using a price comparison site would've found you the same TV on sale at £299.

Example 2: Your car insurance is up for renewal. You spot the Commander Insurance £100 cashback offer on a cashback website, so grab its £540 policy via the site. Yet if you'd used a car insurance comparison website, you'd have found an equivalent policy from Chamberlain Insurance for £370. As Chamberlain is also on a cashback site, you could've got a further £25 off, saving £95 in total.

This is especially important for bigger transactions, where the cost of making a mistake can dwarf the cashback received. So read our relevant guides first, like Balance Transfer Credit Cards, Cheap Car Insurance, Cheap Home Insurance, Best Bank Accounts and How to get cheap broadband.

5. Consider clearing your cookies

Cashback sites track your visits by putting cookies (little bits of info that identify you) onto your computer. Many other sites, like comparison sites, also use cookies.

So when making your purchase, make sure you click through from the cashback site and not from anywhere else, as the general rule's 'the last cookie wins'.

To be doubly safe, especially if you're expecting a lot of cashback, clear your computer's cookies first to ensure the cashback is tracked. Learn more about controlling and deleting cookies at AboutCookies.org.

The top-paying cashback sites
Don't think all cashback sites pay the same. Many pay out 50% or less of what they get paid. We checked out 10 of the biggest cashback sites for the top rates and feedback.

The best sites are those that pay out 100%, so ostensibly give all the money they earn to you.

Topcashback*
THE OVERALL WINNER

If you want the site that pays the most, Topcashback* is the winner. It's free to use and pays out up to 105% of the cashback it receives from the merchant.

That might sound strange, but it's able to do this as it passes on a little of the bonuses it gets for generating lots of sales. It's also the cashback site that gets the best feedback from its users. You can take earnings as cash, or boost returns by swapping cashback for Amazon or M&S vouchers.

How do I join & get cashback?

Choose its free membership. Topcashback has no annual administration fees. New users are are signed up to a one-month trial of its 'Plus' membership – remember to downgrade before the trial is up (which you can do at any time) otherwise you'll automatically be charged for a year's membership.

You can choose to pay a £5 membership fee. Topcashback's Plus membership* gives a 5% bonus on non-exclusive cashback rates, eg, a £100 cashback deal would net you £105 as a Plus member.

Boost returns by up to 25%. Get a payout bonus by exchanging your cashback for gift cards from Amazon, Gap, M&S and more.

Earn cashback in store. Topcashback followed in Quidco's footsteps and offers cashback on certain purchases made in store, see below for more details.

Quidco*
IN SECOND PLACE

Our second best cashback site is Quidco*, which has similar payout levels as Topcashback above. Indeed, the two sites usually compete on exclusive deals.

How do I join & get cashback?

Pick the Basic membership. If you don't pick this, you'll have to pay a fee.

There's a Premium membership available. For £5, Premium members get bonus cashback promos worth £50/yr, higher payout bonuses, exclusive prize draws, a monthly £250 giveaway and ad-free shopping.

Earn around £300 a year. Quidco says that on average its active members pocket £300 each a year.

Boost returns by up to 16%. Get a top-up bonus by withdrawing your cashback in the form of gift cards from Amazon, Argos, Debenhams, M&S and many more.

You can boost cashback in stores. Quidco members can also get cashback in stores from 25+ retailers as well as online. Read more info on this below.

An alternative... if you have (or know) a kid

While the sites above offer standard cashback, if you're willing to put your cashback towards a child's savings – even if those savings sit in your current account – then another option may win.

KidStart
RARE 2% CASHBACK ON AMAZON, PLUS EARN AT JOHN LEWIS, NEXT ETC

It's rare to see cashback sites feature Amazon. Cashback on Next, John Lewis and, for existing customers, Asos shopping is unusual too. But KidStart lets you earn cashback at all these stores, and more than 1,500 in total – the catch is you have to put it towards a child's savings.

But you don't need to be a parent. The child can be yours, a grandchild or a friend's. It can even be a twinkle in your eye that you plan to have one day (though you do need the child's name and actual or expected date of birth to withdraw the cash). You don't need to actually withdraw money to a separate child's account either – you can simply use your own current account.

You MUST be legitimately saving for a child though. KidStart says it has ways of checking and if it suspects you're not, it could wipe the savings in your account.

How much cashback can I get?

KidStart pays 2% on Amazon purchases (though not if you buy or use gift cards or use 'Subscribe and save'). It also gives up to 4% on Next, 3% on John Lewis and 2% on Asos for existing customers. When we checked, the other top cashback sites didn't cover these retailers (except Asos, but other sites only give cashback to newbies).

If you're a regular shopper it can quickly rack up, as MSE Steve's found: "Over the past six years, we've earned a huge £275 cashback for our kids, mainly at John Lewis and Amazon. We started the account before our first child was even born."

That said, KidStart doesn't always win. For example, it pays 2% on Debenhams, compared with up to 6% at Topcashback and Quidco. So always do a comparison, especially if making a big purchase.

How do I join & get cashback?

Sign up to KidStart (it's free). You don't need to add a child's details to start earning cashback – you can add them later.

Log in and click KidStart's link to visit your shop of choice. Your visit is then tracked and an amount is put into your KidStart account once the transaction's processed.

You can withdraw your cash once you've reached the £10 threshold. Before you take the money out you must add a child, enter their name and date of birth, then link that profile to a Child Trust Fund, junior ISA or bank account (though this doesn't have to be the child's – it can be your own current account).

Cashback successes

Plenty of MoneySavers have had huge success using cashback sites. Here are some stories for inspiration:

So far I have got back around £300 from buying things that I would normally have bought and not received anything back for. Things like my garden shed, washing machine, car insurance, home insurance and every day items.

I've made £2,500 from Topcashback alone over the last three years – booked holidays, offered to book hotels for family members for occasions like weddings, and bought all insurance and Christmas and birthday presents.

Have used Topcashback for years and average £300 per year, so very good IMO.

I've been a member with them for almost four years, and I've never had any problems with them tracking or declining any valid transaction ... So far TopCashback has paid me £1,617.88.

Let us know about any success you have using cashback sites, and any other feedback you have, on the Top Cashback Sites forum thread.

How to boost your cashback by £100s more
There are a few ways to boost your cashback:

1. Earn in-store cashback
You can get money back on in-store spending at a few different retailers with both Quidco and Topcashback:

Topcashback. Is our top pick and now it also allows you to earn in-store cashback by registering your debit or credit card and activating offers through OnCard. There aren't a huge amount of offers available through this method, but you can get cashback by spending at big names with a MasterCard such as Debenhams (3%), Cotsworld Outdoor (6%) and Runners Need (6%) through it.

Otherwise, the Topcashback mobile app* lets you earn cashback on your in-store grocery and high street shopping with deals on specific items. Using the app you unlock the offer, scan the barcode of the product and then take a photo of the receipt, and the cashback should be approved fairly sharpish.

Quidco. Register your credit or debit card with Quidco, spend on it, and your purchase is tracked.

Once processed, the relevant amount is paid into your onsite account. There are a number of well-known retailers involved, including Ann Summers (2%), Hotel Chocolat (4%) and Richer Sounds (2%). Learn more about in-store cashback with Quidco*.

An in-store purchase can take up to 21 days to track on Quidco. Keep hold of your receipts, as if a purchase doesn't track you'll need to send a scanned copy of the receipt to Quidco to get it sorted.

With Quidco you can only get in-store cashback – or higher rates of in-store cashback – by 'activating' the deal first on the website or through the iPhone or Android app. You do this by pressing the blue 'activate' button. See the full list* of retailers and offers.

2. Cashback credit cards: 5% spending boost

Cashback credit cards give cold hard cash every time you spend on them. Always make sure you pay them off in full so you're not charged interest though.
There's no conflict between cashback sites and cashback cards, as when you spend on a cashback card, whoever you spend it with, the card will give you some money back. The top card pays up to 5% back on your spending over the first three months. See the Cashback Credit Cards guide for the top payers.

3. Make free cash from cashback sites

You don't have to buy anything to earn cash via cashback sites – you can earn cash just for clicking links on the internet. Cashback websites give you a share of their ad revenue, and sometimes get paid just for generating traffic.

For example, at the time of writing Topcashback pays £2.25 for signing up for a free Experian account . Its Free Cashback* section lists the top offers.

Quidco has a similar page with free cashback offers, which include earning up to £5 for getting a new insurance quote via Quotezone.

4. The big sites will beat the best rates

Topcashback* and Quidco have guarantees that mean they'll at least match other UK cashback sites if you find a higher rate on the same product or service elsewhere.

Topcashback will beat the competing rate by 1% (or 5% for Plus members). You have to submit a claim within four weeks of your cashback tracking. Quidco will double the difference between its cashback rate and the higher one of a competitor, but employs a more strict 72-hour policy for submitting claims.

Other restrictions and limitations apply, so check all the T&Cs before making a purchase on which you're planning to claim.

CHAPTER 26
GET PAID TO HAVE AN APP ON YOUR PHONE

The times are tough and almost all of us need a little extra cash in our pockets. Money earning mobile apps are getting popular by the day. Reason being that you can easily make money on the go and aren't limited to your desktop PC anymore.

So here's a comprehensive guide on these top ten apps.

Cash-for-Apps

Cash for Apps is an app that allows its users to earn money by downloading other apps and running them. How it works is that there's a list of available apps to download and each app has different points that are paid for downloading them. You will earn approximately $.10- $.50 per app. Whats good about this app is that its a simple way to make extra money without having to do anything.

How does Cash-for-Apps Pay

This app pays you in points for downloading its apps. Most apps in the list pay from 10-70 points, this can be earned for either running the app or doing a small task on the downloaded app. These points are then redeemed for gift cards or mobile phone recharge.

FeaturePoints App

FeaturePoints app is another application that lets you earn money or redeem gift cards by downloading other apps. It works the same way as Cash-for-Apps does; but if you are looking to get paid in cash for downloading such apps, this is one of the best applications for it.

Once you download the app on your Android/iOS device, go to the store page that shows you a list of apps to download. Here you can earn points for downloading apps from the list, and you use these app for about 2 minutes to earn your points.

How does FeaturePoints Pay

This app pays you though points. You can redeem these points for cash though PayPal, though gift cards or rewards like Amazon gift card, itunes, Starbucks, etc. The downloadable apps pay you from 50-100 points per download. The user needs to collect 600 points to redeem any reward. Where 600 points equal to $1.

Surveys On The Go

Survey On The Go app is like its name describes it, a survey taking app that pays you in real cash. Here you get paid to take surveys on a variety of topics like entertainment, technology, food, etc. The app works on both Android and iOS devices but its only for the users in US.

So once you download the app and sign up for it, you have to first do demographic surveys for $.50. These surveys will help the app get more surveys for you in the future. There's also a variety of topics you can choose from in the list. You can even turn on your location to get more targeted surveys. Make sure you keep opening the app to check if surveys are available or not.

How does Survey-On-The-Go Pay

This app pays its users through PayPal. The surveys you take can pay anywhere from $0.25 – $5 each, which is more than any other app will pay you. The minimum payout for this app is $10.

CoSign

CoSign is another great app that lets you earn money by uploading photos on social media. It works by taking pictures of products you like or have and uploading them on on social media platforms like

Facebook, Instagram, Pinterest with the description about the product along with its cost. These products can be of any sort, from clothing, to tech products to house hold items, basically just about anything.

After uploading the pictures of these products, you have to tag these products from over 1200 retailers on the CoSign app. This is done by searching for your product by brand name or retailer and drag/drop the correct name on the picture description. So when any of your followers purchase the product displayed, you will earn a commission of 35% of the product price.

How does CoSign Pay

The company pays you through PayPal, Check or gift card. As mentioned before, you earn 35% commission for every product that sells. And you earn points every time anyone views the product or buys it, these points can then be traded for cash. The minimum cash out is $40. So the more products you share the more you'll earn.

Fronto

Fronto is an Andriod lock screen app that pays you to unlock your phone screen and see an ad. Once you download the app, its starts showing you targeted ads on your lock screen. Every time you unlock your phone screen, you interact with the ad and you instantly get paid. How it works is that once you download the app, you fill out your profile along with your interests. The app will then show you ads related to your interests. And every time you unlock your phone, you earn points that can be exchanged for cash.

How does Fronto Pay

Fronto pays its users through PayPal or Amazon Gift card. For every encounter with an ad you earn points. Once you gather enough points, you can exchange them for cash or gift cards.

iPoll

iPoll app pays you to share your opinions about any experiences or products. Basically the app requires you to complete surveys of any kind for market research and pays you cash for your time. There are two types of missions or surveys you can do; one is location based, where you have to go to a specific location/business and complete a survey about your experience. And the second type is to watch a video or complete a survey to earn cash.

How does iPoll Pay

iPoll pays its users through PayPal or Retail Vouchers. The company pays you $5 for signing up with them. And they pay you $0.50 to $3 for every survey you complete. The minimum cash out is $50.

TaskRabbit

TaskRabbit is an app that pays you to perform small tasks for other people. According to your location, the app will show you tasks to perform in your area, you will simply bid on the task you want to perform and complete it to get paid. These tasks can be like picking up grocery, small household repairs, get food and other mundane stuff.

To start on these task, first you have to fill out an application. After that a background check will be conducted and if the company is interested, they will set up a video interview. After that you can begin working as a TaskRabbit tasker.

How does TaskRabbit Pay

The app pays its taskers through PayPal or Check. Although there is no exact amount to performing each task because you have to bid on them and get paid the money to bid on the tasks; there are people who earn \$10-\$20 per hour performing the tasks. The minimum cash out is \$25.

CheckPoints

This app allows you to earn points to check into different stores, watch videos and other stuff. These points can later be redeemed for gift cards. To start making points you have to download the app and get signed up. After that you can make points by going to the "check in" page that displays different stores you are paid to check in at, or watch videos or get paid to sign up on different websites.

How does CheckPoints Pay

CheckPoints app pays though gift cards from stores like Target, Amazon, Walmart etc. You can redeem a $1 gift card for 350 points that you make. You can make 50-100 points watching videos for 3 minutes and 15-25 points for checking in.

Phewtick

Phewtick app that pays you to meet people! You make cash by playing games and redeeming points. How it works is you set up your account on facebook. So once you log in, the app reads your locations and shows you a list of people and their profiles to interact with. The app provides you with a QR code that is to be scanned by the partner to prove they have met. Then you play a game together for points.

How does Phewtick Pay

This app pays you though PayPal or Direct deposit. Where 10 points equal $ .01.

App Trailers

App Trailer is an app that allows you to earn some money by watching videos. If you have some free time on your hands then this app will be great for you. How it works is simple; download the app, login to the system and start watching videos like music, movie or game videos.

You can also earn points by uploading videos and also by getting likes your videos. Once you have accumulated your points, you can redeem them for gift cards or cash.

How does App Trailers Pay

This app pays you either though PayPal or through gift cards from Amazon, itunes, Sephora, Footlocker, etc. Each video length is 30 seconds and you get rewarded 5 points for each video. Where 10 points equal to one cent.

CHAPTER 27
DROPSHIPPING

Drop shipping is an extremely popular business model for new entrepreneurs, especially Gen Zers and Millennials, due to internet marketing skills far outweighing financial capacity. Since you don't need to stock or handle the items you are selling, it's possible to start a drop shipping business with limited funds.

An e-commerce website that operates a drop shipping model purchases the items it sells from a third-party supplier or manufacturer, who then fulfills the order. This not only cuts operational costs, but it also frees up your time to focus all of your efforts on customer acquisition.

If you are ready to start a business that can compete with retail giants, and do so on a limited budget, then follow the six steps below. While it doesn't take a lot of startup funds to launch a drop shipping business, it will require an immense amount of hard work.

1. Select a niche

The niche you select needs to be laser-focused and something you are genuinely interested in. A product range that isn't focused will be difficult to market. If you aren't passionate about the niche you select, you will be more apt to becoming discouraged, because it takes a lot of work to successfully scale a drop shipping business. Here are some points to consider when selecting your niche:

Seek attractive profits. When you are running a drop shipping business model, your focus is on marketing and customer acquisition, so the amount of work required to sell a $20 item is essentially the same as it would be to sell a $1,500 item. Select a niche with higher-priced products.

Low shipping costs are very important. Even though your supplier or manufacturer will handle the shipping, if the cost is too high, it will act as customer repellant. Find something that is inexpensive to ship, as this also gives you the option of offering free shipping to your customers and absorbing that cost as a business expense in order to attract more sales.

Make sure your product appeals to impulse buyers with disposable income. When you are focused on driving traffic to your website, you want to experience the highest conversion rate possible because most visitors will never return. The products you are selling should trigger impulse buys and appeal to those with the financial ability to make a purchase on the spot.

Make sure people are actively searching for your product. Use Google's Keyword Planner and Trends to check some common search terms related to your potential niche. If nobody is searching for what you are planning on selling, you are dead in the water before you even begin.

Create your own brand. Your drop shipping business will have more value if you can rebrand whatever it is you are selling and pass it off as your own. Look for a product or line you can white label and sell as your own brand with custom packaging and branding.

Sell something that isn't readily available locally. Pick something your customer can't find down the street. That way, you become more attractive to a potential customer.

2. Perform competition research

Remember, you will you be competing with other drop shipping operations as well as retail giants like Walmart and Amazon. This is where a lot of potential drop shippers go wrong, because they look for a product that has little to no competition. That's a sign there isn't demand for that particular product.

There are many reasons why a product might not have a lot of competition, like high shipping costs, supplier and manufacturing issues or poor profit margins. Look for products that have competition, as it's a sign that there is a high demand and the business model is sustainable.

3. Secure a supplier

Partnering with the wrong supplier can ruin your business, so it's important that you don't rush this step. Conduct proper due diligence. Most drop shipping suppliers are located overseas, making communication extremely important, both in terms of response speed and the ability to understand each other. If you are not 100 percent confident in the communication abilities of a potential supplier, move on and continue your search.

Alibaba has become one of the largest online resources to identify and communicate with potential manufacturers and suppliers. Make sure to ask a lot of questions and learn what their production capabilities are in the event that your business grows exponentially. You want to be certain they have the ability to scale with you.

Try to learn from other entrepreneurs who have walked this path in the past. There are plenty of information sources available, from business and tech blogs to this subreddit about drop shipping. It's a popular topic that can help you avoid costly supplier mistakes.

4. Build your e-commerce website

The fastest way to launch a website that supports a drop shipping business model is to use a simple e-commerce platform like Shopify. You don't need a tech background to get up and running, and it has plenty of apps to help increase sales.

Even if you have a sizeable budget that would allow you to hire a web design and development company to create a custom solution, it's a much wiser move to use one of the plug-and-play options, especially in the beginning. Once you are established and the revenue is coming in, then you can explore additional website customization.

5. Create a customer acquisition plan

Having a great product and a website is great, but without customers looking to buy, you don't have a business. There are several ways to attract potential customers, but the most effective option is to start a Facebook ad campaign.

This allows you to generate sales and revenue right from the start, which can contribute to quick scaling. Facebook allows you to place your offer directly in front of a highly targeted audience. This gives you the ability to compete with the largest brands and retailers immediately.

You also have to think long-term, so search engine optimization and email marketing should also be a focus. Collect emails from the start and set up automated email sequences that offer discounts and special offers. It's an easy way to leverage your existing customer base and generate revenue without additional advertising and marketing spend.

6. Analyze and optimize

You need to track all of the data and metrics available to grow your business. This includes Google Analytics traffic and Facebook conversion pixel data, if that is your main customer acquisition channel. When you are able to track every single conversion -- to know where the customer originated from and what path they took on your website that eventually led to a sale -- it enables you to scale what works and eliminate what doesn't.

You will never have a set-and-forget advertising or marketing solution. You need to constantly test new opportunities and fine-tune current campaigns, which allows you to know when to optimize or shift campaign spend.

CHAPTER 28
ECOMMERCE

According to the U.S. Small Business Administration, online businesses are growing much faster than traditional brick and mortar stores.

It makes sense.

Local retail shops, DIY craft makers, and even bloggers are starting to sell their merchandise and services online.

What separates the successes from the failures? Among other things, a strategy and an excellent website can greatly contribute to the overall success for business owners. Without these, you may be setting your eCommerce site up for failure by building an eCommerce website that is less than effective. If you want to learn how to create an online store that's successful, our eCommerce website guide is the perfect resource for you.

First things first, you'll need a product to sell to figure before you can start with your eCommerce website building. Once you have your product, you can start creating your online store front and designing your eCommerce website! Click below on any of these subcategories to hop directly to the eCommerce tutorial section you need help with, or simply follow along step-by-step below:

- Create your product.
- Determine pricing for your online store.
- Figure out shipping options.
- Choose your eCommerce platform.
- Pick a domain name and brand.
- Build your eCommerce website.
- Set up your merchant account.
- Add a SSL certificate to your website.
- Start selling online!

1. Decide on your product.

If you've been dreaming of setting up an online storefront for a while, then you may well already have a product in mind that you'd like to sell. Whether it's something you make, like handcrafted furniture or handmade soap, or something you've found a source for at wholesale prices so you can sell it off at a profit, every eCommerce store has to start with a product.

Do some research to make sure your product is viable. Is there already a market out there for your product?

If there is already an established market, consider whether your product is unique enough to break in. Will you be able to compete on pricing?

Develop a MVP and get started.

2. Set your pricing.

Pricing can be one of the hardest aspects to get right when running a new business.

If you price too low, you'll lose money or just barely break even – which won't make the time and effort you put into your online store worth it. If you price too high, you won't make enough sales and still risk losing money on the whole endeavor.

To figure out what pricing that makes the sense you have to first figure out your business' finances. This includes:

- the cost of materials to make your product
- web hosting for your eCommerce site
- taxes
- shipping
- the percentage credit cards or Paypal will skim off the top
- additional marketing and advertising costs

Then figure out how much you want to add on top to pay yourself (and make a profit!).

Pricing pro tip: Before you set your final pricing, research what your competition is charging. You may get to bump your prices up a bit (oh happy day!), or you may have to lower them in order to stay competitive.

3. Research shipping costs and options.

If you're selling a physical product, how will you deliver it to customers?

Your impulse may be to pass on the full cost of shipping to the client, and many online stores do take this route. However, it's important to note that shipping costs can have a strong psychological impact on consumers, with 44% saying they've abandoned an online purchase due to high shipping and handing costs.

Instead, consider offering one of these alternative shipping methods:

Offer free shipping, no questions asked
Offer free shipping and up your product pricing slightly to cover the cost
Offer free shipping for orders of a certain size
Offer a flat shipping fee

4. Choose your eCommerce web hosting.

When it comes to eCommerce, you have two options: use a marketplace that already exists like Etsy or Amazon, or building an eCommerce website and brand that's all your own.

If you want a website and brand that's all your own, many website hosting platforms (including HostGator) make it easy to find compatible eCommerce website hosting options that you can work with in the same space you use to work on your website. This way you can direct people to youronlinestore.com. You look like a real, live store!

An eCommerce software like Magento will make it easy for you to list your products, set your price, and add a shopping cart to the website. They take care of ensuring the process is intuitive for both you and your customers, so you can just focus on selling.

5. Pick a domain name and brand.

This is the fun part for business owners! Just think, what will customers be telling their friends when they talked about that awesome new product they just bought from _____? Fill in the blank with your brand.

Brainstorm words and phrases that say something about the products you'll be selling, and words and phrases that mean something to you. And be sure to stay away from names that have already been copyrighted by other businesses. Follow these top tips for choosing a domain name for your eCommerce website.

6. Build your eCommerce website.

Many hosting platforms can make at least part of this step easier by providing or a merchant site builder you can work from rather than having to build a website from scratch.

At this stage, you'll also need to work on writing web copy that describes your wares and helps persuade website visitors to buy.

Once you set up your site, you have to do more than just add your products. In addition to product pages, your eCommerce website development and planning should also include the following pages:

- A home page where you feature weekly deals and sale items
- An about page with a brief description of what you do
- A contact or customer service page so customers can easily reach you
- A blog where you post updates, industry news, and helpful tidbits
- Aside from these pages, you will also have to consider your website's theme, eCommerce plugin options, Google Analytics, and all

other practical aspects that will help create your online platform.

7. Set up a merchant account.

Online stores need a way to receive money – specifically, a way to receive credit card payments. A merchant account does the very important job of ensuring you can get paid.

You have options that range from big, familiar brand names like Chase and PayPal, to companies more focused on small businesses like BluePay and PaySimple. You will have to pay a small fee to the company in order to get your money, but the ability to accept the money your customers send will make the fees well worth it.

8. Get your SSL certificate.

When you create your site, be sure to install a SSL certificate. These certificates provide the green lock you see next to URLs when you're shopping online, and they keep your customers' private information safe.

PayPal SSL Certificate

If customers are going to hand you their private payment information (or more accurately, enter it into a form on your website), you need to make sure the sensitive details will stay safe. An SSL certificate for your website encrypts all the sensitive information customers provide so that hackers won't be able to grab that credit card information as it's sent over the web.

9. Start selling!

Now it's time to start making money.

Once you launch your online store, you should start thinking about promotion. Content marketing, social media, and paid promotion are all areas worth looking into to start getting people to your website. Check out our post on cheap, easy ways to start marketing your business.

If you're not quite ready to make that level of investment in your online store, start with old-fashioned word of mouth. Talk to your friends about it, mention it to professional acquaintances, and bring it up at any events around town likely to attract the kind of people interested in what you're selling.

Wrapping Up

Brick and mortar business will likely always be around, but the internet gives users access to a larger selection of products and services. Now, the world has access to YOUR products and YOUR services.

Once you have learned how to set up an eCommerce website for your eCommerce business, take a moment to pat yourself on the back. You're an entrepreneur now. Then get back to work!

Are you ready to start selling online? At HostGator, we'll teach you how to build an eCommerce website in no time at all. Start your eCommerce website today by using our step-by-step instructions in this guide.

CHAPTER 29
START A BLOG OR BUY A BLOG

Here is how to make money from a blog:

- Set up your blog
- Start creating useful content
- Get off your blog and start finding readers
- Build engagement with the readers that come
- Start making money from the readership you have through one or more of a variety of income streams

Sounds easy doesn't it! On some levels the process is simple – but you need to know up front that there's a lot to each step and below I'm going to give you some pointers on each including some further reading.

Here's how to make money from a blog.

1. Start a Blog

In order to make money blogging you're going to need to have a blog. While this is pretty obvious it is also a stumbling block for many PreBloggers who come to the idea of blogging with little or no technical background.

If that's you – don't worry! It was my story too and most bloggers start out feeling a little overwhelmed by the process of starting their blog.

2. Start Creating Useful Content

A blog is not a blog without content so once you've set your blog up you need to focus your attention upon creating useful content. What you choose to create will depend a little on the topic that you choose to write about (on that note, most successful bloggers have some focus to their blogging whether that be a niche or a demographic that they write for).

The key with creating content is to make it as useful as possible. Focus upon creating content that changes people's lives in some way will be the type of content that people will value the most and it will help people to feel like they know, like and trust you – which is really important if you later want to make money from your blog.

3. Get off your blog and start finding readers

As you create the most useful content that you possibly can it is easy to get very insular with your focus and spend most of your time looking at building your blog. Many bloggers have a 'build it and they will come mentality' with their blogging but this is a bit of a trap.

If you want to make money from your blog you need to not only focus upon building a great blog but it is also necessary to get off your blog and to start promoting it.

There are many ways to experiment with growing your blog's audience that I've written in previous blog posts and talked about in podcasts (I'll share some further reading and listening below) but it is important to enter into all these strategies remembering that you should not just be looking for 'traffic' but 'readers'.

Start by thinking carefully about the type of reader you'd like to have read your blog.

Once you know who you're hoping to have read your blog ask yourself where that type of person might already be gathering online. Begin to list where they might be gathering:

- Are they reading certain blogs? List the top 3
- Are they participating in certain forums? List the top 3
- Are they listening to podcasts? List the top 3
- Are they engaging on certain social networks? List the top 3

- Which accounts are they following on each of these social networks? List the top 3

Each of these places that you reader might already be gathering has opportunities to develop a presence whether that be by leaving good comments, offering to create guest posts or simply by being helpful and answering questions.

With this list of blogs, focus, podcasts, social media accounts in hand you will have some good spots to begin to hang out and create value.

The key is to build a presence, to add value, to foster relationships – not to engage in spammy practices.

4. Build engagement with the readers that come

With sustained focus upon creating great content and finding readers for your blog you'll begin to notice people visiting your blog and engaging with your content.

At this point you need to switch your focus to engaging with those readers and building community.

Respond to comments, reach out to those readers personally and do everything that you can to keep them coming back again and again by building a 'sticky blog'.

Look after the readers you already have well and you'll find they spread the word of your blog for you and help make your blog even more widely read.

Having an engaged reader is also much easier to make money from.

5. Start making money from the readership you have through one or more of a variety of income streams

OK – the first four steps of starting a blog, creating content, finding readers and building engagement with those readers are important foundations that you really do need to get in place before you'll be able to build long term income for your blog.

There's no avoiding that what we've covered is a lot of work but if you do it well you'll be setting yourself up well and giving yourself every chance of being able to make money from your blog.

With these foundations in place you're now ready to start attempting to make money from your blog but you do need to be aware that just because you have set up your blog, have content and have engaged readers that the money won't just automatically flow.

It takes continued work and experimentation to make money from your blog.

I've written many articles here on ProBlogger on the topic of making money blogging and will link to some suggested further reading on the topic below but let me share a few introductory words on the topic first.

There are Many Ways to Make Money Blogging

One of the biggest misconceptions that I see bloggers having about monetising blogs is that they have to do it in one of a handful of ways. The reality is that there are many ways to make money from blogs.

1. Advertising Income

This is where many bloggers start. In many ways this model of making money from blogs is not dissimilar to how a magazine or newspaper sells ads. As your traffic and brand grows you'll find advertisers will be willing to pay to get exposure to your audience.

While you need decent traffic to do a direct deal with an advertisers there are ad networks (like Google AdSense) that act as a middleman and enable smaller publishers to run ads on their blogs. This is where many bloggers start (I did too).

2. Affiliate Income

A recent survey of ProBlogger readers found that affiliate promotions was the most common type of income that our readers have.

To put it most simply – affiliate income is when you link to a product that is for sale on another site (take Amazon for example) and if someone follows your link and ends up buying that product you earn a commission on that sale.

There's more to it than that but this is another great place to start with monetising your blog as affiliate programs are easy to sign up for and if you have an engaged audience you will find they follow the recommendations that you make on products.

3. Events

While not something most bloggers do I have noticed an increase in the number of bloggers making money by running events.

Alternatively online events or summits are getting more popular.

4. Recurring Income

Another growing category of income that I'm seeing more and more bloggers are experimenting is recurring income streams (sometimes called continuity programs or membership programs).

This is where readers pay a regular recurring amount (usually on a monthly or annual basis) for access to either premium content, a community area, some kind of service, tools, coaching (or some combination of these things).

6. Promoting a Business

Many brick and mortar businesses indirectly make money from their blogs by using their blogs to grow their profile and direct readers to their business.

7. Services

A common way that many bloggers make money is through offering services to their readers. These might be anything from coaching and consulting, to writing or copywriting, to design, training or other freelance services.

8. Products

While I started out making money from my blogs through advertising and affiliate promotions today my #1 source of income is through selling eBooks and courses on my blogs. These 'virtual products' take work to create but have been lucrative for me and many other bloggers.

Products can of course take many forms and income virtual information products like eBooks or courses but also other virtual products like software, reports etc.

The other type of product some bloggers sell is physical products. This is most common when the blogger has a business but sometimes bloggers also create merchandise (T-shirts etc) or other physical products to sell.

Other Income Streams

There are of course other forms of income that bloggers experiment with. Some include asking for donations, syndicating content to other sites and lastly selling their blogs.
Multiple Income Streams
Most full time bloggers make money more than one way and end up with multiple income streams.

Diversifying your income in this way not only is smart and helps you spread the risk from having all your eggs in one basket but it also speeds up the journey to going full time.

CHAPTER 30
ONLINE ARBITRAGE

Online arbitrage (sometimes referred to as retail arbitrage) is, like all sales ventures, based on the concept, "buy low and sell high," but in this case it's "buy lower and sell higher." You buy goods online at a lower price than they're currently selling for on Amazon, and then resell them on Amazon at a profit, taking advantage of that price mismatch.

Unlike some other forms of arbitrage or reselling, in online arbitrage you buy online only, not from brick and mortar stores. And you do so as a consumer, at retail prices, not as a business buying at wholesale prices directly from a manufacturer or distributor.

Online arbitrage is not the same as Amazon-to-eBay Arbitrage, which involves finding items available from Amazon and listing them for sale at a higher price on eBay but not actually buying them until the items you've listed sell on eBay. In online arbitrage as discussed here, the arbitrager buys merchandise before listing it for sale. You can limit your online selling activities to Amazon, or use online arbitrage in addition to selling through another channel, such as your own website or a Shopify store.

In order to list items for sale on Amazon, you'll need to set up a seller account. There is an Individual seller option, but most people who are serious about giving online arbitrage a try will establish a Professional Seller account. You'll need to familiarize yourself with Amazon's rules for selling. You don't want to find that your account is suspended over an infraction of a rule you weren't even aware of.

Here are some ideas that should help you get started on the path to success in online arbitrage.

What to Buy
Where to Buy
How Much to Pay
Automated Tools
Fulfilment by Amazon (FBA)
Keep It Legal
It's a Home-Based Business
Use Social Media
Invest in Your Success
Start Small

1. What to Buy

Aside from price, which we'll look at shortly, the most important consideration in selecting products to buy for resale is that you want to sell them off quickly, not stockpile them long-term in your garage or basement. Two indicators of a product that will sell well are decent product reviews and a good Amazon seller ranking.

Since you will be taking delivery of the goods you buy, you will need to consider your storage capacity as well. If your only storage space is a hall closet in your home, you probably shouldn't be looking to buy and resell pianos or big-screen televisions. Buying smaller items will also help keep your shipping costs down.

Some online arbitragers leverage their knowledge of a particular niche, such as toys or consumer electronics, or high-end cookware, to develop a specialized business. Others prefer to remain flexible and buy an eclectic assortment of merchandise.

2. Where to Buy

In online arbitrage, you buy from online retailers that are known for their low prices and frequent promotions and clearances. In the United States, Walmart.com is a prime example. However, that means that plenty of other online arbitragers will be looking for bargains there, too. You may be better off searching in niche stores, especially if you are specializing in a particular product niche.

3. How Much to Pay

Online arbitragers typically look for items selling at no more than half of their current Amazon listing price. The price difference needs to be large enough to cover shipping charges and your listing fees and still leave you with a good profit margin. Bear in mind that prices can change unexpectedly, turning what looked like a profitable deal into a losing proposition.

4. Automated Tools

Finding arbitrage opportunities could easily eat up every waking hour if you let it. There is simply no way for one person to monitor enough products and enough sources without using some of the many available automated tools designed specifically to support online arbitrage.

Amazon's price tracking software gives you the price history of all of the products sold on Amazon. Amazon price trackers make it easy to distinguish temporary price anomalies from the typical price for a product over time, helping you avoid acting on a short-term price increase that may well disappear by the time you have purchased units to list for resale.

Amazon also offers revenue calculators to help you determine how much you need to charge for an item to cover fees and make a profit. There are separate revenue calculators for North America (US, Mexico, Canada) and Europe.

There are a number of price monitoring tools that yield daily lists of products you may want to consider buying for resale on Amazon. The Web Retailer Directory is a good source of information about arbitrage deal finders. Most of these tools are available for a monthly fee (typically from $20 to $100 per month).

5. Fulfilment by Amazon (FBA)

When you use Amazon's FBA program, you take delivery of the items you have bought for resale, label and package them, box them all up, and ship them to Amazon's warehouse. From that point on, Amazon takes over, assuming responsibility for fulfilling customer orders and providing after-sale customer service. You'll pay the FBS fee, but in the long run, it can save you a lot of time and money that would otherwise go to packaging and shipping each individual customer order. It also means you get to use your hall closet for its intended purpose: storing coats and umbrellas, not merchandise waiting to be sold.

6. Keep It Legal

Some online arbitragers have received "cease and desist" letters from the manufacturers of goods they are reselling on Amazon, raising questions as to the legality of online arbitrage. Rest assured that the practice is legal, based on the legal concept of the "first sale." The first sale doctrine establishes the legality of reselling any authentic item that you have obtained through legal means, the word "authentic" being very significant.

You could find yourself in hot water if you sell counterfeit items even if you buy them from established retailers, believing them to be authentic. If the manufacturer becomes aware that you are selling counterfeits, you could be sued for trademark infringement. The simple solution is to avoid buying designer products that carry major, well-known labels, because those manufacturers keep a close eye on Amazon, eBay, Etsy and other online sellers to try to maintain control over their valuable trademarks and avoid dilution of their brands.

Even so, manufacturers of trademarked goods often distribute their products only through authorized sellers, and if you don't have a distributorship agreement with them, you might receive one of those "cease and desist" letters.

7. It's a Home-Based Business

Another aspect of keeping it legal is to run your online arbitrage operation as a legitimate home-based business. Set up a legal business entity, whether it's a sole proprietorship, a limited liability corporation (LLC), or something else. Get some legal and tax advice to make sure that you're in compliance with applicable local, state, and federal laws and regulations.

Keeping detailed records of your income and expenses will facilitate the preparation of tax returns and give you a realistic picture of your cash flow and the profitability of your online arbitrage activities. Consider using off-the-shelf accounting software to automate your bookkeeping, check writing, and tax preparation.

8. Use Social Media

Successful online arbitragers typically use social media to drive traffic to their Amazon listings, so try to learn something about social media marketing if the concept is new to you. Try embedding a link to your Amazon page in your posts on Facebook, Instagram, Twitter, and any other social media platform you use.

Getting your social media followers to Amazon, which has a higher conversion rate than any other website, should boost your sales significantly, especially if your followers share your posts with others. Try setting up a business page on Facebook and using Facebook ads to direct visitors to your Amazon page.

9. Invest in Your Success

Invest the time to learn more about online arbitrage before diving into it headfirst. There are numerous online resources, from blogs to YouTube videos, to full-blown courses that will help you educate yourself. Decide how much money and time you're able to put into launching your arbitrage business. Be prepared to spend at least a few hundred dollars to get started.

Learn as much as you can about all of the fees and expenses you'll incur so that you can set your pricing to yield a reasonable profit. And understand that online arbitrage involves some degree of risk, most notably the risk that the price mismatch could disappear before you sell out your inventory of an item.

10. Start Small

Try wading before you venture into the deep end of the pool. Once you have a firm grasp of the process, try it out with a few select items, or even a relatively small quantity of one item, to test out your assumptions about demand and pricing. Many online arbitragers work at it for only a few hours a week, regarding it as an additional income stream rather than a primary source of income. Others eventually become full-time arbitragers, but the majority fall somewhere in between. You'll find the involvement level that suits you best once you've gained some experience in online arbitrage.

CHAPTER 31
AMAZON FBA

The Fulfillment by Amazon (FBA) business model continues to grow in popularity, and for good reason. Fundamentally, it's the same as a traditional ecommerce business. But, instead of your having to fulfill orders one by one, Amazon stores your products for you and even picks, packs and ships them out to customers.

This makes it a lot easier for you to build your business without having to worry about the logistics of warehouses, packaging materials, couriers and so on. With private labeling, you also have the opportunity to build your own brand and website, thereby increasing the value of your business.

Raring to go? Here's our basic guide for starting an FBA business.

What Is Fulfillment by Amazon?

The FBA business model allows you to leverage Amazon's robust distribution network and customer base. As noted, Amazon will warehouse your products, fulfill orders and even provide customer service so you don't have to be hands-on with every aspect of the business.

What this means for entrepreneurs is that you can act like a big corporation without the headache of actually being one. You can focus on finding product opportunities while Amazon handles the rest on your behalf.

In a typical ecommerce business, you have to figure out the logistics of sending products to your customers in a timely manner. However, with FBA, Prime members get most orders shipped to their door within two to five days.

Another common challenge with an ecommerce store is that inventorying and listing additional products for sale can increase the complexity of your business. With FBA, all you need to do is ship the products to Amazon's warehouse, and the company will take over from there. You can easily increase your product selection without significantly adding to your workload.

Create an Amazon seller account.

First things first: In order to get your FBA business up and running, you're going to need to create an Amazon seller account. Go to Amazon's website, scroll down to the footer and look for the heading marked "Make Money with Us." Then, click on the link that reads "Sell on Amazon."

At this point, you can either sign up as an "Individual" or a "Professional." When you sign up as an "Individual," you will not be charged a monthly subscription fee. If you're looking to build a business over the long haul, then you'll want to sign up as a "Professional." The first month is free, and after that, it's $39.99 per month plus selling fees.

Other than that, the signup process is relatively straightforward. Follow the onscreen instructions and complete setup.

Uncover product opportunities and establish your private label.

There are a number of different ways to leverage the FBA model, but the most popular way is private labeling. The idea is to establish a brand or label, apply it to your product and sell it on Amazon.

First, you will need to do your Amazon product research. This is the most important step for a variety of reasons. If you enter an unpopular product category and sell a product for more than your competition is selling it for, you could lose money on that product. If you take the time to find a popular product category, do competitive analysis, study product reviews and identify a product that you can improve upon or sell at a better price, you'll have found the sweet spot.

Another popular way to sell products through Amazon is with retail arbitrage -- buying a brand name product and flipping it on Amazon for profit. This is a much easier way of making money on Amazon, at least in the short term.

With private labeling, you need capital. Ordering private label products may cost you several thousand dollars, but if you're looking to build an asset that can later be sold, then this is the direction you want to go in.

Another key piece of the puzzle is your supplier. You can't make money if you don't have products in stock, so you need to ensure that the time delay between the placement and delivery of the order is as short as it can possibly be.

Tips for growing and scaling your FBA business

- Pursue your passion. If you enjoy doing it, you will stick with it for longer. Find a product category that interests and excites you.
- Increase your product offerings. You will need to do proper research for every new product offering you create. Having more

products can reduce the risk of your business becoming dependent on just one product.

- Improve your Best Sellers Rank. BSR is an important metric for both your customers and your sales. This is also a key factor when the time comes to sell your business. Buyers will want to see steady growth in your BSR rank over time.
- Build your brand website. As you continue to expand your private label product offerings, you'll want to build a professional, dedicated site for your business. This gives you another way to market your products, and can also make your business attractive to potential buyers.
- Become an Amazon Associate. Increase your revenues by becoming an affiliate with Amazon. Refer customers to your products from your own site, and start earning commissions.
- Earning potential

How much do FBA business owners earn? What is the earning potential of an FBA business?

Spencer Haws from Niche Pursuits reports he was able to make nearly $40,000 within 30 days of starting his FBA business. Chris Guthrie from UpFuel made almost $3,000 within 30 days. James

Amazio, founder of Feedbackz, went from zero to $50,000 per month in just eight months.

These results aren't necessarily typical, but they do show that it is possible to build a five-, six- or even seven-figure business by leveraging the FBA model.

Final thoughts

Although starting an FBA business will require up-front capital, the effort will be nowhere near as intensive as it would be with a traditional ecommerce business. Getting your business off the ground is the easy part. Finding ways to grow your FBA business is the more difficult part. Take advantage of the resources available to you, and systematize your processes as you go.

CHAPTER 32
BUY EXISTING BUSINESS

Buying a company that's already established may be quicker and easier than starting from scratch.

However, you will need to put time and effort into finding the business that's right for you. Also, the costs involved in buying an existing business can be substantial and should not be underestimated.

This guide takes you through the steps of buying an existing business, including how to assess and value a business and your obligations to any existing staff.

Advantages and disadvantages of buying a business

There can be many good reasons why buying an existing business could make good business sense. Remember though, that you will be taking on the legacy of the previous business owner. You need to be aware of every aspect of the business you're about to buy.

Advantages

- Some of the groundwork to get the business up and running will have been done
- It may be easier to obtain finance as the business will have a proven track record
- A market for the product or service will have already been demonstrated
- There may be established customers, a reliable income and a reputation to capitalise and build on. There will be a useful network of contacts
- A business plan and marketing method should already be in place
- Existing employees should have experience you can draw on
- Many of the problems will have been discovered and solved already

Disadvantages

- You often need to invest a large amount up front, and will also have to budget for professional fees for solicitors, surveyors, accountants etc
- You will probably also need several months' worth of working capital to assist with cashflow

- For a neglected business you may need to invest more on top of the purchase price to give it the best chance of success
- You may need to honour or renegotiate any outstanding contracts the previous owner leaves
- You also need to consider why the current owner is selling up. Think about how this might impact the business and your taking it over
- Current staff may not be happy with a new boss, or the business might have been run badly and staff morale may be low

Decide on the business to buy

Any business you buy needs to fit your own skills, lifestyle and aspirations. Before you start looking, think about what you can bring to a business and what you'd like to get back. List what is important to you. Look at your motivations and what you ultimately want to achieve.

It is useful to consider:

- Your abilities - can you achieve what you want to achieve?
- Your capital - how much money do you have to invest?

- Your expectations in terms of earning - what level of profit do you need to be looking for to accommodate your needs?
- Your commitment - are you prepared for all the hard work and money that you will need to put into the business to get it to succeed?
- Your strengths - what kind of business opportunity will give you the chance to put your skills and experience to good use?
- The business sector you're interested in - learn as much as you can about your chosen industry so you can compare different businesses. It's important to take the time to talk to people already in similar businesses. The internet and your local library will also be good sources of information
- Location - don't restrict your search to your local area. Some businesses can be easily relocated

4. How to value a business

There are several valuation methods you can use to value a business. Your accountant may be able to help. However, a business transfer agent, business broker or corporate financier will be best qualified to provide valuation advice.

Look at:

- the history of the business

- its current performance - sales, turnover, profit
- future projections or a business plan
- its financial situation - cashflow, debts, expenses, assets
- why the business is being sold
- any outstanding or major litigation the business is involved in
- any regulatory changes which might have an impact on the business
- Talk to the vendor and, if possible, the business' existing customers and suppliers. The vendor must be comfortable with you doing this and you must be sensitive to their position. Customer and suppliers may be able to give you information that affects your valuation, as well as information about market conditions affecting the business.

For example, if the vendor is being forced to sell due to decreasing profits, your valuation might be lower.

Intangible assets

Valuing the intangible assets is usually difficult and could include:

- the company's reputation
- the relationship with suppliers
- the value of goodwill

- the value of licences
- patents or intellectual property

Other factors that will affect the value:

- stock
- location
- assets
- products
- debtors
- creditors
- suppliers
- employees
- premises
- competition
- benchmarking - what other businesses in the sector have sold for
- who else in the sector is for sale or on the market
- the economic climate - will any new government legislation have an impact on the business

5. Due diligence

Once an offer has been made and accepted a period of time is allowed for you to access the business' books and records. This is known as due diligence.

It should give you a realistic picture of how the business is performing now, and how it is likely to perform in the future. It should also highlight any issues or problems which might need warranting or guaranteeing.

There are traditionally three types of due diligence. You might need different advisors for each:

- legal due diligence - as part of a sales and purchase contract, the lawyers can check that the business has legal title to sell, ownership of all the assets and that regulatory and litigation issues are fully addressed
- financial due diligence - checking the numbers and making sure there are no black holes or hidden financial issues
- commercial due diligence - finding out the business' place in the marketplace, checking competitors and the regulatory environment

Don't start due diligence until you have agreed a price and terms with the seller. They may agree to take the business off the market during your investigation. This is known as an exclusivity period and the seller will often ask for a down payment to secure it.

The investigation period is negotiable - but most small businesses need at least three to four weeks.

Where to get help

Ideally you should get accountants and solicitors to help you identify risk areas. If it is registered with Companies House, you can also obtain copies of the company accounts, the annual return and the other key documents.

Due diligence is about more than the finances of a business. You need to know exactly what you are getting into, what needs to be fixed, what it will cost to fix, and if you are the right person to take on this business.

Key areas to cover are:

- employment terms and conditions
- outstanding litigation
- major contracts and orders
- IT systems and other technology
- environmental issues
- commercial management including customer service, research and development, and marketing
- You may also need information from external sources such as the landlord, tax office or bank.

6. Buying a business

- An organised approach will help you find and acquire the right business.
- Get professional advice
- Professional help is invaluable as you go through the negotiation, valuation and purchase process.

Research

Research the sector you're interested in, including the best time to buy, and shortlist two or three businesses.

Initial viewing and valuation

Be discreet - the owner may not want staff to know they are selling, but be thorough and record key findings.

Arrange finance

Lenders generally require:

- details of the business/sales particulars
- accounts for the last three years
- financial projections - if no accounts are available
- details of your personal assets and liabilities

Make a formal offer

If you make your initial offer by phone, follow this up in writing. Head your letter 'subject to contract' and include this phrase in all written communication.

Negotiation

Before completing the sale, it may be worth trying to negotiate an overlap period so you have time to become familiar with the business before taking over.

You and your solicitor need to verify the information you have based your offer on.

If you're buying premises, you may want to arrange an independent survey and valuation, even if a lender is also carrying out their own survey and valuation at your expense.

Completion

Even after you reach an agreement on the price and terms of sale, the deal could still fall through. You have to meet certain conditions of sale to complete, including:

- verification of financial statements
- transfer of leases
- transfer of contracts/licences
- transfer of finance
- transfer of existing or new VAT registration

7. Looking after existing employees

There are regulations that govern what happens to employees when someone new takes over a business.

These apply to all employees when a business is transferred as a going concern. This means employees automatically start working for the new owner under the same terms and conditions.

Employment tribunal awards

When you buy an existing business, you might decide you need to employ fewer staff. But be careful about making any changes, as an employee might take a case to an employment tribunal for unfair dismissal or unfair selection for redundancy. It's best to consult a solicitor before making any such changes.

Inform and consult employees

You may want to discuss reducing employee numbers or reorganising staff. However, it's a good idea to wait until you have completed the due diligence period, but before you take over the business. As the new employer you should inform and consult all employees - including employee representatives - who may be affected.

Pensions

As their new employer, you do not have to take over rights and obligations relating to employees' occupational pension schemes put in place by the previous employer. However, if you don't provide comparable pensions arrangements, you could theoretically face a claim for unfair dismissal.

CHAPTER 33
BUY ROYALTIES

Dolly Parton is still collecting royalties from her song, "I Will Always Love You."

It was originally recorded in 1973 and was #1 Billboard country song in 1974 and 1982. Then Whitney Houston covered it for the movie The Bodyguard in 1992 and it reached the #1 spot again and became one of the best-selling singles of all time.

Wouldn't it be amazing to be able to collect royalties on songs like these, forever?

Even if you've never written a song, you can still collect on royalties. If you're looking for an alternative investment opportunity, royalties are worth looking at.

While stock prices constantly fluctuate, royalty revenues have continued to grow.

According to the International Confederation of Societies of Authors and Composers, in 2008 the 2.5 million artists represented by the group collected over seven billion Euros in royalties.

Now You Can Collect Royalties for Songs You Didn't Even Write How is it possible?

There are times when an artist who owns the royalties for a song, and they would rather have some of the money right now. Maybe they want to buy a house, or build their business, or cover immediate living expenses.

Investors who want to have a stable income stream can buy a percentage of those royalties on The Royalty Exchange.

The Royalty Exchange is the #1 marketplace for buying and selling royalties. The company was founded in 2011, and they have auctions and even IPO's on music catalogs like pre-2013 Eminem.

The owner of the royalties puts their work up for auction, with a minimum bid that they will accept. Once the royalties are purchased, the organizations that pay the royalties put the money into an escrow account and the royalties are then paid every quarter or every six months. Buyers get a dashboard where they can keep track of their purchases and earnings.

For example, someone bought 25% of the royalties for the 1984 Alabama song, "If You're Gonna Play in Texas," for $56,000. The website shows that that song earned $4,992 in royalties over the past 12 months.

The royalties for an album of worship music was sold for $122,000. That album earned $20,190 in royalties over the past 12 months.

Sometimes the royalties are auctioned off by a collaborator of the song, or by someone who has inherited the royalty rights.

According to an article called, "Are Music Royalties a New Alternative Investment?" by John Waggoner in Investment News, Tony Geiss, the songwriter for a collection of Sesame Street songs including "Elmo's World" gave his share of the royalties to charity. His estate auctioned them off for $580,000 so that the charities could benefit from the gift immediately.

Royalties can go up because a song was used in a soundtrack or because one of the artists died. Royalties for songs are not correlated to the stock market, which is a big draw for investors.

Get Started on These Platforms

The Royalty Exchange is an online royalty marketplace where you can bid on royalties in many industries such as music, film, TV, books, solar energy, pharmaceutical, intellectual property, oil, gas and more. You pay a 2.5% buyer premium and another 2.5% for the management and payout of your royalty stream.

Lyric Financial is another royalty platform to try. Lyric Financial is a company created to help musicians have the money they need to finance their careers and pay the bills. They give musicians short-term advances on their all or a portion of their royalties. They also offer lines of credit to musicians who earn $100,000 or more a year in royalties.

SongVest describes themselves as the stock market of music. Through their website, you can buy or sell royalties. Fans can finance albums that are being made now through a crowdfunding model, and in return get a percentage of the royalties. The money raised allows the musicians to create and market the albums.

How Can You Tell if a Song Will Earn a Lot of Money?

According to an article on The Royalty Exchange, the most important factor in how much money a song makes is how often it is used. The more popular the song is, the more it is played, and the more money it will make.

In addition to popularity, holiday songs make a lot of money over a long period of time because they are played over and over every year.

If a song is used in a soundtrack to a movie, it will earn more royalties.

And when a song is covered and reinterpreted by a new artist, both the original artist and the new artist will earn royalties.

The top ten highest earning songs are "Candle in the Wind," by Elton John and Bernie Taupin; "The Christmas Song," by Mel Torme and Bob Wells; "Pretty Woman" by Roy Orbison and Bill Dees; "Every Breath You Take," by Sting; "Santa Claus is Coming to Town" by Haven Gillespie and Fred J. Coots; "Stand By Me," by Ben E. King, Jerry Leiber and Mike Stoller; "Unchained Melody," by Alex North and Hy Zaret; "Yesterday" by John Lennon and Paul McCartney; "You've Lost That Feeling," by Barry Mann, Cynthia Weil and Phil Spector; and "White Christmas," by Irving Berlin.

Pension Funds are Increasing their Returns by Investing in Royalties

In his article, "Warren Buffett's Tollbooth Investment Strategy," Simon Black writes that most pension funds are seriously underfunded simply because they get a low return.

When pension managers invest, they are looking for ways to get a safe return. Unfortunately, it's nearly impossible to get a safe return of more than 7-8%.

But royalties are different. Royalties can often bring in as much as 10-25% per year.

You are getting paid for other people to use an asset that you own. Warren Buffett compares owning royalties to owning a toll road. Once you build the road you can collect cash forever just for letting people use the road.

For this reason, many pension fund managers have been adding royalties to their mix of assets as a way to safely boost their returns.

The Canada Pension Plan Investment Board allocated $325 million for a percentage of the royalties in Venetoclax, a cancer drug.

Round Hill Music Royalty Fund owns rights to more than 4,000 songs, including Chris Kenner's Land of a Thousand Dances, which appears in the movie Forrest Gump. According to the CEO of Round Hill Music Royalty Fund, the song generates between $300,000-$400,000 a year.

The benefits of investing in royalties are that you can have a steady income that lasts for the lifetime of the copyright or patent, royalties are not influenced by the stock market and so they are a good way to diversify your portfolio, and there is always the possibility that your royalty will have a revenue spike.

You Can Invest in Royalties in Other Industries

What is a royalty? Whenever the owner of an asset is paid so that other people can use that asset, they are receiving a royalty.

Aside from the entertainment industry, people can invest in royalties in oil, natural gas, and other minerals.

In her article, "Royalties as an Alternative Investment," Enelda Butler explained it this way: "The owner may license the asset to be used by another party, and will be paid a percentage of the net revenues of the asset based on its usage. Royalties can also be used to allow investors in a company to have a percentage ownership of future production or revenues that will be paid at specified intervals like annually, quarterly or monthly."

It's like owning an oil well without all the drilling. Owning and operating an oil well is out of reach for most people.

But you can get a percentage of all the revenue that comes from all that by investing in an oil and gas royalty trust.

In "Energy Investing 101: Tackling Oil & Gas Royalty Trusts," Motley Fool writer Tyler Crowe provides a good primer for people who want to take advantage of these high-yield investments.

Investing in a royalty trust is similar to buying the royalties to a song. The oil company will issue units of a royalty trust so that they can raise capital.

There are several reasons why these investments are worth including in your portfolio.

- They are corporate tax-exempt.
- The distributions count as capital gains, which have a lower tax rate.
- You will become a part owner, which means that you can lower your cost basis by depreciating the asset, delay your taxes and take advantage of tax credits.
- The ten largest oil and gas royalty trusts get returns that range from 8.4% to 28.5%. Royalty trusts are required to distribute all of their cash flow, which is why the yields are so high.
- Oil and gas royalty trusts are more like bonds than trusts. They have a finite lifespan. Crowe said, "It's value slowly declines over time until it's no longer economically feasible to pull oil and gas from the well."

The amount of the distributions vary depending on oil and gas prices, how much the wells are producing and other factors. Although the yields may be high, there is no guarantee that you will earn back the principal. That said, some of the well-established trusts have beaten the S&P 500 for the past 15 years.

Before deciding to invest, the Motley Fool recommends looking at three things. 1) The production mix of the well; what percentage is oil, natural gas, etc. 2) The Payback period; the amount of time it will take to break even. 3) The shelf life of the trust; the total amount of time the trust will be in production.

Royalty Companies in the Mining Industry

In a Stansberry Research article called, "How to Make the Biggest Safest Returns Possible with Royalty Companies," John Doody, the editor of Gold Stock Analyst, explains the benefits of investing in royalty companies.

One of the biggest benefits is that investing in royalty companies lets you enjoy the high returns from the precious metals mines without the risk that can come with mines.

"There's a lot of risk associated with a one- or two-mine company. It's common to see mines encounter difficulties for various reasons, and the related mining stocks might lose 25%, 50%, or more of their value in one day," said Doody. "On the other hand, if a big royalty company had a royalty on that mine, it wouldn't be a big deal, because there would be royalties from other mines that could take up the slack."

Royalties as a Form of Venture Capital Financing

epaCUBE was founded in Dallas, TX, in 2001. It is a SaaS company that provides profit optimization solutions.

They needed funding so that they could adjust their business model and fund new sales and marketing effort. To make this happen, they went to Cypress Growth Capital, who gave them $2 million in 2013.

Cypress offers royalty-based growth capital. The Cypress Growth Capital website said, "Unlike a traditional equity investment, extraordinary growth projections and market opportunity are not prerequisites for royalty-based growth capital. As a royalty investor, our investment success is not dependent on an exit event, like a sale of the company or a public stock offering."

Entrepreneurs and start-ups are turning to a royalty based model of capital funding, like the ones offered at Cypress.

Normally, companies have to give up the control of their company and a chunk of equity whenever they receive funding from investors. But with royalty-based financing, investors get a monthly payout based on the revenue of the company. Rather than get an ownership stake, investors get a guaranteed percentage of the sales.

Royalty Capital Management, BDC Capital and Rockwater Capital are three investment firms that specialize in the royalty-based model.

Diversify Your Portfolio with Royalties

Investing in royalties is a good way to diversify your portfolio because it is possible to get a high return on your investment with relatively low risk.

Musicians occasionally sell all or part of the royalties for their songs and albums, and investors can bid on them on several online marketplaces. Once you win a bid on a royalty, you will receive the royalty checks whenever that song is played. Many pension funds are turning to royalties as a way to increase their yields.

Other industries have opportunities to buy royalties. The oil and gas industry sells royalty rights through oil and gas royalty trusts. Many startups and small businesses are funded through royalty deals where the investor gets a percentage of the revenues that are coming in.

What do you think? Do royalties have a place in your portfolio?

CHAPTER 34
BUY AND SELL DOMAINS

Buying and selling domain names is an exciting adventure that for some seems to conjure up images of finding hidden pirate treasure or guessing the winning combination on the next Powerball. Stories abound of domains that were purchased for $8 dollars 15 years ago being sold today for millions. Of course, that leads the more adventurous of us to wonder, "How can I do that?"

Well, the ocean is big. Your likelihood of cashing in on the motherlode is low, and you're liable to waste a lot of time and money chasing after the wrong ships. You need a map or some other advantage to guide you toward that elusive booty.

Related: The top 25 most expensive domain names

5 tips for buying and selling domain names for profit

Here are some tips to get you pointed in the right direction when trying to buy or sell a domain name for profit:

Narrow your focus.
Find names that offer real value.
Check domain availability.
Evaluate the price.
Get your domains front and center.
Let's dig into each of these tips.

1. Narrow your focus

Buying and Selling Domains Narrow Focus Map

There are millions of domains already registered by someone and endless combinations of available domains to register, especially when you consider the hundreds of new domain name extensions like .app and .club. If you plan on buying a domain to resell it, you should start by narrowing your focus.

What do you know about already that can make this easier? Do you know about pets? Are you in car or home sales? Do you know about education or healthcare? Think about some of the spaces you are most familiar with and start there.

Here's what you DON'T want to do: Target prospective buyers based on their perceived economic status, without any insight into the industry you're targeting. "Lawyers seem to do well," you think, "maybe I should start selling names to them." So you rush out and buy a bunch of domain names you think would appeal to the law firms you've identified as potential buyers. Without knowledge of the space, you may not know that the American Bar Association and other industry-specific organizations set rules that govern some aspects of legal advertising. You're not going to strike gold selling names your target buyers can't use.

Remember to focus on the areas you know well and you will be much more successful than buying domains you think would benefit someone in an industry you know little about.

2. Find names that offer real value

Think of ways that the domains you buy would be a valuable asset to the buyer. Picture someone who would benefit from buying the domain in a space you are very familiar with. If this was you and someone was trying to sell you this name, would it be beneficial for you to own? Be honest. If so, why? If not, why?

Let's play this out with a real example. Say you're familiar with the real estate market in Tempe, Arizona, and you have the opportunity to purchase tempeapartments.com for $200. This might be a good deal. Tempe has a lot of rental property; it's a competitive market; and there's ample turnover in the apartment space because the city is home to a major university. Ask yourself:

How much does one month of rent profit a landlord, property manager or other prospective domain buyer? How about a year's worth of rental profit?

Would you buy this name if you were in the space? If so, why?

What kind of domains are landlords, property managers, etc., using?

How much do they spend on advertising?

How much would this domain help them to sound authoritative in their space?

If you can answer these questions with confidence and know this niche well, you probably already have an idea of who to contact and how to make a compelling case for how this domain could help their business grow.

Related: This entrepreneur spent $900,000 on great.com — Is a premium domain worth the investment?

3. Check domain availability

Now that you have narrowed down what names you should probably be buying, how do you find them?

If the names are taken (as many probably will be), head over to the aftermarket to buy from people who already own the names or who let them expire because they no longer plan on using them.

A great place to look is auctions.godaddy.com.

Use the advanced search option to quickly hone in on the type of names you are interested in. You can narrow the results by price, top-level domain (i.e, .com, .net, .org, .club, etc.), keyword, and many more filters. Using this feature will help you quickly sort through the millions of domains on the aftermarket and find the domain names that best fit your end goals.

4. Evaluate the price

Once you have a name in mind, how do you know if the price is fair? I like to use namebio.com to compare the domain I'm thinking about buying with similar domains that have sold. You can enter the keyword and also use some advanced search features to see a list of names similar to yours, what they actually sold for, and when they sold.

You can also research current domain sales on venues like GoDaddy Auctions and Afternic.

Finally, Ron Jackson issues a weekly report on DN Journal that covers the top public sales of the week. You can use all these resources to help you price your domains correctly.

A great place to look is auctions.godaddy.com.

Use the advanced search option to quickly hone in on the type of names you are interested in. You can narrow the results by price, top-level domain (i.e, .com, .net, .org, .club, etc.), keyword, and many more filters. Using this feature will help you quickly sort through the millions of domains on the aftermarket and find the domain names that best fit your end goals.

5. Get your domains front and center

There are many venues to get your domains out in front of the buying public. You want to consider a few things:

Is the venue trusted and well known?

It's important to feel confident that you will get paid and that the buyer will get the domain name they paid for. Pick a place that has good ratings with recognized bodies such as the Better Business Bureau or licensing from a trusted government source. This will make it easier for the buyer to pull the trigger on the domain purchase as well knowing they can trust the brand that is selling the domain.

A trusted brand is vital when selling a domain.

Is the distribution network strong?

The potential to get your domain name in front of the right buyer is key. Listing in a distribution network such as Afternic can get your domain name in front of millions of potential buyers each month.

Do you know people who could benefit from the domain name? Why not reach out to them and see if they have any interest in using the domain? If you are working in an area of the domain space you are familiar with you should be able to convey the value proposition of your domain name for the potential buyer.

You do not want to start sending spam emails. You want to have conversations with people you know would appreciate the ability to own the domain.

Letting a great name you purchased at a fair price to make a profit sit in your account, instead of getting it in front of the right buyer, is like finally finding that pirate treasure map but framing it to admire in your living room instead of following it to the booty.

Resources to learn more

There is always a learning curve in buying domains with the purpose of reselling them. Don't hesitate to ask a lot of questions to those who went before you, participate in forums such as namepros.com, keep abreast of industry trends via resources like domaining.com, and reach out to the Afternic and GoDaddy Aftermarket support teams.

Attend a conference. By doing so you will really ramp up your knowledge quickly and meet a lot of other professionals who are in the industry. You can also see first hand the tools and services available to you from various vendors in the space. All of these things will help you to be a smarter investor and make the most of your time and money.

CHAPTER 35
RENT A ROOM

The Rent a Room scheme is an optional scheme open to owner occupiers or tenants who let out furnished accommodation to a lodger in their main home.

It allows you to earn up to £7,500 a year tax-free, or £3,750 if you're letting jointly.

You don't have to be a homeowner to take advantage of the scheme. If you're renting you can also lease out a room to a lodger, as long as your own lease allows you to do so.

Opting in or out of the scheme

If the amount you earn from renting out the room is less than the thresholds of the Rent a Room scheme, then your tax exemption is automatic and you don't need to do anything.

If you earn more than the threshold, you must complete a tax return (even if you don't normally). You can then do one of the following:

Choose to opt into the scheme – in which case you need to let HM Revenue & Customs know this on your tax return and claim your tax-free allowance.

Not opt into it – in which case you simply record your income and any associated expenses on the property pages of your tax return.

To ask to be sent a tax return if you don't normally receive one, contact HM Revenue & Customs using the link below.

There's no special form for telling HM Revenue & Customs you don't want to be part of the scheme. If you earn more than the threshold or already complete a tax return you simply declare the relevant lettings income and expenses when completing your tax return.

The rent-a-room scheme and benefits

The rent a room scheme can be a great way to supplement your income and provide accommodation for lodgers. However, the income you get could affect some means-tested benefits.

Housing Benefit and the rent-a-room scheme

How rent-a-room affects your Housing Benefit depends on how the person renting the room is classified.

Boarders: If, along with the room, you are providing prepared food, the renter is classified as a boarder. The first £20 of rental income a week is disregarded along with half of the remaining amount of rent you get.

For example, if the rent is £50 a week, £20 is disregarded automatically, plus £15 of the remaining £30 rent payment.

This means you will have £15 a week income, which could affect the amount you receive in Housing Benefit.

Sub-tenants: If you are only providing a room and no meals, the lodger is called a sub-tenant. The first £20 of rental income a week is still disregarded, but the remaining amount is all seen as income.

In this case, if the rent is £50 a week, £20 is disregarded, but the remaining £30 is classed as income and could affect the amount you receive in Housing Benefit.

If you are claiming Housing Benefit, and rent out your only spare room you won't be affected by the bedroom tax. If you have further spare rooms, you would be subject to it

Universal Credit and the rent-a-room scheme

If you're on Universal Credit, any money you get from sub-tenants and lodgers under the rent-a-room scheme will not be counted as income up to the tax-free allowance of £7,500. This means it is a great way to supplement your income.

However, if you are renting out a spare room you will be subject to the bedroom tax.

Council Tax Reduction and the rent-a-room scheme

If you were living on your own and qualified for the 25% single person Council Tax Reduction and decide to rent out a room, you will no longer qualify for the discount.

Other means-tested benefits and the rent-a-room scheme

If you are getting other means-tested benefits such as Income Support or Pension Credit, any income you get from renting out your room could affect these benefits.

Providing meals and services

You might wish to charge for additional services when you take in a lodger, such as providing meals or laundry services.

The money you receive for these services must be added to the rent you receive to work out your total income. If your total income is more than £7,500 for the tax year (6 April to 5 April), and your overall income is greater than the individual Personal Allowance, you will need to pay some tax.

If you need to pay tax

If your income from your lodger is more than £7,500 for the tax year, you have two options:

Pay tax on your actual profit from the property (which is calculated as income received minus allowable expenses). This is the normal arrangement for a rental business.

Pay tax on the gross (before tax) income minus the tax-free threshold, but with no allowance for expenses.

The simplest way to work out what to do is to calculate what your expenses are. If they are larger than the tax-free threshold of £7,500, then you will be better off with the first option. If they are smaller than the threshold, then go with option two.

You don't have to stick with a single method each year. You can change year to year, so long as you inform HM Revenue & Customs.

Running a business

If you run a guest house, bed and breakfast or provide services such as catering and cleaning as part of a letting business, you can still take part in the Rent a Room scheme.

Advantages and disadvantages of the Rent a Room scheme

The biggest advantage of the scheme is you can earn £7,500 a year absolutely tax-free.

However, this advantage might be outweighed for some people by the fact you cannot claim any expenses related to the letting.

So if you have to spend money repairing wear and tear in the property or replacing a broken boiler, you won't be able to deduct any expense against income if you let out your property under the Rent a Room scheme.

You'll need to work out for yourself whether you will be better off in or out of the Rent a Room scheme.

An example

Frank lets out the spare room in the home he owns for a rent of £200 a week, giving him an annual income of £10,400 – which is more than the Rent a Room allowance.

If he stays in the Rent a Room scheme, he will be taxed at his top rate of tax on the income above £7,500. So if he is a basic rate taxpayer he'll pay 20% tax on £2,900 (£10,400-£7,500). This would result in a tax bill of £580.

However, he could opt out of the scheme and treat his income as a normal rental income. This means he can deduct expenses and only his final profit is taxed.

Over the year Frank's expenses come to £2,000. Once deducted from his total rent, it leaves him with a profit of £8,400. However, his tax bill will have nearly doubled to £1,680 (20% of £8,400).

In this example Frank is better off in the Rent a Room scheme. However, if his expenses were higher – say, £4,500 – he would be better off opting out of the scheme.

The importance of keeping records

It's important to keep records of your income and expenses. Even though you cannot claim expenses with the Rent a Room scheme, you might need those records should you opt out later on.

Before you take a lodger in

There are a number of checks you need to perform before taking in a lodger.

If you are the owner of the property and have a mortgage, you'll need to check with your mortgage lender to make sure you're allowed to rent out a room under the terms of your mortgage contract.

You'll also need to check with your home insurer it is allowed under their terms.

If you're renting, you need to ensure your lease allows you to take on a lodger.

Speak to your lender, insurer or landlord to ensure you can take part in the scheme.

Other ways to boost your income

The Rent a Room scheme is just one way you can bring some money in.

CHAPTER 36
RENT HOUSE

When selling up seems impossible, letting your house can be a handy alternative. Here is what you need to consider if you're thinking of renting out your home.

Do your research

Look at the sorts of properties being let in your area, and how much rent they are asking for.

If you plan to use a letting agent, start looking around at the options in your area, including the service they offer and how much they charge.

If any of your friends or family are landlords, ask them for recommendations.

Weigh up the costs

It's worth doing the maths to make sure it's worth it financially before you decide to let out your home.

Any rental income you receive may be taxed at your usual rate (20% if you are basic rate taxpayer, and 40% if you are a higher-rate taxpayer).

This net figure would need to cover the mortgage payments on your property, at the very least.

Ideally, it should also leave you some surplus for a back-up fund in case you need to do any maintenance and repairs on the property. This could also cover paying the mortgage between tenants when you are not receiving any rental income.

Talk to your mortgage lender

When you decide to rent out your house, you must let your mortgage lender know.
You will usually have to obtain something called a consent for lease from your lender before you can get started.

Sort out insurance

It's very important that your current buildings and contents insurer knows of your intention to let your property, as these policies may need to be amended.

You will also now have to arrange a landlord insurance policy.

Get your property ready

Before you make your property available for rent, you will need to decide whether to let your house furnished or unfurnished.

Other things to consider before any tenants move in include:

- Remove anything from the property that is precious or fragile
- Make sure any repairs on fixtures and fittings have been carried out
- Ensure all appliances are in good working order
- Give the property a mini-makeover to ensure everything is well-presented and up-to-date

Find an agent

You don't have to use a letting agent when renting out your property, but it means you can cut out a huge amount of legwork, as they will:

- Advertise your property for you
- Show prospective tenants around
- Draw up a tenancy agreement
- Deal directly with the tenant on your behalf if you do not want to

Agents will generally charge around 10-15% of the rental income you receive, although you may feel this is worth it for the work they do for you.

Ask your letting agent how much they feel you should charge for rent, but remember this decision is down to you. It may be useful to gather the opinions of two or three agents before you decide.

Vet prospective tenants

You may want to meet potential tenants before deciding on if you would be happy with them living in your property, or you may prefer to leave it to your letting agent, if you use one.

If you use an agent, they can also perform reference and credit checks on potential tenants to ensure everything is above board. Otherwise, you will need to do this yourself.

Find a lodger and rent out a room

If you don't want to move out, you could rent a room in your home to bring in a little extra money.

Under the government's Rent a Room scheme you can earn up to £7,500 each tax year, tax free by renting a furnished room in your family home.

1. Find a lodger: Advertise your room on notice boards or sites like Gumtree or SpareRoom.co.uk.

2. Vet potential lodgers: Ask for references, preferably from a previous landlord, so you can verify their identity and ensure they will make a reliable tenant.

3. Protect your home: Draw up an agreement including rent amount and due date, let period, notice period and house rules.

4. Inform your home insurance provider: This may increase your premiums, but will also ensure you policy is valid and will pay out for any claims you make.

What else should you consider?

The decision to rent out your house will mean you go from being a homeowner and occupier to a landlord. Your new status as landlord will mean you have to:

- Be responsible for all repairs, maintenance and refurbishments
- Fit smoke alarms and extractor fans where required
- Have any gas appliances tested by a Gas Safe registered engineer
- Make sure any upholstered furniture is fireproof

- Arrange an Energy Performance Certificate for your tenants
- Register with the Tenancy Deposit Scheme

As well as these responsibilities you will need to be prepared to be on hand when you get a call from your tenants, as many issues will need attention immediately (a gas leak, for example).

You can avoid this stress by using a letting agent, but this will come at a price.

CHAPTER 37
TAX LIEN CERTIFICATES

A tax lien certificate is a certificate of claim against a property that has a lien placed upon it as a result of unpaid property taxes. Tax lien certificates are generally sold to investors through an auction process.

BREAKING DOWN Tax Lien Certificate

A tax lien certificate is a lien placed on your property for not paying your taxes. Every time your property taxes come due, the municipality will issue a tax lien. When you pay your taxes on time, the lien is removed. If you don't pay your taxes — or don't pay them on time — the town or county will auction off the tax lien certificate to an investor(s). That investor will then pay the taxes on behalf of the property tax owner.

How Tax Lien Certificates Are Sold

Most tax lien sales auctions are conducted by the county or municipality where the property is located.

For a property to be eligible, it must be considered tax-defaulted for a minimum period of time depending on local regulation. Instead of bidding on an amount for the property, the interested parties bid on the interest rate they are willing to receive. The investor who bids the lowest rate wins the auction and is issued the tax lien certificate.

Once You've Bought a Tax Lien Certificate

After an investor places a winning bid for a specific tax lien certificate, a lien is placed on the property and a certificate is issued to the investor detailing the outstanding taxes and penalties on the property. Not all states, counties or municipalities offer tax liens. Some states, such as California, only perform tax sales on defaulted property, resulting in the winning bidder becoming the legal owner of the property in question.

The term of tax lien certificates typically ranges from one to three years. The certificate enables the investor to collect unpaid taxes plus the applicable prevailing rate of interest, which can range from 8 to more than 30 percent, depending on the jurisdiction.

Rate of Return on Tax Lien Certificates

Spurred by the high state-mandated rates of interest, tax lien certificates may offer rates of return that are substantially higher than those offered by other investments. Tax liens generally have precedence over other liens, such as mortgages. If the property owner fails to pay the back taxes, the investor could potentially acquire the property for pennies on the dollar. Acquiring a property in that manner is a rare occurrence, since most tax liens are redeemed well before the property goes to foreclosure.

Associated Benefits and Risks of Tax Lien Certificates

Buying a tax lien certificate can, at times, prove to be an attractive investment. Some of the certificates have a low entry point, meaning you can buy some of them for a few hundred dollars. Compare that to a traditional investment like a mutual fund, which often come with a minimum investment requirement. You also have the option to spread your money around, so you can buy multiple certificates for a low dollar value. And finally, the rate of return (as we mentioned above) is usually pretty consistent, so you're not going to have to worry about the ups and down of the market.

Negative aspects of tax lien certificates include the requirement for the investor to pay for the tax lien certificate in full within a very short period of time, usually one to three days. These certificates are also highly illiquid, since there is no secondary trading market for them. Investors in tax lien certificates also have to undertake significant due diligence and research to ensure that the underlying properties have an appropriate assessed value.

An example regarding the need for due diligence when researching tax lien certificates is a two-acre lot that may initially seem to be a good value, but it's actually a strip of land that is only 3 feet wide by 5 miles long. This renders the land unusable for many endeavors, such as building a home or a business.

CHAPTER 38
EBATES

The Smart Shopper is a blog from Ebates that helps you save money on everything from home and fashion to electronics and travel. We're all about getting you the biggest bang for your buck with coupons, promo codes and discounts at stores you already know and love. Plus, we'll help you out with tips on stacking your savings with Ebates Cash Back and exclusive deals.

What is Ebates?

Ebates is where you can get Cash Back for shopping at over 2,500 stores. Becoming a member is free! Stores pay Ebates a commission for sending you their way, and Ebates shares the commission with you as Cash Back. Get paid every three months, plus earn a cash bonus when you join and shop. Founded in 1998, Ebates has paid members over $1 billion Cash Back. Start getting yours!

How does Ebates work?

Ebates gets a commission from stores when you make a purchase, and instead of keeping it, Ebates share it with you. Find the store on ebates.com, click "Shop Now" and shop like normal on the store site. After you make an eligible purchase, you'll earn Cash Back and get a check or PayPal payment every quarter.

How to use Ebates:

- Shop with Ebates at your favorite stores
- Earn Cash Back on your orders
- Get paid by check or PayPal — no fees, no forms

How to earn more Cash Back at Ebates:

Ebates Cash Back Button: Never miss out on Cash Back! Get our free browser extension to activate Cash Back directly at store sites. The Cash Back Button even automatically applies the best coupons at checkout. Get it here.

- Ebates App: Shop on the go and earn Cash Back anywhere, anytime. Get the free Ebates App for iPhone, iPad and Android for access to App-exclusive deals!
- In-Store Cash Back: You can shop in stores and earn the Cash Back you love! Browse offers, link them to your credit card and shop like normal.

- Cash Back Credit Card: With the Ebates Cash Back Visa® Credit Card, you can earn an extra 3% Cash Back1 on qualifying purchases through Ebates and 1% Cash Back1 everywhere else Visa credit cards are accepted.

- Refer a Friend: If you love Cash Back, so will your friends! Get cash bonuses for spreading the word about Ebates. The more you refer, the more you earn.

- The Ebates Influencer Program: Join our influencer program and get rewarded for being an Ebates ambassador. Enjoy perks like a flat fee for every qualified referral, invites to exclusive events and more.

CHAPTER 39
BECOME A SILENT PARTNER

Many business savvy individuals have considered the thought of becoming a silent partner at one point or another in their careers. The thought of investing in a lucrative business and sharing in the profits without any additional effort is an attractive proposition to seriously contemplate. Basically, a silent partner is an individual who invests capital into a business in exchange for a share in the profits or losses of that business.

Silent partners are not supposed to have a role in the day-to-day operation of the business, and that is where the term 'silent' originates from. They do, however, have a say in anything that affects the management of the company because management and its choice of direction is the reason for the partnership in the first place.

Benefits of a Silent Partnership

There are several benefits that are available to a silent partner that do not exist for other members of the business. Silent partners have little to no responsibility when it comes to the operation of the business on a daily level. Silent partners are brought into a company because of their financial resources, not their knowledge of operations of the company.

Perhaps the main reason individuals become silent partners is the ability to enjoy a passive income stream without having to constantly monitor an investment. The essential basis of a silent partnership is trust in the individual or group that is running the business.

Once trust in the capabilities and direction of the company is established, there is little other responsibility for a silent partner other than to enjoy the profits generated by the company. The key to being a successful silent partner is to completely evaluate all aspects of the company prior to committing to the investment. It is vital to establish the trust needed to limit involvement in the company and act like a silent partner.

Things Can Go Wrong

Not every silent partnership works out as intended, even when all the research has been done prior to the agreement. Even the most brilliantly managed companies can come up against issues that might hinder their growth or cause unseen difficulties. When these situations arise, the common instinct for silent partners who have large amounts of capital invested in a company is to overreact and attempt to involve themselves in the operational aspects of the company in order to correct the situation. This can lead to difficult situations where the silent partner oversteps the boundaries of their role in the partnership and creates a dysfunctional scenario in the operation of the company.

Importance of the Partnership Agreement

Perhaps the most important aspect of becoming a silent partner is to have strict limits of involvement detailed in the partnership agreement. Preventing silent investors from interfering in the daily operations of a faltering company is vital to preventing the possible damage that can occur when the investor involves themselves out of a financial panic.

This is where trust in the direction and capabilities of the management team become so vital to the success of the partnership arrangement. It is important also for the silent partner and the company to have an exit strategy in place should the relationship move in a direction that neither party is happy with. This can be a buyout clause on the part of the company or some form of loss mitigation stipulation for the investor that can be detailed in the partnership agreement. Ultimately, if all parties know the boundaries prior to the agreement and abide by them, trouble can usually be avoided should things not go as planned.

Conclusion

Becoming a silent partner can be an excellent investment opportunity for individuals when the right situation presents itself. As long as the investor spends the time to thoroughly research the company's historical business record as well as their management staff and business philosophy, investing as a silent partner can be a safe and lucrative investment strategy.

Companies with proven track records can be difficult for investors to get involved with because they usually do not require outside financing, but if the opportunity presents itself, the investor should act decisively. Becoming a silent partner is not for everyone, but for those who are comfortable with a hands-off approach to business investing, becoming a silent partner can be a rewarding and lucrative enterprise.

CHAPTER 40
VENDING MACHINES

Vending machines don't always supply the healthiest snacks, but they are indispensable resources for college students and night owls looking for something to tide them over when the nearby stores and restaurants are closed. Vending machines are very easy to use, and within seconds you'll be able to purchase your snack of choice.

Using a vending machine

As most vending machines take cash only, make sure you have the funds necessary to purchase the snacks inside. Most vending machines allow you to use any combination of one-dollar bills, quarters, dimes and nickels to purchase your snacks. Larger bills, pennies, Sacajawea dollars and other odd bits of change are generally not accepted.

Look at the snacks and/or sodas inside the vending machine, or, if the actual snacks cannot be seen, the pictures and/or lists of available snacks and/or drinks depicted on the machine. Each item will have a price listed next to it. Decide which item you would like to purchase, and take out enough money to pay for the item. If the machine indicates that you must use exact change, count out the amount exactly equal to the price listed next to the snack. If the machine has no such indication, you will usually be able to pay an amount more than or equal to the listed price.

Insert your money into the vending machine. The machine will have a marked slot for coins and, if it accepts dollar bills, a separate, lit up, large horizontal slot for dollar bills. If you have a dollar bill you wish to use, make sure it's smooth, as vending machines often reject wrinkled or torn bills, and feed it face up into the horizontal slot. If the machine doesn't take your bill, try using coins instead, or smooth your dollar bill a second time. Feed any coins into the coin slot. Sometimes your coin will be rejected, and will fall down into the change dispenser near the bottom of the vending machine. If this happens, tap your coin onto metal and try again. Continue feeding bills and/or coins into the machine until you have paid the necessary amount to purchase the product. The machine will usually have a digital display to indicate how much money you have paid.

To tell the machine which product you want, you will either have to type in a number or press a button. On most soda machines, different types of sodas are marked on their own button. Press the button that goes with your beverage of choice. Most snack machines have letters and/or numbers that correspond to each snack. Look at the snack you want, and type the letters and numbers connected with that snack into the keypad on the front of the vending machine.

If all goes well, your snack will dispense. You will usually be able to see or hear the snack falling into the retrieval unit near the bottom of the machine. Push in the door of this retrieval unit, if a door exists, and retrieve your snack or drink.

Tips & Warnings

- Sometimes, after paying and selecting your snack, the machine will indicate that they are out of the selected product. In this case, you may select an alternate snack using the money you have already paid, or you can hit the coin return button to get your money back.
- Sometimes a snack will get stuck in a machine during the dispensing process, after you've already paid for it. In this case, you may write to the manufacturer listed on the side of the vending machine to request a refund.

CHAPTER 41
ATM BUSINESS

W e're all looking for a way to generate income passively. This is a myth and it will probably lead you through very dark entrepreneurial places. The pursuit of the unicorn or "mythical passive business" has led to many jaded entrepreneurs. The first thing to remember is that there is no such thing as a passive business. Entrepreneur is an euphemism for janitor because you're going to sweeping up all the worst jobs that no one else wants to do.

ATMs or automated teller machines are seen everywhere but have you ever thought about the company or entrepreneur that operates that machine. There is an entire industry structured around the ATM business. Typically the fees for an atm ranges between $1.00 to $8.00 dollars. The national average for atm fees were $1.97 in 2008 and $4.35 in 2014. ATM fees are increasing at a significant rate over the last ten years. But, how much would you really earn from an ATM?

How much will you make with ATM fees?

ATM fees are split between various parties or partners in the ATM ecosystem. The three main parties in every ATM business are the ATM owner, the venue owner and the ATM processor. The ATM owner ("you") are the one that's buying the machine and placing it at a specific venue or place. The venue owner is the person you've contacted and negotiated with to place your ATM machine. Lastly, the ATM processor is the company that is handling the processing or paperwork to document and allow the ATM to function. These three parties are the ones that will share the fee that everyone pays.

ATM processor contracts will typically provide terms in the form of a "surcharge rebate of X% and a fee between $0.10 to $0.50 per transaction." What does this mean? A surcharge is the "ATM fee" you charge to use your ATM to withdraw cash. The surcharge rebate is the ATM processor referring to how much of your "ATM fee" is returned to you. You should expect a 100% surcharge rebate or a full return of your ATM fees charged. ATM processors may attempt to eat into your profits by providing a percentage less than 100% or by adding "network accessing fees." (E.g., $0.25, $0.50 or $0.75)

The venue owner will typically receive $0.50 per transaction. Obviously, this amount is a negotiation between you and the venue, so the cost per transaction could vary drastically. If the venue is highly desirable, you may be willing to offer up to

50% of the ATM fee or surcharge fee because it would generate a significant amount of fees. But, the typical fee share is $0.50 per transaction.

Sample Annual Gross Profit for Fees

The average ATM customer nationally withdraws $60 dollars per transaction. You'd expect an ATM to have between 8 to 10 transactions on an average daily basis. This would mean that $600 dollars are withdrawn per day. Your fees collected based on $3.00 per transaction would be $24 dollars – conservatively. Assuming your ATM processor fee is $0.20 per transaction, the ATM processing cost is $1.60. Assuming the venue owner cost per transaction is $0.50, their fees are $4.00. The total in transaction fees deducted is $5.60. Your gross profit is $18.40. Your gross profit per 30 day month is $552. Annually, this ATM would generate $6,624 in gross profit.

CHAPTER 42
CROWDFUNDED REAL ESTATE

The JOBS Act in 2012 was HUGE because it made it legal to crowdsource funding online. Shortly after, access to both debt & equity real estate deals exploded for investors.

Since 2012, over 100+ real estate crowdfunding sites have come into existence. A good number of them have already closed shop with new ones appearing on a weekly basis. So how do you determine what the top real estate crowdfunding sites are? Honestly, that's a tough task.

Well, I've been involved in real estate crowdfunding since 2014 and have been able to perform my own due diligence on a good number of those 100+ sites. I'm a fully subscribed member to all of the ones mentioned on my list and I keep a close eye on all of these platforms to invest in new deals. In future posts, I'll review each of these crowdfunding sites in more detail.

The factors that went into making up this list include:

- My own personal experience with the sites as an investor
- Reputation amongst experienced investors in the space
- Financial stability and market share of the sites

EquityMultiple

This platform is one of my more recent favorites because some of the big deals I've found on their site. They focus mostly on commercial real estate deals, both debt & equity. They might have a slightly lower volume at this point than some of the other sites, but they say it's due to their extremely stringent vetting process. I'm okay with that because ultimately it all comes down to how well the platforms vet the deals. To make it even more special, they personally co-invest in every deal, adding some of their own skin in the game.

Rich Uncles

Don't mind the funny name, this crowdfunding site means serious business and hopes to have you cash-flowing passive income immediately. They have one of the most (if not the most) experienced management team among all crowdfunding sites.

Rich Uncles has two different offerings: A REIT that is focused on commercial Triple-Net properties and the other and newest offering is a REIT that is focused on Student Housing, a sector that I think is extremely intriguing. In fact, I've invested in it myself. Minimums are $500

Alpha Investing

Wish there was a concierge service for crowdfunding where you have direct access to a private manager and are able to gain exclusive access to vetted deals? Alpha Investing is a private capital network that connects accredited and professional investors to institutional-quality, private real estate investment opportunities. Access is available by invitation or referral only but I've secured that invitation for PIMD readers that go through this link.

What makes this platform special is that each investor has a direct relationship with a principal at the firm, and they are always available to speak directly about any issue. My most recent crowdfunding investment was through this platform and I've experienced this concierge service firsthand.

CrowdStreet

CrowdStreet launched in 2014 and very quickly revolutionized the commercial real estate industry. They focus on providing their investors with direct access to a range of vetted, institutional-quality commercial real estate (CRE) opportunities and all the online tools needed to manage those investments. What sets this platform apart is that they make investing in CRE accessible, transparent and efficient by directly connecting individualinvestors with CRE investment firms seeking capital for their projects.

PeerStreet

This site has a great source of deal flow. They focus mostly on residential debt, but you'll occasionally see a multifamily or commercial deal. They typically partner up with other lenders and provide the platform for them to get the funding. Gets high marks in the industry for transparency and excellent management.

RealtyMogul

RealtyMogul is one of the earliest players in the space. They specialize in a variety of deals – larger commercial equity deals to mobile home park funds to their well-known MogulREITs. MogulREITs are known to provide steady, reliable returns for as little as $1000. They provide access to real estate crowdfunding for both accredited and non-accredited investors.

They market themselves as the alternative to investing in stocks and bonds. They provide access to private market real estate through their eREITs and eFunds. You can build a portfolio using the various products to meet your goals. Some are available to non-accredited investors.

RealCrowd

This site specializes in connecting investors to vetted syndicators (focusing mostly on commercial real estate equity deals) and large real estate funds. If you're looking for extremely passive ways to get involved in real estate and get your money working for you, check out their offerings. Their deals have higher minimums though, typically $25-50k. My first deal with a syndicator was found through this site.

Alphaflow

One concern I have with crowdfunding is that in order to mitigate some risk, I feel like I have to invest in multiple deals at the same time and it's sometimes a lot of work to make that happen and keep track of everything. Alphaflow takes your investment and basically buys fractional shares of crowdfunding deals and you end up invested in over 70-100 loans at once. In some ways, it's like a mutual fund for crowdfunding deals.

Real Estate Crowdfunding Summary

Real estate crowdfunding has really shaken up the real estate investment landscape by dramatically increasing the level of access to deals for the average investor. It helped me dip my toes into the real estate investing world and has now become a significant portion of my personal portfolio. In fact, I've invested nearly $300,000 in crowdfunding deals over the last three years.

Obviously, it's not without risk and if/when there's ever a downturn in the housing market, you will likely see some more publicized losses. However, the better the platform, their management, and their vetting process is, the better off you'll be.

CHAPTER 43
LICENSE A BUSINESS IDEA

I f you've got a great idea for a product or service but don't have the means or the will to sell it yourself, fear not. You have the option of licensing your product, service or idea to another company instead. Stephen Key inventor, licensing expert and author of the book "One Simple Idea" shared some tips for licensing products and services in a phone interview with Small Business Trends. Check out the top tips below.

Tips for Licensing Your Product or Service

Consider the Amount of Work You Want to Do

According to Key, the main benefit of licensing your product or service rather than just selling it yourself is the amount of work involved. With licensing, you can sign your idea over to another company and let them do all the work. But you have less control. So before making your decision, you need to really think about what is more important to you.

Research Other Patents

So you've got an idea and you want to license it? Great. But before licensing your product or service, you first need to research your idea to make sure that it's not already patented by someone else. To do this, you really just need to Google your idea.

Find a Small Improvement

Even if you find some similar items out there, that doesn't necessarily mean you're out of luck. You can still be competitive in the marketplace if you just have an idea that's slightly different than others out there.

Key says, "You don't need to reinvent the wheel. You just need a good idea that gives people a small improvement over an existing idea."

Don't File Too Early

Key says that one of the biggest mistakes he sees people make is filing for patent protection too early in the process. In fact, though he holds many patents, he said that they're not absolutely necessary depending on the type of idea you have. And if you're still working on developing and testing your idea, you might find that you want to make changes that don't fall within your original patent. So filing more than once can be very expensive.

Consider a Provisional Patent

In some cases when licensing your product or service, Key recommends looking into a provisional patent application. It can give you a little bit of room to make changes and really flesh out your idea before filing an official patent application.

Be Your Own Expert

The process of patenting and licensing can be complicated, so it can be necessary to enlist the help of an attorney. But Key cautions against fully relying on someone else for this process. Before getting into the process of licensing, you need to really decide what it is you want, what you think you can get, and research all of the different factors that go into the licensing process.

Find Your Market

Key also thinks it's a good idea to find out if your product or service will actually sell before paying for an official patent. You can pitch the idea to companies early and see what kind of reception you get. If no one is interested, you can save yourself the time and money of patenting your idea.

Create an Ad

To really market your idea to companies, Key suggests simply creating a one-sheet advertisement that gives the basic information about your idea. You can hire a freelancer to create an image of your prototype and then offer all of the basic information.

Use Multimedia

You can also create a video ad to send to companies so that you can gauge their reception of your product or service.

Reach Out to Multiple Companies

Another big mistake that Key says he sees people make all the time is giving up on their idea too quickly. Reaching out to one or two major retailers with your idea isn't enough. If a few people say no, that doesn't mean it's hopeless. So before you even start, create a long list of companies that you can reach out to. And try not to get discouraged early on.

Keep It Specific to Your Niche

When deciding on companies to pitch, it helps to think about where you'd expect to find a product like yours if you were out shopping. The more specific you can get, the bigger your chances of gaining some interest in your offering.

Find the Right Contacts

You also need to research who within the company would be best to contact with your idea. Don't just settle for a general contact form unless it states very specifically that that's where the company wants you to send licensing requests. Instead, you can use tools like LinkedIn to find people who work in marketing or similar areas for the companies you've chosen.

Ask About Their Process

When you first make contact with those people, you don't need to rush into pitching your idea. In fact, it can be more beneficial for you to start a conversation with them first. Tell them that you love their company and then mention that you have an idea you may want to license. Ask their process for doing so rather than just sending your idea and getting ignored.

Study the Language

Licensing your product or service can be a complicated game, especially when it comes to all the different terminology. Key says that it's an important step to study the language of licensing when you first start considering it. And then continue to learn about it throughout the process.

Research Constantly

Whether it comes to the language, your target companies, or just fleshing out your idea, the process of licensing your product or service takes a lot of research. And since every entrepreneur's experience is different, there's no one right way to go about it. Whenever you're looking for answers though, you have search engines to help you find them. So don't be afraid to search for even the smallest things to help with your licensing journey.

Key says, "The Internet is the largest library in the world. You can pick any topic and no matter what, you can find something related to it from multiple sources. Even if you're looking for a licensing agreement, you can just type in "licensing agreement checklist" and you can get an idea of what your agreement terms would be and what should go into your agreement."

CHAPTER 44
MAKE 401(K) PASSIVE INCOME

A recurring question that comes up each year is how much can I contribute to a retirement plan? That question is primarily a function of how much money you earn. A frequent area of confusion is what type of income can be used as the basis for a 401k, Profit Sharing or Defined Benefit Pension contribution. The purpose of this article is to explain the difference between "earned" versus "passive" income. Let's define what each of these are.

Earned Income

Earned income, simply put, is income one earns from actively working. Think of this as a salary or earnings from work done, even if self-employed. A general rule of thumb is that if the income is subject to FICA / Medicare taxes, then it is considered earned income in the eyes of the IRS.

Passive/Portfolio Income

Passive income is income that comes from not actively working such as income from investments, including dividends, rental property income, or earnings from which you are not materially involved (e.g. returns from investment in a company).

Passive Income Cannot Be The Basis of Contribution

It is a common mis-held belief that retirement plan contributions can be based on total income (that is, earned income plus passive income), but this is not true. Retirement plan contributions can only be based on earned income subject to FICA and Medicare taxes. Where it gets a little tricky is with the K1. Some K1s that are generated only report passive income. But there are K1's that are subject to self-employment earnings. Pension professional and actuaries annually request W2's, Schedule C's and K1's. With the K1 we specifically are looking at Box 14 of the K1 (2016): self-employment earnings. This income CAN be used as part of the pension / profit sharing calculation. Frequently only Box 1 is filled in and that's where the confusion and frustration sets in with CPA's, financial professionals and their clients. K1 Form 1065 is available from the IRS (2016) here.

Example:

Client earns $120,000 through earned income e.g. W2, K1 or possible a combination of both.

Client earns $50,000 through passive income e.g. rental income

Total income = $170,000

The total basis of retirement contribution is $120,000, not $170,000. The percentage of income contributed should be only based on earned income.

CHAPTER 45
YOUTUBE CHANNEL

YouTube is currently the most powerful video-sharing platform in the world. Since its launch in 2005, it has produced numerous millionaires, with the highest-earning star pulling in $12 million in revenue in 2015 (Forbes). Plus, according to YouTube, the number of channels that hit six figures in annual earnings through the platform is doubling each year.

We rounded up ideas from the pros to show you first how to make money on YouTube, plus some tips on how to make sure your channel is a success.

1. Try to Make Videos That Don't Have Too Much Competition

Find a topic where there aren't many other videos and then exploit it. For example, if you try to review tech gadgets, your video will be buried under the many other reviews that flood YouTube. But, if you make something more creative, like "15 Apps That Make You a Genius," chances are you will rank higher in searches in the relevant categories. Always try to find unexploited sub-niches within your niche on which you can create videos.

2. Be Consistent with Your Videos

YouTube is paying less and less for views these days. Fortunately, you can stack different business models to maximize your income. To start, focus on making as many high quality videos as you can and be regular in your schedule. These will need to be mostly reviews, advice and experience-based videos for this tactic to work. When you have lots of videos, you'll show up in all kinds of searches. Makes sure you enable ads on your page and then recommend affiliate products in your videos. To use this strategy, find a product on Amazon or Clickbank, review it in the video, then include a link in your description and make sure you tell people to click the link in the description. When they buy the product, you get paid a commission.

3. Create and Sell Information Products

If you know a professional skill, you can teach it to make money. If you are a graphic designer, you can teach graphic design. Even if you don't have a skill you can teach, you can learn a new skill quickly. And don't worry about not being an expert.

Once you know what skill you will be teaching, start creating free YouTube videos on the subject. For example, if you are good with Photoshop, make videos on how to edit pictures or design logos in Photoshop. To get views on your videos, make a list of all the people who are making Photoshop tutorials. Once you do that, make another list of the top five videos of these competitors. All of these videos have been proven to work. If you make similar videos with similar titles and similar video tags, you have a very high chance of getting discovered.

Once you have at least five to six thousand YouTube subscribers, you can launch an information product. Basically, a premium video course on Photoshop where you teach your subscribers the basic. Because you have already helped your subscribers with the free videos, they will be likely to buy your video course.

4. Make Money with Video Blogs

With a video blog, you will generate income by creating work from your expertise. The video blog places you as a subject matter expert and people want to work with the best. When a viewer begins to need services around information you have already talked to them about, they will come to the experts first. They may come to your YouTube channel for something that they cannot complete on their own. Now that you have provided them with advice on a topic, they complete the task successfully. They will now come back to you on bigger projects or smaller ones they don't have time for.

The nice thing about a video blog is it is for anyone in the services industry. You can be an auto mechanic, marketing agency, doctor/physician, in home improvement, and so on. Anyone who provides a service to a consumer can talk to show their expertise on topics. People are doing much of their research prior to purchasing these types of services, so why not show the consumer your expertise and why they should buy your service over anyone else's. Buying a product is usually just price, but when buying a service, you want to know who you are working with.

5. Become a Bitcoin Expert on YouTube

Talking with my group of entrepreneurs, we have discovered that we have something in common: we all want to invest in bitcoin, but we do not know exactly how. Virtual currencies have become a revolutionary concept in the field of monetary transactions. But because the change was so abrupt, there is still a great lack of understanding about this new way of doing business.

It could be possible sell traffic to exchanges that buy and sell cryptocurrencies and then, if the channel reaches enough subscribers and visualizations go up, the main source of income would be the platform itself.

6. Become a YouTube Partner

Today, anyone whose account is in good standing can become a YouTube partner through expressly allowing YouTube to place advertising in, on, and around your video content. Google makes money from the views of these ads and partners can then earn a percentage via a Google AdSense account. Exactly how much money a partner can make varies enormously and depends on a range of different factors. Find out how to become a YouTube Partner in this article.

7. License Your Video

In a digital era where everyone can create and distribute media, the rules of engagement between the media industry and individuals seem ever more confusing. But once you have this down, it will be easy to start earning from your video's rights. You can either wait for media representatives to reach out to you about using your video, or you can upload it on a marketplace like Jukin. Find out all about video licensing in this article.

8. Promote Your E-commerce Website Through YouTube Videos

YouTube really is one of the most effective and cheapest ways to market your e-commerce store.

People are highly visual and watching a video on what a product actually looks like, how easy it is to use, and how it can benefit them. How other individuals have experienced good results with your brand (customer testimonials) can go a long way towards attracting more interest and attention, compared to the written text. This, in turn, can boost your sales in your online store. Read this article to learn how to sell products from a WordPress website.

9. Create Reviews and Earn Through Affiliate Marketing

I have found that reviewing products and offering people bonuses to buy from them through your link underneath the YouTube video is a great way to make money as an affiliate marketer using YouTube.

You can leverage the YouTube videos to get people to know, like and trust you, which makes it a lot easier to sell something. Plus, the built-in audience of YouTube, being the number two search engine on the planet, and the results which tend to rank highly on Google (since they own YouTube) help you naturally get traffic to your videos, which can bring in more profits for you.

10. Promote Your Channel as a Brand and Sell Merchandise

Once you build a good level of recognition and engagement with your audience, you can take it up a notch by establishing your channel as your own personal brand. You can sell branded merchandise, such as shirts, mugs, umbrellas, or items that are more relevant to your niche.

A good example of this is fitness guru Cassey Ho, who was able to turn her Blogilates YouTube channel into branded activewear, gym bags, sports bottles, etc.

11. Start Teaching via YouTube Videos and Link Them to Your Paid Online Courses

Share any business-related knowledge that you possess that isn't common knowledge for the average person but something they would likely pay to learn. Examples include how to leverage LinkedIn effectively for your small business, how to write blogs to get noticed by bigger publications, or something simple like accounting.

You can then easily create your online course on a site like Teachable—they will host your classes, provide all the payment gateways and everything else you need to run your business. All you have to do is get people there by advertising on places like YouTube, Google or Facebook. After that, the business runs completely on its own and you can collect monthly passive income.

12. Manage YouTube Channels

If you are knowledgeable about how to operate a YouTube channel and how to use the different features of the platform, you can work as a manager for an account. YouTube has added a feature wherein one account can be managed by several people. It depends on your agreement with the account owner, but some of your functions could include uploading videos (you can use Hootsuite to schedule your posts), responding to and leaving comments, thinking of video ideas and titles, writing the video descriptions and including links, and promoting the videos on various social media platforms. You can create an account on freelancing platforms, such as Upwork or Fiverr, to offer your video creation and editing services.

13. Buy Helpful Videos That People Will Want to Use and Resell Them

To be able to update their channel regularly, some YouTube account owners may consider looking for existing videos that they can buy and post on their page. This provides an opportunity for experienced and creative videographers to sell their work. Webinars and video training courses are especially profitable and marketable. You cannot sell your videos directly through YouTube, but you can promote through the platform by giving a sneak peek of what you do and then linking to where they can buy the full video.

14. Post Sponsored Reviews

YouTube allows sponsored content, but make sure that you comply with the site's terms and guidelines regarding videos of this nature. Keep in mind that companies are willing to pay you for your video reviews because of the high level of credibility that you have built with your followers, so be honest in your reviews and opinions. Do not push a product that you personally do not want to use.

Remember that your viewers would love to hear your real experience with the brand and not some sort of canned marketing pitch.

15. Become a Freelance Video Creator/Editor

Remember that making money on YouTube does not necessarily mean appearing in front of the camera. There are opportunities to work and earn income behind the scenes too. One way is by creating and editing videos for other people. This is similar to ghostwriting—you make the content based on your client's or employer's requirements, and then they post your work under their name. Getting ghost workers is how successful people usually keep their YouTube channels and blogs updated in the midst of all their work commitments. You can market your video-making skills as a freelancer. Fit Small Business shares the ultimate guide on how to become a full-time freelancer.

16. Have a Unique Personality and Capture Attention

Here's a list of the commandments you need to follow to be successful on YouTube. These are the basics! Once you get more involved with YouTube, then you'll understand more about them:

- Make your profile and channel artistic
- Create a ritual with catchy phrases or slogans
- "Call to Action"—tell your viewers to subscribe
- Collaborate with other creators
- Create content based on the comments your fans write
- Come up with original and clever titles for your videos
- Make your thumbnail interesting— something that grabs people's attention
- Write descriptions with a hook—don't say too much or too little
- The most important thing: good image and audio

17. Be Visible: Upload One Video per Week

Upload a video at least once a week and let your subscribers know about it. Respond to their comments, let your fans get in touch with you, and build your fan base. Mention in advance when you're uploading a new video—date and hour, if at all possible. You need to fall in love with your project, and you need to be persistent. These things, like anything else, take time. Remember, no one gets to one million followers overnight.

18. Channel Your Originality and Creativity

Don't rehash other people's video content. Besides the possibility of getting your YouTube channel gutted for violating intellectual property rights, your audience will figure it out after a while and walk away.

19. Focus on Something You Feel Passionate About and Don't Make It About the Money

YouTube is like any other business: you need to be persistent and bring something new to the table. There are thousands of YouTube channels out there. The hugely successful ones are the ones who came first and who did it because they loved it, without expecting anything in return.

YouTube, like any other social media outlet, is about passion and doing it because you love to produce videos and you are creative. Making digital content is like that hobby that you need to turn into your daily work and maybe one day make a living from it.

20. Use Your Available Tools and Equipment Before Investing in More Expensive Ones

Start with your phone. Don't spend $5,000 to buy a 5D camera that you have no clue how to use. Your smartphone's camera is perhaps one of the best cameras out there—the trick is in the lighting.

With good lighting and your phone, you can produce something that could look almost as good as anything made by an award-winning director. Start simple and make it grow. It's like going to the gym: make it a habit and once you notice that you love it, get the equipment you need.

CHAPTER 46
GOOGLE ADSENSE

Google AdSense is a advertising program that allows you to run ads on your website or blog, or YouTube videos, and get paid when when visitors click on them. The ads are generated from businesses that use Google's AdWords program.

For new websites or blogs, the AdSense program can be one of the fastest ways to generate income, which is why it's so popular.

But while AdSense is free and easy to use, there are aspects you need to understand about it, and things you can do to maximize your success with it.

Pros and Cons to Making Money with Google AdSense

The Google AdSense program has several great advantages including:

- It's free to join.

- Eligibility requirements are easy, which means you can monetize your website or blog even when it's new.
- There are a variety of ad options and several you can customize to fit the look and feel of your site.
- Google pays monthly (if you meet the $100 threshold) by direct deposit.
- You can run ads on several websites from one AdSense account.
- There are options to run ads on mobile devices and RSS feeds.
- You can easily add it to your YouTube and Blogger accounts.

With that said, there are a few drawbacks to AdSense as well:

- Google can terminate your account in an instant, and it's not very forgiving if you break the rules.
- Like all forms of online income, you need traffic in order to make money.
- When people click on an AdSense ad, you do make some money, but your visitor also leaves your site, which means you lose the opportunity to make money with higher paying affiliate products or your own products and services.

- It doesn't necessarily pay more than other similar programs.

AdSense is a great monetization option, but it's not a get-rich-quick or make-money-doing-nothing program. Further, Google has a lot of rules that aren't always noticed upfront. As a result, many website owners have found out the hard way that they'd violated a Google policy, and have lost their account forever.

Types of AdSense Ads

Google offers a variety of ad types to run on your website, including:

Text: Text ads use words, either as an Ad Unit (one offer) or a Link Unit (list of offers), and come in a variety of sizes. You can customize the color of the box, text and link.

Images: Image ads are graphic ads. They come in a variety of sizes. You can choose an option that mixes both text and image ads.

- Flash
- Video
- Rich media ads include HTML, Flash or other interactive feature.
- Audio

- AdSense for Search allows you to have a Google search box on your site. When a user enters a term and conducts a search, a search results page opens with AdSense ads. You can customize the color scheme of the search results page to harmonize with your web site.

Google AdSense Payments

Google pays monthly through direct deposit or check, but will not issue an AdSense payment until your earnings reach or exceed $100. If you don't earn $100 in one month, your earnings roll over and are added to the next month. Each time you reach the $100 threshold, Google will issue a payment on the next payment period. Through your AdSense account, you can see your current earnings, what ads are generating the most clicks, and more.

Making Money with AdSense

Making a significant amount of money with AdSense requires a plan. Here are tips for maximizing AdSense revenue:

- Read and adhere to Google's rules. Webmasters must comply with Google's webmaster policies as well as the AdSense program policy.
- Don't click on your own ads or ask others to click on them. Incentivizing clicks, buying Pay

Per Click (PPC) space, or using a program designed to drive traffic to AdSense pages are against the rules. Remember, Google isn't very forgiving about breaking the rules, so be sure to adhere to them.

- Have great content your target market wants to read. Ultimately, money is made, whether through AdSense or other monetization methods, by providing valuable content and quality traffic to your blog or website.

- Use honest, organic traffic building website marketing techniques, especially search engine optimization and article marketing.

- Make sure your website/blog is optimized for mobile (responsive). The number of people who use mobile devices is high. Also make sure you're using responsive ads, so Google can send appropriate ad sizes to mobile devices viewing your site.

- Test ad types and placement to find the options that lead to the most income. Start with standard sizes (300×250, 728×90, and 160×600) as there will more ad options for Google to run.

- Max out your ad placement. You're allowed 3 standard ad placements per page. Use them all for maximum benefit.

- Have ads above the fold (the part of your page first seen without scrolling).

- Have a leader board ad below your header/logo instead of at the very top of the page, where it's more likely to be noticed.
- Include in-content ads for viability.
- Monitor your results. Google can overwhelm you with tools and feedback, but do your best to check out what it says about your results so you can make the most of your effort.
- Read email from Google, especially if it's sending a warning about something it doesn't like on your site. Failure to deal with Google's complaints will lead to termination of the program.

Advanced AdSense Tips

Once you have ads running on your site, you'll want to make sure you getting the most of your AdSense program. Here are some additional tips to consider when you're ready to boost your AdSense income:

Run Experiments - You can A/B test your ads through AdSense.
Experiment with link and box colors - If you're colors match your theme, consider changing them up to see if it impacts results.
Enable placement targeting - This allows advertisers to choose where their ads appear.
Set up custom channels so you can get a better sense of what's working and not working

Dealing with Competitors' or Questionable Advertisements

If you offer products or services on your website, you may find that some ads Google delivers come from your competitors. Another issue that can occur is ads that may not be completely legitimate or they might offend your market. To prevent these offers from showing up on your site, Google AdSense allows you to block up to 200 URLs from appearing on your site.

The challenge of this is two-fold.

You don't know what ads are running on your site until you see them there. Plus, with each page load, and depending on the visitors browsing history, the ad may not show up again or it might appear in a different spot.

Since you can't click on your own links (to the get the URL), you need to be careful about obtaining the URL to block. The best way to get the link so you can block it in AdSense is to right click the link, select "Copy Link Address," and paste it into a document or text editor (i.e. Notepad). The Google URL is really long, but you're looking for the section that identifies the advertiser. Copy that link, and paste into your AdSense blocked ads account.

Other Programs Besides AdSense

There are many ad network programs similar to AdSense, such as Media.net and InfoLinks. Some might require a traffic threshold, so you'd need to wait until your site is established before being accepted. Most have similar rules to Google, such as a limit to the number of the network's ads per page (usually 3) and termination for clicking your own ads. In most cases, you can run different ad networks on your site without violating terms of service, but you'll want to read the rules of each network before doing it.

Further, you want to avoid your site becoming so overwhelmed with ads that your readers can't find the content.

Other Income Options besides Ad Networks

Ad networks, especially AdSense, are great options because you can join as a new blogger or website owner, and are easy to use. But they're not the only ways to make money from your website. In fact, as your site traffic grows, other monetization options might be better. Here are some other money-making ideas you can use instead of, or along with, ad networks.

Affiliate Marketing: Like ad networks, affiliate programs are usually free to join and easy to add to your website.

Sell Your Own Product or Service: When you have a readership and social media following, you have an audience that trusts and likes you. As a result, they're more open to buying directly from you. Creating your own product or service, as opposed to promoting someone else through affiliate marketing, can earn you significantly more money. This is especially true with information products or online courses that are inexpensive to create and sell. Other options include ebooks and freelance services.

Coaching or Consulting: As an expert in your topic, you're in a good position to help people beyond the information you provide on your website/blog, to offer more in depth help through coaching or consulting.

Sponsors: When you have a good amount of traffic and terrific influence over your audience, other companies will pay to sponsor your website. They can sponsor your entire site, which would cost them more, or a single page. Some just have advertising.

As you can see, there are many ways to earn income from a website or blog. But many require that you have traffic and an audience that is paying attention to you before they make any money. This is where AdSense is a good beginning monetization option. You don't have to create anything, it's free to join, and it's easy to add the ad code to your website.

CHAPTER 47
CREATE MANUFACTURE AND SELL YOUR OWN INNOVATIVE PRODUCT

You could argue that there are only two kinds of businesses – the ones that spring up because there's a demand, meaning that these enterprises already exist and the innovators, who've created something or developed an improvement on something, and just need to get their idea out there.

So, if you are looking to start a business selling your new innovative product we've produced a guide to getting started on your business selling your new product.

First things first; Market Research. Research your Market

Make sure people actually want to buy your product. Just because it's new and different, it doesn't mean it'll automatically sell. There may be a niche out there for people who need a toaster that also prints photos, but you'll never know if there is or if there's even a big enough niche unless you do your research.

Surveys, public demos and events are always a good way to mingle with a consumer base, show off your new device and see if people like it, or even take a gander at stuff that the customers are interested in. There's an abundance of source material; Use It!

Next you need to develop your product.

Ideas are the backbone of business. However you can't just go out and make your fortune from an idea, that's just not done, you need to work on it, fine tune it, and figure out the flaws and problems with the original idea. That's only the beginning of the development stages. Once you have a coherent idea for your product, you have to start the more in depth development. Design, functionality features and even the colour schemes. It all needs to be on point, to maximise the appeal.

Now that you've gone through the development stage, you need to sort of back track and check out the customer market.

Source Funding.

Arguably the most gruelling task you'll be asked to do is to source the funding for your product. There are numerous ways to do it, but of course, the most common would be investment, subsidies and crowd funding. There are other ways, like loans etc. Just remember however that these all come with their own legal and financial ramifications down the line, so balance your finances against what you stand to lose before making any rash decisions. There are plenty of tips and advice out there to think about when looking into financing your new business.

Understanding what you're selling and who you're selling to.

This isn't the longest step, but it's one of the most important. You need to know what you're selling, and who will be buying it. That's simple, questioning people, and getting feedback from your customers is par for the course.

Make sure that the product works, is to a high quality and to customer satisfaction.

Unless you're a really talented business person, (and a criminal) you can't sell people nothing. Make sure your product is up to snuff, and make sure you've made stock to sell. No product; No business.
Market your Product. Market your Product

Now the work really gets heavy, getting the word out and promoting your product. This is usually one of the more comprehensive tasks that startups have to undertake when selling a new product. Nobody knows what it is, or how useful it is. You have to make them understand that they NEED this. This is basically up to you to determine. You can utilize

Social Media, paid advertisements online or television and radio, even promote it throughout startup sites and other promotional outlets. Oh, and feel free to find out about our own Startup publicity offerings too.

Online SalesSelling your Product.

There are an abundance of choices that you can take when deciding how to sell your new product. Supplying it to outlets and stores is an option, or if you're focussing on something a little less mass produced or personalised, there is a large community of people who use sites like ebay, Amazon and Etsy to sell their wares themselves. Each has their own benefits and pitfalls so make sure to do your research. Another important thing to remember here are the legal ramifications of sales. Most sites keep you in check, but it's best to self check in order to avoid a legal disaster.

Making sure your product doesn't break copyright or patent laws in the territories you're selling to or from is always a good place to start. From there you should also make note of any import fees, taxations and other problems that may arise from your shipping locations. This should all be reflected accurately and fairly in your price after shipping and taxes are calculated. You don't want to lose money, nor do you want your customers to get upset when they have to pay more money than they expected for import charges etc.

Developing and growing your Product / Brand. Develop and Grow

This is far from the final step, but it is one that will be happening throughout the life of your product. You've been selling, doing well and getting the product out there, Great! But is your product actually perfect? Are there no improvements to be made? If not, then congratulations, you deserve to win every business award ever, but if that's not happening for whatever reason, maybe you should look at your product and expand on it. That's not all though, your brand is just as important. People won't buy from a brand they don't believe in. Make sure there's always improvements to social networking, promotion and sales pitches and make sure the customers are aware of how good your product is. With success and growth comes the expansion of your products. An expanded range of products, home website and order page and even self sustained development are just a few of the perks you can look forward to.

CHAPTER 48
CREATE BUSINESS SYSTEM AND FRANCHISE IT OUT

American business franchises account for well over $1 trillion in revenue.

The following table illustrates that American franchises have an enviable rate of success compared to other American businesses. Franchisers provide their franchisees with three advantages that most entrepreneurs do not have: an established business system, a profitable plan and financing. Of these three advantages, the critical differentiator is the established business system, what I call a Business Operating System.

The news and our neighborhoods are filled with stories of companies going out of business or reducing their workforces significantly. However, you might be hard pressed to find a McDonalds, Starbucks, Subway or any other franchise who has closed one of its locations in your neighborhood. So, what can we learn from the successes of the American franchise business?

Business Operating System

A Business Operating System (BOS) is your company's unique way of doing things--how it operates, goes to market, produces and deals with its customers. An effective BOS transcends the people who are doing and managing the work, and is more valuable as a result. A business that effectively operates without you is always more attractive to public and private sources of capital.

In order to create an effective BOS it is key to view your product as the business itself rather than the commodity/service you produce. This paradigm enables the leader to think of the business as a model for 100 others just like it. For example, McDonald's commodity - hamburgers and fries--are not claimed to be the best. However, McDonald's product--its business operating system--is undoubtedly one of the best.

Although many companies spend the time and resources needed to create their BOS, they are disappointed with the results. This is because the components of a BOS are held together by The X Factor. The X Factor is the same thing that sets great companies apart from their competition. I am frequently asked, "How do Southwest Airlines and The Container Store achieve outstanding results and create such a great place to work?" A closer inspection reveals that their success is less about incredibly innovative management practices and all about The X Factor--discipline.

Great companies create and reinforce a rigorous discipline about the little things that affect their customers, employees and shareholders. They have instilled a discipline in their business (via a BOS) and reinforced discipline at a personal level (via their cultures). Personal and organizational discipline help breathe life into your BOS and enable you to sustain it over time, making it the way you do business rather than just a set of hollow procedures.

Components of Your Business Operating System

It is important to create each BOS component to be scalable, up or down, for future growth or contraction. The components are interrelated as with any living system. Therefore, the successful leaders address all components and understand how they affect each other.

A description of the five components is presented in priority order for effectively creating your BOS.

Processes
Systems
Roles
Skills
Structure.

1. Processes

Underdeveloped work processes are the most common risk factor for growing companies, and are the first thing that will crater a company in tough economic conditions. In addition to traditional work processes, we include other processes like communication, decision-making and conflict resolution. It is easy to say, "We need a new system". However, effective leaders have the discipline to resist the illusion that a new system will solve their problems. Streamline your manual processes before changing technical systems. Companies who jump into a new system typically automate their own inefficiencies. This is why Processes should be the first BOS component you create.

Effective processes are:

- Clear
- Replicable
- Documented
- Supported by tools
- Easily accessible.

2. Systems

This component addresses hard and soft systems including: technology, financial, marketing, operations and people. A hard people system is your payroll and human resources information system, whereas soft people systems include performance management, selection, compensation and development systems. Well-designed and applied systems create predictable customer and employee experiences and also enhance your operational efficiency.

Looking at the 80/20 Rule, the 20% of the most effective employees (who produce 80% of the results) inevitably use some kind of a system to enhance their effectiveness. A client recently had to let go of 70% of its sales force and found that the remaining 30% actually accounted for 90% of the company's revenue. Sure enough, the remaining sales people were disciplined in using a system of prospecting, qualifying, proposing, presenting and closing business.

3. Roles

Defining clear roles is a big challenge that requires significant personal discipline. You should write a job description (even if a brief one) for all roles within your desired BOS. Remember to focus on the role itself, not the person. At the early stages of your BOS, one person may play multiple roles. By creating the roles first, you acknowledge this. As your company changes, predefined roles will enable you to make more effective decisions about which roles an employee should continue or discontinue doing and who you should add/delete from the payroll to effectively implement this change.

Resist jumping to the structure component when defining roles--again this requires personal discipline. This step is about defining the required roles to accomplish your company's mission, not how those roles relate to each other.

4. Skills

Now that you have clear roles that your business requires, you can more precisely match the necessary skills to each role. Effective processes and systems will ensure the highest and best use of your talent. Your systems and processes should be created for the lowest common denominator so they are not people-dependent. This will free up your employees' minds and time so they can focus on more creative, proactive ways to improve your business. It is common to see talented employees who are underemployed because they are using excess time trying to figure out how to get their work done.

When you fill your roles, it is important to match the role requirements with the employee's skills and natural style. Ensuring a skills match has obvious benefits. Matching the role with the employee's natural style is subtler but is often even more critical. This can be achieved via a simple style assessment and helps the employee be successful. We all can remember a time when we were in a role for which we were not ideally suited, resulting in greater stress and lower productivity than we (and the company) would prefer.

5. Structure

The key to an effective organizational structure is to design it before you need it--then grow into it. It takes great discipline for leaders to design the other four BOS components before they design their organizational structure. In fact, tinkering with structure is one of the great executive past-times. Unfortunately, this tinkering typically ignores the other, more substantial components.

Structure dictates process. That's why I have outlined the sequence of BOS components in this order. If you create a structure first, your business process will be constrained by your structure and may not reflect the needs of your business and customers. Defining your processes and systems first, as we suggest, results in an organizational structure that supports the way you do business rather than constraining it.

Winston Churchill said, "For the first 25 years of my life I wanted freedom. For the next 25 years I wanted order. For the next 25 years I realized that order is freedom". Your BOS will provide you and your business the order and freedom to work on your business rather than in it.

Although I suggest a particular sequence for creating your BOS, most companies have naturally created one or more of the five components. Since each component may be developed at different levels, it is helpful to prioritize the readiness of each component.

CHAPTER 49
RESELL ON EBAY

Check your favorite eBay category and see what the hot-selling item is. Better yet, go to your favorite store and make friends with the manager. After you're armed with the information you need, search out that item for the lowest price you can, and then give it a shot on eBay.

Keep these shopping locales in mind when you go on the eBay hunt:

Upscale department stores, trendy boutiques, outlet stores, or flagship designer stores are good places to do some market research. Check out the newest items and then head to the clearance area or outlet store and scrutinize the bargain racks for brand-name items.

Discount club stores such as Sam's Club and Costco made their mark by selling items in bulk to large families, clubs, and small businesses. In case you haven't noticed, these stores have upscaled and sell just about anything you could want.

Dollar stores in your area. Many of the items these places carry are overruns (too many of something that didn't sell), small runs (too little of something that the big guys weren't interested in stocking), or out-of-date fad items that need a good home on eBay.

Garage, tag, moving, and estate sales offer some of the biggest bargains you'll ever come across. The stuff you find at estate sales is often of a higher quality. Keep an eye out for "moving to a smaller house" sales. These are usually people who have raised children, accumulated a houseful of stuff, and want to shed it so that they can move to a condo in Palm Springs.

Liquidation and estate auctions are two types of auctions where you can pick up bargains. Before you go, double-check payment terms and find out whether you must bring cash or can pay by credit card. Also, before you bid on anything, find out the hammer fee, or buyer's premium. These fees are a percentage added to the winner's bid; the buyer has the responsibility for paying these fees.

When a company gets into serious financial trouble, its debtors obtain a court order to liquidate the company to pay the bills. The liquidated company then sells its stock, fixtures, and even real estate in a liquidation auction. Items sell for just cents on the dollar, and you can easily resell many of these items on eBay.

Estate auctions are the higher level of estate garage sales. Here you can find fine art, antiques, paper ephemera, rare books, and collectibles of all kinds. These auctions are attended mostly by dealers, who know the local going prices for the items they bid on. But because they're buying to sell in a retail environment, their high bids will generally be the wholesale price for your area.

Newspaper auction listings are an excellent source of merchandise for resale, particularly the listings of liquidations and estate auctions and the daily classified section, which often has ads that announce local business liquidations. Liquidation and estate sales are professionally run, usually by licensed liquidators or auctioneers, and involve merchandise that may be new but is always sold in lots.

Going-out-of-business sales, some of which run week by week, with bigger discounts as time goes by. Don't be shy about making an offer on a quantity of items.

Flea markets or swap meets in your area may have some bargains you can take advantage of.

Gift shops at museums, monuments, national parks, and theme parks can provide eBay inventory — but think about where to sell the items. Part of your selling success on eBay is access. People who can't get to Graceland may pay handsomely for an Elvis mini-guitar with the official logo on the box.

Freebies are usually samples or promotion pieces that companies give away to introduce a new product, service, or, best of all, a media event. Hang on to these! If you receive handouts from a sporting event, premiere, or historic event — or even a collectible freebie from a fast-food restaurant — they could be your ticket to some eBay sales.

For example, when Return of the Jedi was re-released in 1997, the first 100 people to enter each theater got a Special Edition Luke Skywalker figure. These figures are still highly prized by collectors and when the next part of the Star Wars saga was released, the prices on this figure went up yet again.

57. Design T-Shirts, Mugs and Sell via online marketplaces like Zazzle or Cafepress

Design t-shirts to sell online - 8 companies that pay!Have you ever read a funny slogan or an inspirational quote and thought, "I wish I had a T-shirt that said that!"? I would say most of us (including myself) have. As you might have guessed, this post is going to highlight several sites that pay you to design T-shirts. So if you're someone who is forever having creative flashes and you also happen to be a fairly decent designer, there's potential for you to earn money here!

Today I did lots of digging around and found quite a few sites you can use to get paid to design T-shirts. I want to say upfront that most of these only offer a chance to get paid — you'll have to have a "winning" design, or your shirt will have to receive enough interest from potential buyers. Even so, it may be fun to try out if you think you'd be good at it.

Ways to Design T Shirts to Sell Online
Teespring
Use their easy online designer to create a T-shirt. Set your price, a goal, and then if you collect enough pre-orders, they will manufacture and ship the T-shirt to buyers. One of the best things about this site is that you keep ALL of the profit on T-shirt sales. However, there is of course a chance you won't get enough pre-orders for Teespring to decide to print and ship the shirt. This site is open internationally, although you do have to have a Paypal account for collecting payments if your shirt is sold.

So do people actually make money on Teespring? Looks like it! Here's a pretty impressive claim.

SellMyTees

This is another website that will provide you with an online shop for selling your designs on T-shirts. Note that while they do have a free plan for sellers which lets you open up a small basic shop with 20 designs, they do offer paid (monthly) plans as well.

SellMyTees pays monthly via Paypal or check, your choice. There is more info on how payment works here.

Threadless

This is an online T-shirt shop featuring designs from many independent artists around the world. Threadless has an ongoing design challenge that you can submit your own designs to.

Members of the Threadless community are allowed to score the designs submitted, and if yours is one of the best of the best, it will be manufactured and sold. You'll get not only a cash prize for having your design selected, but you will also receive ongoing royalties from sales of your design.

In addition, you can set up your own artist shop on Threadless.

Spreadshirt

Spreadshirt allows you to create your own T-shirt designs, upload them, and sell them (pending approval from Spreadshirt). You can also open your own shop on Spreadshirt and sell lots of different designs. According to Spreadshirt, if you sell a $20 T-shirt, you'll get to keep $12 for yourself. They do not charge any fees.

Payments are made quarterly via either bank transfer or Paypal as long as you have $25 in commissions pending. If you have more than $100 pending, you can request a payment monthly.

SpreadShop

This site makes it possible for you to open your very own T-shirt store. Plus there are no fees — the site is completely free for you to use. There are two ways to earn here — by being a marketplace designer and setting your own prices based on what you think your designs are worth, or you can become a shop owner and earn an commission off each sale of your products.

TeePublic

Create your own design for a T-shirt, upload it, and it immediately will go up for sale. For 72 hours, the shirt you design will be priced at just $14 but will go up after that so they encourage promoting it heavily during the first three days. You can check out their commission rates here.

Zazzle

You've probably heard of Zazzle — it's very well-known. You can put your artwork not only on T-shirts, but also on coffee mugs, calendars, posters, and more. Zazzle allows you to open your own online store and also set your own royalty rates for your creations.

I've actually written a review of Zazzle if you'd like to learn more about how it works. Or, if you'd like, go ahead and check out their website here.

CafePress

This is another site very similar to Zazzle and about as equally popular. With CafePress, you can create designs and put them on T-shirts, posters, coffee mugs, etc. and then sell them. You can get your own online branded shop through CafePress. They will handle marketing for your shop and then you can earn royalties on all sales.

I also have a review of CafePress if you'd like to learn more about it, or go ahead and get started with them here.

I've always thought that I'd love to create some designs for sites like this and just see what happens. It could, at the very least, result in some extra fun money here and there. Sadly, I don't have time to try it these days. If you try it — or if you have already tried it — please leave a comment below and let us all know how it went for you.

CHAPTER 50
GIVE AWAY FREE INFORMATION
AND ASK FOR DONATIONS

When it comes to asking for donations, most of us head for the hills.

We get it. It's intimidating to ask other people to part with their hard earned cash. They might ask, "Why?" And we might not have a great answer.

At its heart, fundraising is helping others connect an existing passion directly to your cause. We don't convince donors. We help them realize that they already care.

Once donors believe that your cause truly matters, giving almost becomes an afterthought. Of course they'll give! The question simply becomes how much to ask for.

But until then, you won't have to sweat your fundraising ask if you follow these seven tips:

1. Research Your Donors to Read Their Minds

The words you want them to say: "Wow, it's like he read my mind!"

How do you get to that point? You research your donor as an individual, but you also have a broad depth of general research on the kinds of people who donate to your nonprofit as a whole group.

You need to be able to answer these questions if you want to get into a donor's heart:

What kinds of words do they use? What do they talk about when they're feeling passionate?
What do they care about? What other causes are they a part of?
Do they have a history of giving?
What are their common objections, fears and concerns about giving?
Thanks to the web, we have more access to information about our donors than ever, as well as the ability to survey our donors and examine how they talk about our cause.

Note, however, that if you survey your donors or ask questions of a potential donor, you have to learn to read the answer behind the answer.

We have to address the fears and risks every donor feels, even if the donor herself can't identify them out loud. And then, we get to connect their existing passions and desires to your NPO, using the same language they use.

In other words, understand your donor base so well it's like you've read their minds.

Don't worry, this is easier than it sounds if you follow the next six tips...

2. Practice, Practice, PRACTICE – And Then Practice Some More

The best way to dominate your donor visits, get more funds and create real, lasting connections with your nonprofit ... is to PRACTICE every aspect of your ask.

In other words, by the time you are actually sitting in front of a prospect, you should have rehearsed the many paths the conversation could take MANY times before. Understanding your talking points, how you'll graciously address common objections and the exact way you'll frame your ask allows you to stop thinking about these things and just focus on talking with the donor.

Practice your ask. Can't emphasize it enough.

Run through how you'll call them on the phone. Plan on how to structure your meeting. Decide how long you'll small talk at the beginning, and how to transition smoothly into the ask itself. Leave no stone unturned!

The key to this:

- Practice out loud.
- Then, practice in front of a mirror.
- Then, record yourself on video practicing.
- It's painful, but you'll learn things about your delivery and be far more confident and free when it comes to actually making the ask. Don't skip this step.

3. Never, Ever Surprise Your Prospect

If your potential donor is ever surprised you're asking them for money, something is deeply amiss.

Make it clear in your first call or contact that you're interested in talking to them about your cause and how they might be able to get involved. Make it clear that, while you're interested in them as a person, there's a deeper purpose for your visit. That way, they'll be able to prepare their response, objections and questions.

4. Stop Being Boring (It Isn't Worth It)

Boring feels safe. No presenter who just reads bullet points off a PowerPoint instead does it because they want their audience to eagerly contemplate running from the room.

Nope, they do it because it feels safe. Reading a PowerPoint feels like an easy way to tell your audience all the info they want and be sure not to forget anything important. But instead, you fail to keep your audience engaged.

The actual way to be safe is what we discussed above: PRACTICE. Then you won't need slides, and you can focus instead on not being boring.

Don't be scared of sounding weird or too forward by asking things like, "What do you think is the biggest challenge we face in this area?" Provoke interesting reactions that are memorable, not boring, formulaic encounters.

Of course, your real goal is to make your donor both catch your enthusiasm and feel understood. But to get there, you need let yourself be not-boring enough that they can have fun talking to you.

5. Ask for Advice – You'll Usually End Up with Money

The old fundraising maxim applies here:

"Ask for money, you'll get advice. Ask for advice, you'll get money."

What most people truly want is to be heard. Asking for advice means that they will freely tell you the secret thing they are most passionate about, as well as their biggest fears about giving.

And most importantly, the donor will feel valued and important. Which they are! They're the ones whose enthusiasm makes changes happen in the world. So ask them for their input and impressions.

For more tips on the advice visit, check out Gail Perry's great article on how advice visits can open any door in town.

6. Your Secret Weapon is Pointed Silence

Our culture HATES silence. We want to fill it. This is one reason why extroverted salespeople and fundraisers can do worse than introverts.

But often times, the most important, meaningful thing – the thing your prospect REALLY wants to tell you – won't be said if you quickly fill the silence.

Bad Fundraiser: "What's the most important thing about the environment to you?"

Donor: "Well, I think environmental damage is a pretty big problem. We're hurting the environment forever and we don't even realize it!"

Bad Fundraiser: "Yeah, you're so right! That's why our Program X is so important! Let me tell you... [Donor hears: "blah blah blah"]

NOOOOOOOO—don't do this! Your funding for next year will die a thousand painful deaths.

Here's how that conversation could have gone:

Superman Fundraiser: "What's the most important thing about the environment to you?"

Donor: "Well, I think environmental damage is a pretty big problem. We're hurting the environment forever and we don't even realize it!"

Donor: [feels like he should talk because of the silence] "... yeah! It's really crazy. In fact, the other day I was thinking about when I was a kid and would go out and look at the stars in the country and see meteors and all kinds of awesome stuff. But now that the city is so big, and there's so much light pollution and smog, when I go out with MY kids to our cabin we're lucky to see anything. It's so sad."

WOW. And you were about to start making a generic appeal about one of your programs, totally at random! Now you have so much material to work with, and know exactly the RIGHT program to talk about.

Your donor has practically sold themselves, all because you shut up! You're fundraising for this guy's kids' happiness now, not your program!

Too many advice-givers say "just listen better!" but fail to tell you that means "shut up and allow silence, even if it feels awkward at first." Great journalists love this technique – it gets them the best interviews and quotes.

By the way, this works in discussions of all kinds – whether you're negotiating a contract, your salary, trying to understand your significant other or asking for a donation. Use strategic silence next time you talk with anyone. Its effects feel almost magical.

7. Ask for a Specific Amount (Don't Make Your Donor Do Any Work)

Finally, always ask for a specific amount to contribute to the cause.

Why is this important? Because it takes the burden off of the donor to figure out what size of a donation is necessary. They don't know anything about your campaign goals. You do. So help them out. Don't make your donor do the work.

CHAPTER 51
BUY DOMAINS AND PARK THEM

After just about two years with increased focus in the online sphere of content and technology, I realised that in many ways, digital businesses can be very reflective of more traditional operations. Take for example domain flipping which to my mind is similar in concept to property flipping.

In property flipping, you buy a property such as a house or apartment at a good price and resell it at a higher price. Domain flipping works on much the same principles and can be just as stunningly profitable, if not more so.

Here are some examples of domain names that were flipped for massive sums;

Insure.com was sold for $16 million
360.com went for $17 million
Insurance.com was flipped at a whopping $35.6 million
Those figures look wonderful, don't they? But before dashing in and buying up domain names like crazy there are a couple of things you need to know about the domain flipping business.

Learn How to Estimate the Value of a Domain Name

Buying domain names is not as simple as snapping up random names and hoping they all go up. To put it succinctly, there is a subtle art as well as a bit of science behind the madness. The best domain flippers put in a lot of thought and knowledge to their purchases.

If you think putting a price tag to a domain is like gambling, you are wrong. Seasoned domainers put a domain through an appraisal process before investing. Several professionals and companies offer this service. The valuation is based on parameters such as age, length, search popularity, e-commerce potential and likely future valuation.

These are factors you need to consider:

1. Extension

The .something is the extension of a domain name, otherwise known as the top-level domain (TLD).

Not all TLDs are equal and some are more valuable. For example, in considering TLDs alone, a country level domain (such as .za) would not be as valuable as a standard .com TLD.

2. Length of name

While ThisSpaceForSale.com might sound like a good idea, domain names that are shorter often demand premium prices. Take for example sex.com which was sold for $13 million. A single word domain often commands an awesome price.

3. Composition of domain name

Similar in concept to length of name as mentioned above, having a domain name that doesn't include hyphens or other unusual characters is better.

4. Existing similarities

Going back to the principle of willing buyer, willing seller, the have value, a domain name must have a potential buyer. Consider the permutations and possibilities of similarity the domain name you're interested in snapping up has and compare that to potential buyers.

5. Pizzazz

Normally, when buying your own domain name, people are encouraged to choose something quick and snappy. The reason for that is because it has pizzazz. I call the appeal of a domain name as it's pizzazz, since that is the potential it has as a brand.

Think about Nike for example; short, sweet, and today a global multi-billion-dollar brand.

There are of course other considerations when choosing a domain name to buy, so a bit of research and experience is in order before you embark on your new domain flipping business.

Domain Flipping Does Carry Some Risks

Again, like property flipping, there is an inherent risk in domain flipping. I am certain that there are those out there who make money out of domain flipping, but in all honesty, hitting the jackpot with a name is really touch and go.

Even worse are those who don't go into the business prepared and end up with a bunch of albatross domain names. These are domain names that you can't even pay someone to take off your hands.

Let me make this clear: Like any other business, domain flipping requires knowledge, experience and a bit of luck. Do not go into the business expecting to turn into a millionaire overnight!

Prepare yourself as if you'd be embarking on any other business. Know the trade, know your own limitations, be aware of capital requirements, etc. In short, treat it like reality instead of a pipe dream.

Getting Started Tips

As mentioned earlier, knowing the potential value of a domain name is an invaluable skill. By adhering to basic guidelines such as those I listed above and through some of your own research, you'll be able to pick names that offer you a higher chance of flipping them more easily. Remember, a net profit of $100 is still a profit, you must start somewhere.

Aside from places where you buy and sell domain names, there are some companies around that support the business of domain flipping. GoDaddy is one of the bigger names out there that does. There, you can not only trade domain names but also park those you've bought. The buying, parking and selling is relatively painless and all you must give up is a small percentage of your selling price.

Size does matter

To be in the domain flipping game, you'll need to be prepared to hold a significant number of domain names in your portfolio. These domain names need to be parked properly so that even if you only sell a fraction of them, the others may give you an opportunity for some revenue.

Make sure that people know your domains are for sale and what the price is! You won't believe how many people I've encountered who just bought domain names and sat on them, hoping for a sale. How, I have no idea. So, make sure you don't make that mistake and list your domain for sale along with the right price tag.

Know the right price for your domain.

Not an easy task, but this will make sure you don't get burnt in any deal you make. Calculating an estimate can involve many factors, such as the value of the name, potential market and more. Some companies such as SmartName can help you value your domains, but are a bit fussy when accepting clients.

GoDaddy on the other hand has a free domain valuation tool that's open to everyone. I recommend you give it a try first and perhaps use something like that as a second opinion. It'll help with the learning curve.

Flipping Your Domains

1- How to buy domain names

There are domain names and there are domain names.

The difference is that you must buy the latter on sites that specifically cater to domain names that are already owned. Sort of like buying a used property from another buyer, rather than the property developer.

Domain Market Place

Domain Marketplaces are simply lists of available domain names and their prices
Two good examples of places where you can buy domain names which are already owned are on Namecheap and GoDaddy. Both sites have domain marketplaces that are like property listings. You can browse and purchase them on this marketplace.

Premium Domain Market

Some premium domains on sale found on Brand Bucket.
Another alternative is Brand Bucket which offers a more selective choice of premium domain names. These domain names are specially handpicked by domain name purveyors and could be a very useful resource if you're shopping for something unique.

One more example of an upscale domain name source is BuyDomains.com which lists the cream of the crop. Through this site you can just enter the domain name you want and even if it's not available it could help facilitate a purchase.

To search and buy a domain name, enter a keyword into the search box.

Here are some "wonderful" domain names I found. Note- My dear colleague Azreen Azmi talked about how to buy a domain name from an existing owner here – do read it if you need the step-by-step guide in buying a pre-owned domain.

2- How to sell domain names

The Direct Approach

In the same way as selling a car, you can reach out to potential buyers and act like the used car salesman. This requires quite a bit of extra research and legwork, but it might be a good way of getting rid of a more niche domain.

For one thing, you can target your sales pitch and skew it correctly. For another, because you know it's a niche, you can bump up the price a little bit. Lastly, by selling the domain directly, you won't have to pay a cut to a middleman such as a domain marketplace.

GoDaddy has a free domain appraisal tool.

Domain Marketplaces

Just like a property listing, except much simpler, domain marketplaces are basically massive lists of domain names that are up for sale. The process of using them is simple. Buy a domain and park it, then list your domain on the marketplace for a price you're willing to let it go for. Once the domain is sold, the marketplace takes a cut and then passes on the remaining funds to you.

Different domain marketplaces charge different percentages of commission and have their own terms and conditions. For example, some require exclusivity, which means if you're listing a domain with them, you can't list it anywhere else. Here are some domain marketplaces to check out. Take some time to find one that's right for your needs.

Flippa

Website: https://www.flippa.com

A site that brands itself as an entrepreneur's marketplace, you can get more than just a domain name from Flippa. In fact, you can buy an entire online business through Flippa by browsing as many as 5,000 new business and domains that go on sale here daily.

Sedo

Website: https://sedo.om/us/

More than just a domain name marketplace, Sedo allows you to engage the services of a domain name broker. These experts can help you find the right domain names not just for your business, but even marketing or campaign-specific domain names.

Conclusion

Having read through what I've written here, I hope that you take away the key element that I've been trying to instill, and that is to be realistic. There is absolutely no problem with having lofty aspirations and dreaming of the mother lode but do take a sensible approach as a whole.

If you respect the domain flipping business and treat it like any other money-generating venture that you would enter, you'll stand a fighting chance. As long as you stay afloat while in the business, there's always that chance of that ten-million-dollar sale dropping into your lap some day!

CHAPTER 52
SOCIAL MEDIA INFLUENCER

An influencer is a user on social media who has established credibility in a specific industry. Social media influencers have access to a large audience and can persuade others by virtue of their authenticity and reach. Since the rise of social media, influencers have become a major trend. These are 'ordinary' people who have earned a substantial following due to their expertise and transparency. They are being used more and more by companies to grab the attention of millennials as this group is less receptive to traditional marketing techniques. Brands purposely seek out influencers who create content that subtly pushes a product or service. The partnership between the brand and influencer is mutually beneficial. The company successfully reaches their target audience while the influencer is paid and continues to grow their following.

Now, trying to become a social media influencer is an even more onerous venture. You have some work to do before you'll be able to get 9.2 million views on a video of you reading mean comments about your dog like the aforementioned Miss Marbles or even the 11 million views on how to make "galaxy slime" from

DIY channel, Threadbanger. The road to those number of views is a long one, but it's not impossible to be an influencer in your industry with the right approach.

By following the steps below, you'll be on your way to growing your following, attracting the attention of brands and successfully becoming a social media influencer.

01. Find your topic (and get obsessed)

The first thing you want to do is find the subject that you'll be covering across your social channels. The more specific, the better, as there will be less competition. However, try not to choose a subject that is too niche, as you may end up tweeting yourself into a corner. Find something that you're genuinely interested in that has a following of its own and dive into it. It can be a passion from childhood, a hobby in which you've developed outstanding skills, or your professional expertise: the important factor is to be passionate about what you're going to talk about. Bringing the passion has two major benefits: first, you won't get bored, and it will tell in your videos, tweets or other outlets. Secondly, passion is a strong engine for quality: the more adamant you are about your topic, the more convincing you are.

Once you know what you're going to cover, consume everything about the subject you possibly can. Stay on top of your chosen topic by following related news and blogs as much as you're able to. If there's something new in the industry, you want to know about it and you want to be able to give your two cents on your social channels. Assess your perspective by getting the story from many outlets and see how your opinion or view differs. Highlighting this difference allows you to stand out and provide valuable information to your audience.

02. Make a plan

Once you've chosen a topic and are well seasoned in the subject, it's time to strategize. This includes making a plan with your content strategy and answering questions like: what is your persona? Your message? The tone that resonates with your target audience? This is also the time to get all of your ducks in a row to organize how and when you will produce, edit, and publish your content. Making a schedule at least a month into the future will allow you to easily maneuver choppy waters if you run into hiccups at the beginning of your journey. Do your research on what's the acceptable number of times to post per day on Facebook, Instagram, YouTube and Snapchat. Dig even further to find out what days and times are most popular (for your audience) to post as well. Knowing these things ahead of time will help you define your schedule going forward.

03. Get social

If you really go all-in to become a social media influencer, you will need to find the networks that fit within your industry and target audience. It may be best to start with one or two major channels (like YouTube and Instagram) in the beginning. The idea is to stay consistent, so it's important to not take on more than you can bear. Still, it's recommended to sign up to all networks in order to secure your user handle. For each network that you sign up for, write up a solid biography with relevant links to your other social channels or website so your audience can easily find you. It should feel like you are EVERYWHERE. Keep the same tone and description across all the platforms that you open. Also, when signing up to social networks be sure to go for the "business" account if available. These types of accounts provide much better metrics to track your posts and allow you to create paid promotions when you're ready.

Wix: How to become a social media influencer

04. Remember: content is king

Hope you like creating content, because that's really what being a social media influencer is all about, and it will be around 90% of what you're doing. Here are some key factors to keep in mind when planning your content:

Consistently produce content: Social media moves fast and if you think you can go a week or two without posting and expect the same following when you return, you might want to reassess your goals. Your content should also remain fresh and relevant. This means identifying trends you see on social media with others in your industry and responding accordingly with content of your own. It will likely take some time, but you'll need to find a balance of trending content and content that is uniquely yours to share on your channel. Keeping up with trends is one thing, but your biggest challenge may actually be to know the trends before they are labeled as "trends".

Mind your hashtags: Hashtags (represented by the symbol #) allow you to further your reach to people also following that hashtag – they're essentially a universal language that allow you to pop up in places you might not, normally. Researching trending and relevant hashtags is important, which will require you to do some digging within posts that cover your chosen subject. Hashtags on both Twitter and Instagram are very much worth your time to get right, but surprisingly, they don't matter on Facebook and YouTube for the success of your posts. Also, note that depending on the network you're posting to, the number of hashtags is also important. Curious to know more about this magical symbol and its power?

Find out more in this complete guide on everything you need to know about hashtags.

Experiment with all types of formats: It's 2018 and social networks have considerably evolved, coming up with new revolutionary ways to post your content. Instagram is no longer just for photos but also for posting Stories – which are photos and videos that disappear after 24 hours but have amazing exposure potential. Another example: almost all social networks have some sort of "live" option that will stream what you're doing in real-time (something you should be taking advantage of). The "live" craze looks like it won't be stopping anytime soon and for good reason. Influencers can use live streams to give their audience a glimpse of what goes on "behind the scenes," which can help build trust between them and their customers. For a budding social media influencer like yourself, a live video can show your followers a more personal, off the cuff presentation.

Even if hosting live streams or other less traditional posting methods don't become your primary method, a social media influencer should be well rehearsed with the tools they are given. Meaning, you should at least know what they do and how to use them. Knowing the tools of the social media landscape is what sets you apart from an everyday user and an influencer.

05. Build your community

An important part of building a following is engaging with them. There are a couple of ways to do this, for example: responding every time someone comments on one of your posts is simple but shows your audience that you're a "real person." You'll also want to invite your audience to engage with you and let them know that you would like to hear from them by telling them to leave a comment or ask a question.

Going back to the "live" way of doing things, it provides an opportunity for your audience to reach out to you in the most direct way possible. Host a Q&A or even ask your audience for advice on something to let them know they are being heard. If you're producing video content, end a video by posing a question and start your next video with some of the answers you received. A community heard is a community that feels loved.

Wix: How to become a social media influencer

06. Don't buy your followers

Hey, you know what's a terrible idea? Buying your followers, that's what! The road to whatever success you're seeking is likely a long one, but buying followers to give the illusion that people like what you're doing not only sets you up for failure, but it's also just lame. Don't do it, as it will only hurt you in the long run. It's important to stay open and honest with your following. Even if that means starting small, it will only be a matter of time till your following grows and blossoms into a loyal and trusting community.

07. Network IRL (In real life)

A long time ago, there was this old-fashioned concept where people would gather in the same location and talk to each other face to face. On purpose! In fact, if you look for them, you can still find these "analog" social gatherings. Attending networking events is a great way to get to know others in your industry, which could help spawn a future collaboration.

08. Further your reach with a stunning website

Just because you're aiming to be an influencer in social media doesn't mean your presence should stop there. Having a website or blog (or a website with a blog) gives you yet another place for people to find you. Having a blog dedicated to the happenings in your industry will only further solidify your place as an influencer. Plus, you can easily share your blog posts to your social channels. Creating a website is easier than ever thanks to all the available ready-made templates

If you have unique content shared across multiple social channels, your website can be a great place to showcase it all together. For example, take food blogger and Instagram influencer, Jeremy Jacobowitz from Brunch Boys – his website is home to his blog posts, YouTube feed, links to his social media and press coverage. Now that's the way to do it!

Wix: How to become a social media influencer
Rhett & Link

09. Get active on forums

If there's a dedicated forum(s) to the industry or subject you cover, make your presence known there. Not only can you help share your knowledge (and links to your social channels), you may end up learning a thing or two from other industry experts while you're at it. While being active on other forums is great don't let that stop you from creating your own. You can keep the conversation going by adding Wix Forum to your website.

10. Collaborate with other influencers and brands

While your primary focus, in the beginning, should be to create and release great content and slowly but surely bud out your community, you will eventually want to look into collaborating with others. Whether it's another influencer in the same (or different) industry, or a business looking to tackle your target audience's demographics, partnering up can be a fun and mutually beneficial endeavor. If you already have an idea of who you'd like to collaborate with, be sure that they align with your values and have a similar following (you want to appeal to their audience and vice versa).

Before jumping off the deep end, be sure you've waded the water first. Follow them on their social channels and engage accordingly. Be tactful and not tacky. Don't come off as super "extra" to your potential collab partner. You're trying to show genuine interest and respect, so don't go overboard with comments and emojis. Pitch them with a proper email or DM. Be upfront, state your intentions, show enthusiasm, and be as personable as possible.

CHAPTER 53
INVEST WITH A ROBO ADVISOR

A new type of online software has emerged that can help you manage your investments. These software products are called "robo advisors."

A robo advisor can be a good solution for someone who does not want to hire a financial advisor, doesn't have enough assets to hire a financial advisor yet, or for someone who has typically been a do-it-yourself investor, but no longer wants to select investments, rebalance, and place trades on their accounts.

Robo advisors can automatically select investments and build a diversified portfolio for you. Once your funds are invested, on an ongoing basis, the software automatically makes changes to the investments to align your portfolio back to a target allocation. Some robo advisors even make trades automatically to help reduce your tax bill—a process called tax-loss harvesting.

If you are a do-it-yourself investor, these low-cost online robo advisors can help you build a better portfolio. Here's how they work.

What Fees Are Involved

With a robo advisor you pay a service fee and you pay the expenses of the investments used.

Each robo advisor has a reasonable service fee that may be structured as a fixed monthly fee or as a percentage of assets. With robo advisors that charge a fixed monthly fee, the fee typically ranges from about $15 per month to $200 per month depending on portfolio size. With a percentage of assets structure, you'll see fees in the range of about .15% to .50% of your account size per year. If you had a $100,000 a .50% fee would equate to $500 a year.

You also pay any expenses associated with the investments used by the robo advisors. For example, mutual funds and exchange-traded funds have expense ratios. That type of fee is taken out of the assets of the fund before any returns are allocated to investors.

Many of these online portfolio solutions offer a free trial period so you can see how it works before you are charged.

Benefits of Using a Robo Advisor

One of the biggest benefits of using a robo advisor is to avoid costly investing mistakes. It has been documented many times over that one of the biggest reasons investors get poor outcomes is due to their own behavior. Investors make emotional decisions at market highs and market lows and based on gut feelings. Software does not make these kinds of mistakes.

Another benefit is reduced stress. Once you open your account the robo advisor software automates the whole process. You no longer have to worry if you should make changes to your portfolio, or wonder if you should invest more in technology or less in financials. You don't have to log in and place trades. You don't have to worry that a broker or other financial sales person is making a recommendation that is not in your best interest.

Who Robo Advisors Are Best For

Robo advisors can be a great solution for beginning investors, young professionals who want to put their portfolio on "automatic," and for investors that have a relatively simple situation.

Investors who have stock options, need to coordinate company benefit packages and 401(k)s with other accounts, or who need a customized approach to the tax impact of investing may find that an automated solution is not ideal.

What Investments Are Used

Most robo advisors use mutual funds or exchange-traded funds to build the portfolio, not individual stocks. Rob advisors typically follow an index fund or passive investment approach based on modern portfolio theory research. This research says the most important factor is your allocation to stocks or bonds. Then you focus on which underlying stock asset classes, such as large cap, small cap, or international. Then you focus on which underlying bond asset classes, such as short, intermediate, or long-term.

With a robo advisor, the software does all this for you.

How Taxes Work on a Robo Account

If you have an IRA, Roth IRA, or another type of tax-deferred retirement account, there are not tax consequences to be concerned about with an automated process. With these types of accounts, you pay no tax until the day you take a withdrawal. Rollovers or transferring your account from its existing place to a robo advisor does not count as a withdrawal.

If you own investments that are not tucked inside a retirement account then you receive a 1099 form each year that reports the interest, dividends, and capital gains. You report those on your tax return and pay tax on these types of investment income.

Robo accounts most typically must be funded with cash. If they do allow you to transfer in existing investments, those investments are likely to be sold unless they are investments already used in the robo model portfolio. If these investments are not inside retirement accounts when they are sold any capital gains or losses will be realized. If it was a gain, this may result in a larger-than-normal tax bill during the year that you transition to the robo advisor.

More About Robo Advisors

A robo advisor is not a financial planner. Some robo advisors have additional software tools that can help you project how your accounts will grow, but you do not receive customized planning advice on how much to save, whether to use a Roth IRA or Traditional IRA, how to allocate investments in other accounts like your 401(k), etc.

Some robo advisors offer live assistance (this usually costs slightly more), while others interact with you almost exclusively through the web. If you like hand-holding and a familiar voice to talk to, a robo advisor is probably not for you.

In addition, once you are near retirement, the allocation models used in the robo advisor tools may not help you align your investments for the withdrawal phase. At that point, you may want to seek the services of a professional retirement income planner.

Where to Find a Robo Advisor

Below is a list of popular robo advisors. Some offer more human assistance than other.

- Asset Builder
- Betterment
- Personal Capital
- MarketRiders
- Rebalance IRA
- Schwab Intelligent Portfolios
- SigFig
- WealthFront

CHAPTER 54
INVEST IN DIVIDEND PAYING STOCKS

Looking for an investment that offers regular income? Dividend stocks can be a good choice.

Dividend stocks distribute a portion of the company's earnings to investors on a regular basis. Most American dividend stocks pay investors a set amount each quarter, and the top ones increase their payouts over time, so investors can build an annuity-like cash stream.

Dividend stocks tend to be less volatile than growth stocks, so they can also help diversify your overall portfolio and reduce risk.

How to buy dividend stocks

We'll cover two ways to invest in dividend stocks here: Through exchange-traded funds that hold these stocks, and by purchasing individual dividend stocks. Let's start with dividend ETFs, since they're the easiest entry.

Investing in dividend stocks through ETFs

Like much in the world of ETFs, dividend ETFs offer a simple and straightforward solution to getting exposure to a specific investing niche — in this case, stocks that pay a regular dividend.

A dividend ETF typically includes dozens, if not hundreds, of dividend stocks. That instantly provides you with diversification, which means greater safety for your payout: Even if a few of the fund's stocks cut their dividends, the effect will be minimal on the fund's overall dividend. A safe payout should be your top consideration in buying any dividend-paying investment.

Here's how to buy a dividend stock ETF:

1. Find a broadly diversified dividend ETF. You can typically find dividend ETFs by searching for them on your broker's website. (No broker? Here's how to open a brokerage account.)

Probably the safest choice is a low-cost fund that picks dividend stocks from the S&P 500 stock index. That offers a broadly diversified package of America's top companies. You may want to also restrict your search to commission-free options, so you don't pay a commission each time you buy or sell the ETF.

2. Analyze the ETF. Make sure the ETF is invested in stocks (also called equities), not bonds. You'll also want to check the following:

The dividend yield. This is how much a company pays out in dividends each year relative to its share price, and is usually expressed as a percentage. Generally, higher is better, though anything above 3.5% should be examined more closely to assess the safety of the investment.

5-year returns. Generally, higher is better.

Expense ratio. This is the ETF's annual fee, paid out of your investment in the fund. Look for an expense ratio that is under 0.50%, but lower is better.

Stock size. Dividend ETFs can be invested in companies with large, medium or small capitalization (referred to as large caps, mid caps and small caps). Large caps are generally the safest, while small caps are the riskiest.

3. Buy the ETF. You can buy ETFs just like you'd buy a stock, through an online broker. A good approach is to buy them regularly, to take advantage of dollar-cost averaging.

Why you should buy an ETF: The biggest advantage for individual investors is that you can buy just one ETF and don't have to track dozens of companies, which is what you'd have to do if you buy dividend stocks yourself. Buy your dividend ETF and then add money to it regularly.

Investing in individual dividend stocks

Building a portfolio of individual dividend stocks takes time and effort, making it more complex than investing through a dividend ETF. But by picking and choosing your dividend stocks, you have the potential to personalize a portfolio and find higher dividends than in an ETF.

Before buying a stock, you'll need to analyze the company and industry, evaluate the safety of the dividend and then determine how much to buy.

Here's how to buy a dividend stock:

1. Find a dividend-paying stock. You can screen for stocks that pay dividends on many financial sites, as well as on your online broker's website.

2. Analyze the company. This step is probably the hardest but the most important. To make sure you choose a healthy company that can sustain its dividend for years, you'll need to spend a lot of time understanding the company's financial statements and industry.

3. Analyze the safety of the dividend. What is the payout ratio? That is, what percentage of income does a company pay in dividends? The lower it is, the safer the dividend and the faster the dividend can grow over time. A payout ratio over 80% is generally a red flag, but even that is just a rough benchmark. In some industries, you don't want a payout ratio above 50%.

4. Decide how much stock you want to buy. You need diversification if you're buying individual stocks, so you'll need to determine what percent of your portfolio goes into each stock. If you're buying 20 stocks, you could put 5% of your portfolio in each (or buy 25 stocks at 4%, 30 stocks at 3.3%, etc.). However, if the stock is riskier, you might want to buy less of it and put more of your money toward safer choices.

The No. 1 consideration in buying a dividend stock is the safety of its dividend. So when buying a dividend stock, it's absolutely crucial that you not be a "yield pig," focusing only on the highest dividend yields. A high yield often signals that investors are skeptical of the company's ability to sustain the dividend and that it may be in danger of being cut. That skepticism drives down share price, and a lower share price pushes the yield ratio higher.

If the market thinks the dividend will be cut and it is cut, the stock will go down and you'll lose money.

Plus, you'll have a smaller dividend. So you get hit two ways.

Why you should buy individual dividend stocks: You like the challenge of combing over the market for attractive stocks and don't mind — even enjoy — spending the time to do it. If you're good, you'll likely be able to build a portfolio of dividend stocks that offers a higher yield than what you could find in a dividend ETF.

CHAPTER 55
INVEST IN INDEX FUNDS

Everyone gushes about index mutual funds, and for good reason: They're an easy, hands-off, diversified, low-cost way to invest in the stock market.

When investors buy an index fund, they get a well-rounded selection of many stocks in one package without having to purchase each individually. And because these funds simply hold all the investments in a given index — versus an actively managed fund that pays a professional to do the stock picking — management fees tend to be low. The result: Higher investment returns for individual investors.

Lastly, index funds are easy to buy. Here's how it's done.

Step 1. Decide where to buy

You can purchase an index fund directly from a mutual fund company or a brokerage. Same goes for exchange-traded funds (ETFs), which are like mini mutual funds that trade like stocks throughout the day.

When you're choosing where to buy an index fund, consider:

Fund selection. Do you want to purchase index funds from various fund families? The big mutual fund companies carry some of their competitors' funds, but the selection may be more limited than what's available in a discount broker's lineup.

Convenience. Find a single provider who can accommodate all your needs For example, if you're just going to invest in mutual funds (or even a mix of funds and stocks), a mutual fund company may be able to serve as your investment hub. But if you require sophisticated stock research and screening tools, a discount broker that also sells the index funds you want may be better. (If you don't have a brokerage account, here's how to open one.)

Commission-free options. Do they offer no-transaction-fee mutual funds or commission-free ETFs? This is an important criterion we use to rate discount brokers. (The selections at Charles Schwab, E-Trade, Fidelity and TD Ameritrade are worth checking out.)

Trading costs. If the commission or transaction fee isn't waived, consider how much a broker or fund company charges to buy or sell the index fund. Mutual fund commissions are higher than stock trading ones, about $20 or more, compared with less than $10 a trade for stocks and ETFs.

Step 2. Pick an index

Index mutual funds track various indexes. The Standard & Poor's 500 index is one of the best-known indexes because the 500 companies it tracks include large, well-known U.S.-based businesses representing a wide range of industries.

But the S&P 500 isn't the only index in town. There are indexes — and corresponding index funds — composed of stocks or other assets that are chosen based on:

Company size and capitalization. Index funds that track small, medium-sized or large companies (also known as small-, mid- or large-cap indexes).

Geography. These funds focus on stocks that trade on foreign exchanges or a combination of international exchanges.

Business sector or industry. Funds that focus on consumer goods, technology, health-related businesses, for example.

Asset type. Funds that track domestic and foreign bonds, commodities, cash.

Market opportunities. Emerging markets or other nascent but growing sectors for investment.

Despite the array of choices, you may need to invest in only one. His Royal Investment Highness Warren Buffett has said that the average investor need only invest in a broad stock market index to be properly diversified. (For more, check out our story on simple portfolios to get you to your retirement goals.)

However, you can easily customize your allocation if you want additional exposure to specific markets in their portfolio (such as more emerging market exposure, or a higher allocation to small companies or bonds).

Step 3. Check investment minimum, other costs
Low costs are one of the biggest selling points of index funds. They're cheap to run because they're automated to follow the shifts in value in an index. However, don't assume that all index mutual funds are cheap.

Even though they're not actively managed by a team of well-paid analysts, they carry administrative costs. These costs are subtracted from each fund shareholder's returns as a percentage of their overall investment.

Two funds may have the same investment goal — like tracking the S&P 500 — yet have management costs that can vary wildly. Those fractions of a percentage point may seem like no big deal, but your long-term investment returns can take a massive hit from the smallest fee inflation. Typically, the bigger the fund, the lower the fees.

The main costs to consider:

Investment minimum. The minimum required to invest in a mutual fund can run as high as a few thousand dollars. Once you've crossed that threshold, most funds allow investors to add money in smaller increments.
Account minimum. This is different than the investment minimum. Although a brokerage's account minimum may be $0 (common for customers who open a traditional or Roth IRA), that doesn't remove the investment minimum for a particular index fund.

Expense ratio. This is one of the main costs are subtracted from each fund shareholder's returns as a percentage of their overall investment. Find the expense ratio in the mutual fund's prospectus or when you call up a quote of a mutual fund on a financial site. For context, the average annual expense ratio was 0.09% for stock index funds and 0.07% for bond index funds, versus 0.82% for actively managed stock funds and 0.58% for actively managed bond funds, according a 2016 report from the Investment Company Institute.

Tax-cost ratio. In addition to paying fees, owning the fund may trigger capital gains taxes if held outside tax-advantaged accounts like a 401(k) or an IRA. Like the expense ratio, these taxes can take a bite out of investment returns: typically 0.3% of returns when invested in an index fund, according to a 2014 study by Vanguard founder John Bogle. Fund tracker Morningstar calculates the tax-cost ratio, which shows the percentage by which a fund's performance has been reduced by taxes.

Other things to keep in mind

Index funds have become one of the most popular ways for Americans to invest because of their ease of use, instant diversity and returns that typically beat actively managed accounts. Some additional things to consider:

- Is the index fund doing its job? Your index fund should mirror the performance of the underlying index. To check, look at the index fund's returns on the mutual fund quote page. It shows the index fund's returns during several time periods, compared with the performance of the benchmark index. Don't panic if the returns aren't identical. Remember, those investment costs, even if minimal, affect results, as do taxes. However, red flags should wave if the fund's performance lags the index by much more than the expense ratio.

- Is the index fund you want too expensive? Invest in an exchange-traded fund that tracks the index. Instead of having to buy the main-course mutual fund, you purchase just a slice of the fund.
- Want to buy stocks instead?
- New to investing?
- How much will you need to retire?

CHAPTER 56
INVEST IN CRYPTOCURRENCIES &
EAU-COIN/GELT

The question that prospective crypto investors rightly ask themselves is how much to invest in the sector.

The burgeoning crypto universe is susceptible to market fluctuations, partly due to its relative infancy. As such, investors should always retain a cautious attitude toward their investments.

With this in mind, it's important to consider several factors:

Decide which kind of cryptocurrency you're interested in.

As important as it is to decide how much to invest in cryptocurrency, it is also necessary to be strategic in understanding the fundamentals of a digital asset, as this can play a major role in the level of risk involved.

Fundamental analyses are the best indicators for long-term investors, so you'll need an understanding of how a coin or Initial Coin Offering (ICO) functions, its history and what it brings to the table before choosing to participate in its development.

It might be best to look at the purpose of the cryptocurrency you're interested in, how long it has been in the market, its market capitalization and its underlying tech solutions. Cryptocurrencies that solve problems are less likely to fail than those that are essentially ICOs.

Also, the longer a cryptocurrency has been in the market, the more trusted it is.

Decide what type of investment you're after.

Naturally, you'll want to create a plan if you want to enter the crypto market. The question is whether your trades will be short-term or medium- to long-term endeavors. This is an important consideration that affects the amount of money you'll place in your investments. If the plan is to trade regularly, then understanding market trends, the culture driving the markets and the mentality of investors is a step in the right direction.

If you want to go further, then studying up on market indicators, fundamental and technical analyses, incoming market-moving events, general tech news and developer announcements — among other things — is the next step to up your game.

Remember: crypto market statistics matter.

As I mentioned previously, gauging market behavior during different time periods is part of a well-ordered strategy. While this might be confusing to follow up on at times, market dynamics shouldn't be overlooked — especially if you plan on trading in the short term. To make it simpler, streamline your cryptocurrency choice to the ones you prefer, look up their charts and try to spot trends via market indicators.

Find out whether the digital asset is widely accepted and trustworthy.

As in most markets, trust is crucial for prospective investors. In order for someone to put their money behind a cryptocurrency or ICO project, that person must, through some process of their own, conclude that they trust the idea enough to put their money behind it. In the crypto universe, one could predicate this process on three key factors about new technology billionaire philanthropist and entrepreneur Peter Thiel has discussed: a unique idea (that offers tangible solutions), incremental improvement (which requires a good development team), and the ability to coordinate complex ideas.

In reality, these three points are the best indicators a long-term investor can consider in regard to cryptocurrencies.

In a talk at the Economic Club of New York in March, Thiel analyzed the trustworthiness of cryptocurrencies by drawing parallels between Bitcoin and gold. Both are considered a store of value, are not backed by any government, have unclear inherent values and are immutable in different ways.

Take a look at the major crypto players so far. www.eau-coin.ic

In any field, learning from the knowledge of predecessors can never hurt, but it can help. Cryptocurrency is no exception. In fact, this move might be more important due to the market's volatility, as a small mistake could cost a fortune or your entire holdings.

The most common saying by crypto investors and finance experts is that you should only invest money you are willing to lose. Put into perspective, this translates into a low percentage of your net worth. The question is: Do they really do as they say? Crypto millionaire Erik Finman, for instance, invested $1,000 in cryptocurrency when he was 12 years old. He had very little money, yet he went for a high-risk,-high-reward strategy and earned millions in the process.

At one point, Jeremy Gardener invested most of his stock holdings in crypto investments and has since become a millionaire.

At the end of the day, these individuals took huge leaps by investing in cryptocurrency. Even so, the important thing about their investments is that they were willing to lose the money.

Invest the right amount of money.

The rule of thumb that you should "only invest what you are willing to lose" is nigh on impeccable. Think about it this way: If you woke up one morning with your investment in a shambles, would it make you unable to pay your bills the next month? If so, you're investing too much. Of course, losing money will always hurt. But if you invest properly, it won't be a devastating event if the worst comes to pass.

Workforce development is a topic that impacts every corner of the United States, so it is appropriate that a national initiative and its new book reflects this massive undertaking.

The Federal Reserve System's Investing in America's Workforce is just that. This week marks the release of the initiative's three-volume book Investing in America's Workforce: Improving Outcomes for Workers and Employers, which is available as a free download. More than 100 authors representing the different stakeholders in workforce development contributed their ideas to the goal of changing the public conversation about workforce development.

"We pulled together some of the best thinkers and authors and practitioners in the United States to contribute their thoughts on a range of issues," contributor and editor Carl Van Horn said.

The sprawling 1,130-page report leaves nothing related to workforce development untouched. Well-publicized issues centering around the impact of technology on the workforce and the skills gap are joined by lesser-known topics like improving the employment of disabled people and bridging the digital divide. Altogether, it presents the entirety of work in America and how to get more workers engaged in the red-hot economy.

"Even though the top-line number of unemployment is low, the reality is underneath that, there are still millions of people who are working part-time but want a full-time job, who are long-term unemployed, who are contract workers or gig workers who really need a better job," said Van Horn of the imperative to improve the lives of all workers.

Lennon, whose previous work with JP Morgan Chase & Co. was featured in a December 2017 article, examined the role of technology in connecting workers to jobs in an article with co-author and JP Morgan Chase & Co. vice president of global philanthropy Sarah Steinberg. From social media networks to mobile applications, technology has more potential to increase efficiency in the labor market.

They acknowledge that job matching technology has drawbacks that transfer problems from the offline world to the online world, including hiring biases and restricting access for lower-income job seekers. They suggest that to unlock the potential of technology for American workers, it must be equitable and affordable.

Tyszko, who serves on WorkingNation's Advisory Board and was interviewed by Ramona Schindelheim about the USCCF's Opportunity Project in February, wrote about the changing skills market and the inability for current systems to keep pace with employers' needs.

He argues that new organizational models, such as the USCCF's Talent Pipeline Management initiative, are improving how employers signal their skill needs to educators and workforce developers. The role of intermediaries like USCCF in linking the employment and educational world will be vital for the workforce to adapt to changes brought on by technology.

Van Horn's chapter eloquently summarizes the future all Americans must prepare for, in whatever shape it will take due to automation and artificial intelligence. Beyond the dire predictions of wholesale replacement of human workers, Van Horn writes that the future of work is uncertain, but American workers still face dangers of structural unemployment and another economic downturn.

CHAPTER 57
LICENSE YOUR PHOTOS

Copyrights give the owner the exclusive right to do, or to authorize others to do, specific things with their photographs. Copyright law effectively gives you, the copyright owner, a legal monopoly on the use of that image. Specifically, when you own the copyright to a photograph, you have the sole right to:

reproduce the copyrighted work;
display the copyrighted work publicly;
prepare derivative works based on the copyrighted work; and
distribute copies of the copyrighted work to the public by sale or other transfer of ownership, or by rental or lending.
These are known as the "exclusive rights," and you may assign, sell, transfer, or give them away. When you assign, sell, transfer, or give others only some of your exclusive rights (not the entire copyright), you are licensing them.

Creating a license
To create a license, think about the "five Ws": who, what, when, where, and why. In the above example, "you" is the who; "borrow the car" is the what; "the

park" is the where; "today until 5 p.m." is the when; "to play tennis with Taylor" is the why.

To license the copyright for one of your photographs, for instance, you could say: "I grant to the ABC Company (who) the right to reproduce my photograph of the sleeping grizzly bear (what) for the August 2015 issue (when) on the cover of "Wildlife" magazine (where). The "why" could be money—for example, "for $1,000," and/or "with the photo credit of 'Copyright 2015 Jane Doe' included in the magazine's masthead."

Licenses for copyrights are designed to exclude. If the use isn't explicitly included in the license, then the user doesn't have the right to use your photograph in any other way. Therefore, it can be good to include "all other rights are reserved" in your license.

Your license shouldn't be different for a friend's use of your photo. If you want to share your images with friends, tell them that the photos are for personal use only and to let you know if they want to use them for anything else.

In addition, the nonprofit organization Creative Commons offers free copyright licenses to "provide a simple, standardized way to give the public permission to share and use your creative work—on conditions of your choice." Creative Commons' license terms can be customized to a certain extent and may help you to create a license to fit your needs.

Put the license in writing

Some photographers grant exclusive licenses so that only the licensee has the right to use their photograph in a certain way or for a certain time. Exclusive licenses must be in writing. You can grant non-exclusive licenses orally, but it's best to put all licenses in writing. It minimizes confusion and gives you something concrete to rely upon if a dispute arises.

License checklist

When you license your photographs to others, consider including the following items:

- Who are you giving the rights to?
- What specific rights are you granting?
- Are you authorizing print and/or electronic rights?
- If you grant electronic rights, what kind? CD? Web?
- For what time are you granting the rights?
- Will the rights be exclusive?
- How will the rights be used? In what market or industry?

- What territory do the rights cover? North America? English-speaking countries? Worldwide?
- Are there any work-for-hire implications?
- How will you be paid? By a flat fee? By royalties?
- If paid by royalties, how will the royalties be calculated?
- When will you be paid?
- Will you allow the user to alter your photograph for the use?
- Will you require certain items to be included with the use? Copyright notice? Photo credit?
- Do you want samples of the use?
- Retain all other rights; you never know what future usage technology will bring.
- Make the license subject to being paid in full: "No rights are granted to Client until Photographer has received payment in full."

To be sure that every important aspect of licensing is addressed, ask an attorney who is familiar with these issues to review your license. Always having a license—especially a written one—is important for protecting your copyrighted work.

Regardless of the scenario, Van Horn argues that policymakers are slow to respond to widespread unemployment, resulting in the United State's meager investment in job training programs compared to other developed nations. Without sufficient action to remedy this problem, the millions of under- and unemployed workers will suffer the same fate as what befell workers during the Great Recession.

"We do not know whether the current bundle of technological changes, including artificial intelligence, semiautonomous vehicles and the Internet of Things, will eliminate more net jobs than previous innovations. However, those who have limited formal education or skills and who are not retrained for new opportunities will likely be at risk of losing jobs and remaining unemployed," Van Horn writes.

Instead of viewing job training as a social service, Van Horn told WorkingNation that he wants the public to look at investing in workers as the solution for continued economic growth. With low unemployment and the skills gap contributing to a shortage of qualified workers to fill a record six million job openings, there is room for more Americans to enjoy the benefits of the expanding economy now.

"It's not charity. It's a good economic decision because it not only benefits that person [but] that family, that community and the entire economy," said Van Horn, "It's not acceptable to have a large number of people who are underemployed or unemployed."

CHAPTER 58
SELL DIGITAL ART FILES

Are you a graphic designer? Perhaps you have landscape or animal photography you would like to sell online? The Internet can be a difficult place for entrepreneurs with digital art to sell because it is easy for people to download your work without paying for it. An image you upload on your site might be listed in Google Images. From there, a person could easily download it. If you wish to sell digital art online, you need to find a safe and secure platform. Here are the 10 platforms through which you can sell digital art:

1. PayLoadz: PayLoadz is at the top of the list because of its secure storage and delivery features. To sell your art, all you need to do is upload the digital art files, and PayLoadz takes care of processing payments and delivering files to buyers. Begin with a free account and, after you start making money, you can convert to a paid account that provides advanced features to grow and manage your sales.

2. Esty: Etsy is a marketplace for creative and handmade goods. While the focus is on selling handicrafts and handmade products, you can sell

your art using this service. Etsy charges a per-item listing fee plus a commission on each sale.

3. DeviantArt: DeviantArt is a community for artists to exhibit and promote their work. The artwork on deviantArt is sold as prints and in the form of art gifts such mugs, calendars and greeting cards.

4. Imagekind: Imagekind offers unlimited uploads, a dedicated URL and a global audience to display your digital art.

5. Redbubble: Redbubble is an art community and marketplace for wall arts and other art-based products such as T-shirts, stickers and calendars.

6. Zazzle: Zazzle is an e-commerce store with a designer twist. Zazzle allows designers, photographers and artists to upload their work and earn royalties when their work is sold as design elements on different products.

7. EBay: People who use eBay sell digital art, prints and original artwork. Artists can set up their work for sale through the auction or fixed-price modes.

8. Renderosity: The Renderosity marketplace is open to anyone who sells high-end digital art. The service is primarily focused on selling 3D art and graphics.

9. E-junkie: E-junkie is similar to PayLoadz regarding functionality. The pricing, however, is based on the number of products and storage space.

10. Tradebit: Tradebit provides you with an open platform to publish your digital art and a tool for marketing.

66. Create an Ecourse
Developing an eCourse on any topic or in any subject field requires many of the same things as developing a regular course; it is only the delivery that changes. Keep that in mind as your look at the following 5 tips for creating your eCourse like a pro.

5 Tips To Create Your First eCourse Like A Pro

How To Create Your First eCourse Like A Pro

If you are entering the world of eLearning as an instructor, you have probably read a lot about it, including a number of articles and posts that provide tips for creating, delivering, and evaluating your course. Still, you are nervous – it's the first time for you, and you want to get it right. Here are 5 key tips that will help you create an eCourse like a pro:

1. Find Some Good Models.

Concept of distance elearning and education and ecourse creating

Take a look at some other successful online programs and courses. There are many websites offering free coursework, such as Khan Academy and Academic Earth. You will be able to access a course similar in topic area to yours and get a feel for how it is structured. If you have already taken a great eCourse yourself, then you already have a good model.

2. Organize Your eCourse Content.

Concept of distance learning and education. Online tutorial and video course, research and graduation, science and webinar, digital elearning, test and literature. Set of thin, lines flat icons

Whether you are offering a 3-week mini-course or a full-length semester class, the process of organizing your content will be the same. You will need to develop the following:

Learner Outcomes (Course Goals).
What do you want the learner to know or be able to do at the end of your course?
Course Overview.
A short written piece explaining the nature of the course and the course goals (a bit like a course description in a course catalog).
The Units Of Study.

This is the course broken down into logical sections with learner outcomes for each unit.
Your Lesson Plans.
The individual lessons within each unit, including objectives, learning activities, and a method for evaluating student mastery (assignments, a paper, quiz, etc.).

Suppose, for example, you are developing a course on personal finance. One of your units will probably be "Establishing A Budget", with a very practical learner outcome – development of his/her own budget based upon all of the elements (income, expenses, necessities, near-necessities, luxuries, balancing, etc.).

This unit will probably include explanation of terms, the process for budget development, and then, of course, the evaluation component – an assessment of each student's developed budget.

3. Content Delivery.

Content delivery

There are a couple of things to be mindful of as you plan your delivery. Learning activities must be student-centered and you should rely less on texts and lengthy reading assignments in favor of different modes of content delivery and skill practice. Take a lesson from the courses at Khan Academy – there are no textbooks.

Engaging the student.

A lot of setting up your course will involve the "housekeeping" tasks of setting up your platform – apps, tools, dashboard, and methods of communication. After that, however, you must think long and hard about making your lessons engaging and enjoyable – yes, enjoyable. Learning is no longer a matter of quiet students sitting at desks and listening to a teacher drone on and one. Students need to interact personally with their learning, so keep that it mind. You need high quality materials – videos, props, tools, and apps– and you need enthusiasm when you are presenting. If you use podcasts, charts, infographics, slides, videoconferencing, etc., all should be planned with learner needs in mind, not yours. Again, you can learn much by studying how others develop activities that are engaging and motivational.

Platforms for assignment completion and submission.

It goes without saying that you need an easy method for students to get their assignments to you. Using a platform like Google Docs is really a necessity. Be aware that your students will be at many different levels of technology skills, so you may have to point them to tutorials for using the platforms you have chosen.

Lessons in small chunks.

While you want to maintain high expectations for your students, you do not want to so over-burden them that they drop out. Plan for small chunks of learning at a time. When they are successful with these smaller lessons, they are motivated to keep moving on.

4. Keep It As Social As Possible.

Keep content social

You don't have a classroom in which students can interact. But you can emulate that classroom if you have the right tools in place. It is not good for students to feel isolated in their learning, so discussion boards, video conferencing and other tools like Skype should be incorporated.

Collaboration during learning has always been far more effective than individual, isolated learning. If you need help setting all of these things up, make certain that you get that assistance. You don't want to have "fails" once the course is launched.

And as much as students should be interacting with each other, they should also be interacting with you.

Students need relationships with their teachers as much as they need them with one other. The best method is to establish times when you are available to answer emails and times (office hours) when you are available via Skype or come other video platform. It is also important to check in on discussion boards and add your encouragement and support.

They need to feel that you want them to be successful. And when students need some individual assistance, you need to be available during your scheduled times.

5. Evaluation: This Is A Two-Way Street.

Students should know from the beginning how they will be evaluated and what assignments/projects will bear what type of weight. If, for example, you are teaching a course on business writing, you may want to opt for a pre- and post-test situation. Final evaluation will be based on the degree to which they improve writing skills over the duration of the course, as opposed to "one size fits all" criteria. Other types of courses will involve established criteria by which all students will be assessed. And if you are using quizzes and exams, be certain that they are designed to test the learning objectives, not nit-picky details that don't matter.

You must have a method by which students can provide feedback to you. If there are portions of your course that "bombed," you need to know that. A survey that is completed anonymously will give you the information you need to make course modifications.

CHAPTER 59
TURN ACTIVE BUSINESS TO PASSIVE

So many of us physicians never make the transition from having active to passive income. Mostly because we've never been exposed to it or even thought about it. Well, I know I think about it quite a bit and I appreciate a physician who understands how to make this a reality.

This guest post comes from Sylvie Stacy, a preventive medicine physician who blogs about career fulfillment and lifestyle design for medical professionals at Look for Zebras. She has some great actionable tips that you can start implementing now. Enjoy!

Not every side hustle can be a passive source of income. In fact, most of them aren't. Passive and active aren't two discrete boxes into which each income source can be placed. Income generation is more like a spectrum. When it comes to side hustles, the most obtainable opportunities tend to fall toward the active side.

Telemedicine, freelance medical writing, selling health products, and the like are all means of earning active income, regardless of whether we do them alongside a 9-5 or whether we rely on the cash to pay our bills. They take time, drain our brain power, and demand critical thinking. Even passive sources of income, such as royalties, are only available to those who've put in the active work up front to create valuable copyrighted material.

Fortunately, there are steps you can take to shift your side hustle from active toward passive.

Consider Your Exit Strategy from the Get-Go

When you're thinking about starting a new side hustle, take some time to ponder how and why you'll stop doing it. This may seem like its dramatically jumping the gun. (It's not.) Or it might seem like something that only a venture-backed Silicon Valley startup should be doing. But it can really benefit a lowly part-time physician endeavor, too.

If your side gig exit strategy is nothing more than to taper and discontinue as you lose interest or prioritize another obligation, chances are it will be active income all the way until you stop. But if you plan ahead for an exit, you'll naturally increase the likelihood of your gig becoming passive.

Consider these approaches hustle-halting:

Establishing a licensing agreement
Passing the hustle along to a family member
Posting your online business to a marketplace for sale
Selling the rights to your intellectual property

All of these options require that, at some point, the hustle no longer depends on your own time and actions in order to generate income.

Avoid Trading Your Time for Money

Work that results in you being paid by the hour means that all income generated is active. We can't increase the number of hours in the day. And most of us have the mental capacity to only dedicate a certain amount of time to a side hustle – especially when we're trying to balance it will a full-time job.

There are a couple of ways to get around this and make the income at least slightly more passive. First, charge for contracted work on a "per project" or flat fee basis rather than an hourly rate. Another approach is to develop some sort of package or bundled service that you offer. As an example, this could take the form of a written report to go along with consulting work.

MLG real estate investingAutomate, Delegate, and Eliminate

When taking on a side hustle as supplemental income, most of us are tempted to do it with as little out of pocket expense as possible. It's a hustle, after all. However, spending money to automate, delegate, and eliminate activities will make your income increasingly more passive.

As you go about your income-generating pursuit, pay attention to whether the "passivity" component has plateaued. Then determine why. If you're spending time on tasks that could be completed with software or another tool, consider implementing that tool. Many minor challenges in the day-to-day work of your gig could potentially be delegated to an assistant or a sub-contractor. You might also find yourself wasting time on activities that don't actually add value to what you offer and don't increase your returns. These can be eliminated entirely.

As a bonus, doing this will afford you the time to consider how you can generate even more income. This will make up for the extra money you've spent on automation and delegation.

Help Potential Clients or Customers Find You

Many physicians looking to make extra income end up tracking down one job after another, as a series of one-off paychecks. This can take many forms – freelance projects, expert network engagements, or taking online surveys, to name a few. Not only is the work itself active, it takes time to find and secure each job.

Having clients and customers reach out to you is a huge step toward transitioning active income to passive income. You can facilitate this by marketing your service or product. Build a website and start a blog, buy ads in relevant publications, or ask past customers for referrals. There's no need to get fancy – even a thoughtful and thorough LinkedIn page can be beneficial.

Don't Make It All About You

Consider these small business names:

Joe Sixpack, MD Consulting

Jane Smith Medical Writing

These folks are probably generating active income. The individual is the business. They are the face of the business, and they are what comes to mind for customers who think of the business. This is precisely what some physicians want – and that's fine! But this can make it difficult to turn your income into passive earnings.

There are a few ways to help prevent this (aside from selecting your business name carefully). Offer something more than just your expertise. Build a brand. Use repeatable, systematic approaches in your work.

Ask yourself, "Could someone else take over my side hustle right now and be successful?" The answer doesn't need to be yes, by any means. Contemplating this question, though, can help you make changes and put processes into place that expedite earning income that is more passive.

Rich Uncles Student Housing

Follow Your Passion

This tip may be an obvious and trite one, but it's important. Do something that fires you up. The more passionate you are about your work, the more it will be reflected in your results. As you find yourself overloaded with opportunity, you'll have no choice but to streamline practices, hire help, or find other ways of turning some of the active components of your income into activities that don't rely on your time or energy.

To make a broad generalization about the points above, think about your side hustle as a true business. You'll be more likely to push the needle toward the 'passive' side of the active-passive income spectrum.

CHAPTER 60
SELL OWN PRODUCTS ONLINE

If you are looking for a way to earn income from home, consider selling products online. Whether you only sell occasionally, such as when you clean out your closet, or you have a home-made craft or other product to sell, selling online is convenient and potentially lucrative. Learn how to sell your products in established marketplaces, such as eBay or Etsy, or create your own website with a storefront. Find effective ways to promote your product, and set up a payment gateway account.

Method 1 Selling on eBay

1. Choose a product to sell. The most popular items in eBay's marketplace are electronics, clothing and accessories and collectibles. Sell used items from your home, or sell new items for a profit.
Popular electronics include laptops, game consoles, televisions and cell phones. Sell new, used or refurbished electronic items.

Used and new designer suits, shoes and handbags sell well. Wedding dresses are also popular.

Popular collectibles include remote control cars, American Girl dolls, new and vintage Lego sets and action figures, stamps and trading cards.

2. Set up a seller account. Select a username and password. Confirm the contact information eBay has on file for you. Provide a valid credit card, debit card or bank account information for paying seller fees. Select the payment methods you will accept, such as Paypal, merchant credit cards or payment on pickup. Although it is not required, it is recommended that you get PayPal verified.

Pay insertion fees when you list an item. The amount depends on the category of the item and the selling format you choose. You are responsible for these even if the item doesn't sell.

Pay final value fees when the item sells. These are calculated as a percentage of the total amount of the sale.

Getting Paypal verified means that you have complied with PayPal's verification process to establish your identity. This process increases your security.

3. List your item. Write a description of the listing. Post pictures of the item. You can post up to 12 pictures for free. Price your item. Decide how much you will charge for shipping.

Follow eBay's suggestions for writing the listing description based on successful listings of similar items. Or, write your own original listing description. Describe the item using straight-forward language. Connect with interested shoppers by selecting the most relevant category and using descriptive keywords.

Take several photos of your item from different angles.

Research active and completed listings for similar items to determine a fair price. Recommendations for shipping prices are provided by eBay.

4. Promote your items. Write a blog post to notify readers of your sale. Post on Facebook and Twitter to let your followers know you are selling on eBay. Drive more traffic to your eBay store with promotion boxes. These are graphic displays that advertise featured items and sales. You can use eBay's guided setup to create a promotion box, or you can create your own design.

5. Manage your listing. Check the "Sell" section of your "My eBay" dashboard to see if anybody has viewed, bid on or purchased your item. Revise your listing if you think you need to. Answer questions from potential buyers. Establishing trust make them more likely to buy from you.

6. Complete the sale. Provide excellent customer service in order to receive positive feedback. Communicate with your buyer about shipping. Make sure you have received payment before you ship the item. Package your item securely and with care. Create a shipping label and packing slip on eBay.

Creating a shipping label on eBay is free and convenient. Just print it out and tape it to your package. Tracking and delivery confirmation information are uploaded to eBay so you and your customer can track the package.

Method 2 Selling on Etsy

1. Sell handmade goods, vintage items or craft supplies on Etsy. Etsy prides itself on being a unique marketplace. They are committed to selling items that buyers can't find anywhere else.

- Familiarize yourself with their requirements before listing on Etsy.
- Handmade items must be made or designed by you. Outside manufacturers of handmade items must comply with Etsy's ethical manufacturing guidelines.
- Vintage items must be at least 20 years old.
- Craft supplies include tools or materials used for the creation of a new handmade item.

- You cannot resell handmade items that you did not create yourself.
- aising money for charity on Etsy requires that charity's consent.

2. Join and set up shop on Etsy. It is free to become a member and create a shop. Give your shop an original, interesting name that customers will remember. Choose a name that reflects your style and refers to the product you are selling. Announce your new shop on social media. Post about it on Facebook, Twitter and your blog to direct traffic to your shop

3. Add listings. Sign into your account and go to Your shop > Quick links > Add a listing. Click on the "add photo" icon to add photos to your listing. The first image becomes your thumbnail. Give your item a descriptive title with searchable terms. Use dropdown menus to select the type of item and category. Write a thorough description. Set the price. Set your shipping price

4. Pay seller fees. Each item listing costs $0.20 USD. Listings remain active for four months or until the item sells. Transaction fees are 3.5 percent of the final sale price. Fees are accrued to your seller account monthly. You need to have a credit card on file for paying seller fees.

5. Get paid. Etsy provides a direct checkout service. Customers from anywhere in the world can pay in their local currency. Funds are deposited into your account in your local currency. You can also accept payments from Paypal, checks or money orders.

6. Market your shop. Participate in social media to promote your items for free. Use Facebook, Twitter, Tumblr and Pinterest to advertise your shop. Join an Etsy team. These are groups of members who support each other to grow their businesses.

Use Promoted Listings, Etsy's on-site tool for advertising your shop and products.

Method 3 Building Your Storefront

1. Create a website to sell your product professionally. If you feel confident enough about your business to branch out on your own, develop a website that acts as a storefront for selling your products. Learn about the ins and outs of designing and hosting a website. Organize your site to guide customers through categories of products. Write content to promote your products. Get paid through a payment gateway account and merchant credit cards.

2. Register a domain name. This is the web address of your online business. Find a name that isn't already taken. Most registrars charge a fee for claiming the domain name. You will need a credit card or PayPal

account to pay this fee. Domain name registrars include GoDaddy, Namecheap, 1&1 Internet and Dotster

3. Choose hosted shopping cart software if you are not confident with technology. They will manage the hosting, security and coding if you do not know how to do it yourself. They typically offer a user-friendly, non-technical interface. You can quickly upload your products, connect to a payment processor and start selling. However, you may not have much flexibility to modify the functions they provide. You will receive technical support from support staff. Examples include Shopify, Bigcommerce, Wix, Weebly, and Squarespace

4. Choose self-hosted open source shopping cart software if you can manage the hosting, security and coding yourself. These are standalone programs that require you to install them into your own host. You can design them to operate the way you want them to. Choose from several advanced features that let you customize your customers' shopping experience. You must manage all of the technical aspects yourself or hire someone to do it for you. Examples include Magento, Word Press with WooCommerce and Open Cart.

5. Choose a web host if you are using a self-hosted open source shopping cart software. A web host gives you space on the internet and support for building

your ecommerce site. You will have to pay for site maintenance, search registration and site development.

Free web hosts are available, but you have to deal with disadvantages. These include advertising on your page, a limited amount of web space (typically under 5 MB) and limits on file sizes and types. Also, they may be unreliable and slow which may cost you customers.

Choosing a commercial web host has advantages. They are faster and more reliable, and you can purchase enough bandwidth to transfer more data to customers, such as music and videos. You can purchase more web space and they offer technical support. Also, you can have email addresses at your own domain.

Choose a web host that lets you set up a secure SSL server. This gives you a website that begins with "https://" instead of http://. Expect additional charges, but you will need this if you plan to accept credit card payments

6. Choose a template for your website. Your software may offer hundreds or even thousands of different templates. Choose one with background graphics and visual images that give your website the image you desire. You may even find graphics that reference the product you are selling. Many templates are free.

However, consider paying for a premium template to find one that fittingly complements your business.

7. Choose advanced tools to expand your website. These are provided with your software. If your business is small, you may be able to manage processes like shipping and bookkeeping manually. However when your business starts to grow, you may want to automate some of these functions. This frees you up to deal with the other administrative and operational issues of your growing business. Shopify and Bigcommerce both offer apps that can increase their capabilities

8. Organize your website. Think about what your website will look like and how you want your customers to use it. Determine the location and size of your logo and other visuals. Create menu selections that guide your customers through the pages of your online store. Start with a home page, and choose other menu selections and submenus that organize the information on your website. Identify the kind of information you want on each page. Your software will give you options for setting up your storefront with different formats and styles.

9. Develop content. Ecommerce content creates a superior shopping experience for your customers. Most of your content will be unique product descriptions and customer reviews. But it may also include buyer's guides, videos, photographs or

comparison tools. Do keyword research to identify terms your customers search for and use them in your content. Balance usefulness with relevancy. You don't want to go overboard and clutter your site with too much information. Give your customers a satisfying experience that convinces them to purchase.

10. Obtain a merchant account from a bank. This gives you the ability to process credit cards. Go to a bank with whom you already have a relationship. If you have credit cards and business accounts there, they will likely give you a merchant account because of your long-term relationship with them. If they won't give you a merchant account, apply at another local bank. Offer to move all of your business accounts there to persuade them to give you merchant status.

11. Choose a payment gateway account. This is an online transaction processor that lets you process credit cards from online shoppers. It handles verification and transfer requests. It communicates with the shopper's bank to authorize the credit card in real time. If you don't have a merchant account, they offer packages that let you set up a merchant account and accept payment. The most popular providers are PayPal, Authorize.net, Cybersource and Verisign. You pay a monthly processing fee based on the number of transactions per month, and

you also pay a fee of from 3 to 5 percent per transaction.

Method 4 Directing Traffic to Your Site

1. Use contextual marketing. Collect data about your customers and their behaviors. Use this data to create customized and relevant content. Time the delivery of this content to take advantage of your customers' shopping habits. For example, if your target customers are teachers supplying their classrooms, you would want to know when they are most likely to shop for supplies. Gather this information from online profiles, surveys and browsing activity on your website. Marketing automation systems are available to help with this process

2. Use user generated content (UGC). On ecommerce sites, this is typically found in the form of customer reviews. Shoppers trust consumer reviews more than traditional marketing and advertising. They believe that reviews from real customers are more authentic and believable. Display customer reviews prominently on your site. Having them has been proven to translate into increased sales.

3. Develop engagement-based loyalty programs. Encourage customers to leave reviews by creating badges, leaderboards and user profiles. This not only increases the quantity of reviews, but also the quality. Customers have an incentive to write longer, more

detailed reviews. They will also include other content such as photos and videos. These reviews make shoppers more likely to purchase because they will trust customer reviews more than other content.

4. Offer customers the ability to shop in their native language. Shoppers prefer a native-language shopping experience. More than two-thirds of online shoppers have native languages other than English. This includes customers both in and outside of the United States. Providing the ability to shop in their native language gives customers a more satisfying experience. This translates into increased sales.

5. Perform A/B testing. This is the process of comparing two versions of a web page to see which one performs better. Show two variants of an element on your website to similar visitors at the same time to determine if one results in more sales

For example, test two "Add to Cart" button designs for your website. Option A is your existing button, and option B is the new design you want to try. Direct live traffic on your site to either option. Determine which button generated more clicks. Other elements to test include layout, pricing, promotions and images.

6. Start an email list. One of the most effective online marketing techniques available is also one of the oldest – digitally speaking, of course. What is it? Email! When you get people to sign up for an email

list, you're building a group of potential customers who are already engaged enough to want communication from you. With an email list, you can keep interested people aware of new products, sales, deadlines, and more so that they're more likely to make purchases. How likely? According to a survey from Marketing Sherpa, businesses report a 119% ROI for their email campaigns. That's sure to help you sell products online.

7. Share your expertise in a blog. Want to sell products online? People have to trust you. How do you get that trust? Start writing. It's not as easy to quantify the ROI that businesses see from blogging and other forms of social media, but it's clear that engaging potential customers in this way can definitely help raise brand awareness, cause people to see you as an expert in your field, and make them more likely to think of your store when they need products like the ones you sell. You just have to be smart about it.

For example, if you sell mainly gardening products online, your blog shouldn't be an explicit advertisement for those products – instead, offer DIY tips, talk about industry trends, and share examples of awesome gardens you find. The idea is to present your company as one that knows all about gardening.

When it comes right down to it, the best way to sell products online is to reach qualified leads in any way that you can. Get the right people coming to your shop and the sales will come.

CHAPTER 61
LAUNCH A DATING WEBSITE

You've always had a knack for matchmaking at dinner parties, so why not offer your talent to a wider market by launching an online dating site? When done right, these sites can be lucrative and require minimal effort to maintain.

Markus Frind, founder and CEO of PlentyOfFish, says he brings in more than $10 million a year (at least half is pure profit) working for just an hour a day. If you want to start your own moneymaking site for love connections, try these five strategies.

Find the right niche. At this point, there are so many big players in online dating (PlentyOfFish, Match.com, and eHarmony among them) that it's tough to gain traction in the general marketplace. To find your audience, focus on building and marketing a site that fits their needs, however quirky they may be. Trek Passions, for example, helps lonely Trekkies find love. Keep in mind that the narrower your focus is, the more limited your audience and income potential will be.

Decide on a business model. Online dating sites can operate on either an advertising- or a subscription-based model — or a combination of the two. PlentyOfFish.com has attracted more than 30 million members primarily because it's a free ad-supported site; however, it doesn't make nearly as much money per member as a subscription-based site like Match.com, which has just 1.3 million paying subscribers, but brings in nearly $350 million in annual revenues. If you're planning to launch a smaller-scale site, a subscription-based model will likely be more profitable. However, when customers pay to use a site, they expect more from it, so don't skimp on tools and services.

Perfect your algorithm. Online matchmaking services typically ask users to fill out questionnaires about their lifestyle, hobbies, work, and other interests. In some cases, these questionnaires are extremely comprehensive: eHarmony asks each user to fill out a 400-question psychological profile in order to receive matches. Think about what values will be the most important to your potential users — and how you should rank their matches. Once you've determined your algorithm priorities, hire a programmer to set up your search tool (unless you have the know-how to do it yourself).

Lure in your customers. No one wants to join a dating site that very few people use, so you'll want to wage a strong marketing campaign and provide added incentives to sign up initial members. Ask all of your single friends and acquaintances to join the site, and, if your business model is subscription-based, offer discounted memberships to the first several hundred people who sign up. Once your site is populated, you'll be able to promote it more successfully through targeted advertising methods, such as Facebook and Google keyword ads.

Maintain quality control. No, that doesn't mean kicking out the ugly people (unless you're BeautifulPeople.com). Online dating sites must be prepared to cope with sexual harassment and other forms of online abuse, as well as privacy concerns. Set up a system that allows users to flag others for bad behavior, and rescind the membership privileges of abusers. Of course, you can't control what people do after they decide to go out on a date, so work with a lawyer to create a membership contract that will release you of any liability for the real-world results of your online matchmaking.

CHAPTER 62
SURVEYS

The anonymity that the Internet provides makes it the ideal environment for asking your customers what they really think about your business, product, or service. An online survey can reveal customers' true opinions, as well as enabling them to share ideas with you in a safe and comfortable environment. Setting up the best online survey is easy when you use these six steps to guide you in the process.

1. Decide on your research goals

Before you can start your research, you will need to form a clear picture in your mind of the expected outcome. Do you need feedback on a product or your service? Is the information you are looking for of a general nature or very specific? Do you have a particular audience in mind, or will you be sending out online surveys to the general public? The answers to these questions will help you to decide how to target your survey.

2. Create a list of questions

There are many different types of questions that can be used on a survey, like open questions, closed questions, matrix table questions, and single- or multi-response questions. Most people who take part in surveys prefer short multiple-choice questions. When writing the questions, keep the language very simple and avoid ambiguity or double negations. One of the benefits of designing an online survey is that participants don't have to fill in questions that are not relevant to them. Based on their answers subsequent questions can be skipped using logic and piping, improving response rates.

3. Invite the participants

There are many ways to invite people to take part in your online survey. Who you want to take part in your survey will help you to decide on the best contact method. You can send an email to your subscriber list, post your survey on Facebook, send surveys by sms or design a banner that can be displayed on other websites if you wish to cast a wider net. If your research goals require targeting a specific audience you can buy responses from a dedicated consumer panel.

4. Gather your responses

It is important to monitor your response rate, as your final sample size will depend on how many participants complete your survey. In many cases you can increase the response rate by offering an incentive to the participant, for example, you can offer a gift, the chance of winning something in a lottery, a donation to charity, or a points accumulation system where participant can save up points that can be exchanged for gifts. Another way of increasing the response rate of your survey is by promising to share the results with your participants.

5. Analyse the results

Visualise your data by presenting the results in charts and graphs, as this will help you quickly reference your results in reports. You can also make use of text analysis and word clouds on open ended questions to pick out common response trends. You can also print out the data in the form of a spreadsheet, which can then be exported for further analysis. With online surveys the gathered data is stored automatically, so you can start analyzing the results straight away. In most cases, you can already see preliminary results when the survey is still open.

6. Write a report

The final step in conducting online surveys is to write a report explaining your findings and whether they have met your research goals. A successful survey will provide reliable answers to the questions you had about your business, product or service. Allowing you to take data-driven actions based on hard evidence. Used correctly online surveys can effectively measure customer satisfaction, get feedback on products or services, and reveal key influences in your area of research.

The process for conducting an online survey is easy and inexpensive. SmartSurvey can provide you with all the tools needed to help you in designing your survey. Most businesses' needs can be met with simple and short online surveys that target a specific group of customers. The results, on the other hand, are priceless because they will help you make important decisions about your business.

CHAPTER 63
GET OUT OF DEBT

To get out of debt, you need a plan, and you need to execute that plan. That's why we've created this simple, six-step, get-out-of-debt checklist that can help you leave that financial burden behind you.

As you work on your plan, you'll need to make all necessary adjustments to your budget along the way so you don't overspend and slide back into debt. Plus, if you don't have an emergency fund, consider setting some money aside in savings beforehand.

Keep this checklist someplace where you'll see it often (like your refrigerator door, or your vision board if you have one), and make it your goal to check a task off the list each day (or each week), depending on how quickly you want to become debt-free.

What Is the Best Way to Get Out of Debt?

If you want to do this right, you want to make sure that you know where you stand before you start. You need to have a complete picture. Here's what you need to do:

Make A List

Having everything written out in front of you is really the key to success here. Plus, once you've written it all out, and it's right there in black and white, it may not seem as insurmountable as it did before.

Make a list of all your debts: name of creditor, interest rate, balance, minimum monthly payment.
List how much you'll need to pay in order to zero-out the cards' debt within three years, as found on credit card statements.
Remember to include loans not listed on your credit reports (e.g. family loans, medical bills).

Lower Your Rates

Paying high interest rates on existing debt causes your debt to really mount, and makes paying it off much more difficult. If possible, you want to lower those interest rates. Here's what to do:

Based on your credit, you may qualify for much better interest rates on credit cards.
Open a free account with Credit.com and see what kind of low rate balance transfer credit cards you can get.
Check out student loan consolidation and Income-based Repayment at StudentLoans.gov.
Call your card issuers to ask for lower rates on credit card balances.

Consider a consolidation loan and/or balance transfers to pay off high-rate credit cards at a lower rate.

Find out if you can refinance a high-rate auto loan.

Get Your Number

Once you know what your total payoff number is, you'll have a real, complete goal to work towards.

Total the three-year pay-off amount for all your credit cards.

Add the monthly payments for all other debts.

Write down the result: Your Total Monthly Payment.

Plan Your Strategy

There are plenty of ways to attack this problem and you'll likely approach this using a variety of tools and methods. Plan your strategy carefully.

Determine if you can afford to pay the Total Monthly Payment until your debt is paid off.

If not doable, contact a credit counseling agency and/or bankruptcy attorney for advice. Remember though, bankruptcy has a huge impact on your credit score, and if you're able to work out a payment plan with your creditors, it can be avoided.

If doable, decide which debt to pay off first (highest interest rate or lowest balance?) — "target debt." This is also known as the "snowball" or "avalanche" method.

Set up "auto pay" for required minimum for all debts except target debt.

Pay as much as possible toward target debt until paid off.

Choose new target debt and pay extra toward that one, and so on.

Monitor and Adjust

Once your plan is set, don't get too comfortable. You'll need to track your behavior closely to make sure you're making progress, and you'll want to make adjustments when necessary.

Monitor your credit score each month to see if your credit score improves (over time it should).

As your credit score improves, reconsider a consolidation loan or balance transfers to save money often spent on interest charges for remaining debts. (Your interest charges are often listed on your credit card statement.)

Stick with your plan until your debt is paid off.

Create an Emergency Fund

You may think that while paying off debt, you don't have money to save, but this is essential. Life happens, so if anything comes up, like a job loss, medical bill, or car repair, you're covered. The suggested amount is three to six months' worth of expenses, but if that's not immediately possible, aim for one months' worth – that's a great starting point.

See which expenses can be cut out of your budget. If you eat out multiple times a week, see if you can cut it down to only once a week (everyone needs a little bit of money for fun).

Automate your savings. See if your employer will let you contribute part of your paycheck to a savings account. The ideal amount is 10% to 20%, but if you're trying to get out of debt, this might not be possible. See if you can start with 5% each paycheck.

If you can't automate your savings from your paycheck, have your savings automated from your checking account each payday. That way, you don't accidentally spend this money and you won't miss it.

If you receive a bonus or a pay raise, see if you can afford to contribute some of that money to your emergency fund.

As you begin to work this system, keep in mind that it's not easy. Just like losing weight, losing your debt takes work, but if you genuinely want to slough of that stressful debt, your perseverance can make it happen. And don't fret if you need to make adjustments along the way. This isn't about a quick fix, it's about changing your habits and behaviors so you can achieve your financial goals.

CHAPTER 64
WRITE ONLINE REVIEWS

Online shopping has many pros and cons as you have probably experienced. On one hand, you can shop in the comfort of your home or on the go. On the other, you can never really be sure of the quality of the product... until you receive it.

Because customers can't see or test the product before buying, it means they will almost always read product reviews first.

effective-online-reviews-amazon.jpg

In addition to popular review sites such as Amazon, Reddit, or Trust Pilot, a lot of people are even turning platforms like YouTube for expert reviews of technical products like laptops or smartphones.

All of these online reviews help a person choose the perfect product without testing it in real life. It also helps companies grow their following and brand awareness.

The power of good online reviews

Statistically, more than 90% of people go through reviews of a product before even going to the company's website.

For this reason, it's vital for your products to have an ample number of reviews, especially if it's new. A high number of positive reviews will help people discover it more quickly.

What's more, Google uses the reviews to rank the same products in order, from most popular to least popular. Customers then follow the reviews to choose their product, thereby, increasing the click-through rates to your website. Sounds simple right?

There's one caveat though: the reviews need to be good and authentic.

It goes without saying, but customers will trust the products with the most favorable reviews. However, if the reviews smell fake, consumers can sniff it out within seconds and quickly dismiss them. For this reason, businesses need to encourage more good online reviews, and people need to write them.

3 reasons why you should write good online reviews

You may think that a lot of people who write online reviews are being paid or compensated in some way. The truth is, many of them actually do it for selfless reasons, and here are some of the key ones:

1. Sharing is caring

How many times have you avoided buying a sketchy product thanks to good, honest reviews? A number of people that write them genuinely do it to help others make good decisions. Why not do the same for them?

2. Better products

Good reviews help companies improve their products. It's basically free user feedback! So, clearing stating what you don't like about a product and why will allow the company to understand exactly what they need to change.

3. To restore faith in the review system

According to Spectoos, a percentage of people out there actually write good reviews so they can "reinforce the interdependency of the review system". It makes sense because if we want to benefit from good reviews, we need to write and encourage to write them.

It sounds simple, but you can't how do you write a good and credible online review? In this blog post, we'll be exploring 5 tips which can help you.

effective-online-reviews-yelp.jpg

Tips to follow when writing reviews

We have come up with some special tips that will bring the X-factor in your reviews. As everyone and their grandmas are writing reviews, you need to have some secret ingredient in your review to stand out.

#1: Avoid promotional jargon

Always remember while writing the review that you are not advertising the product. There is a special team dedicated to that. What the company and customers want is honest reviews about what happened when you used the product.

For example, if you are reviewing a face mask that sold on AliExpress , you should include things like how it made your skin feel, did you have reactions to it, etc.

A generic statement like, "It is the best product. It's better than anything out there!" isn't descriptive enough and over-promotional. You need to stay in a neutral position in your review even if it IS the best face mask you've ever used.

Here are some key points to keep in mind when you write your next review:

It should sound like an anecdote or personal experience
Provide proof like screenshots, product shots, or before and after shots
If you didn't like the product, try not to overemphasis on the fact that they should buy it – Just give your opinion and let your readers decide

#2: Be responsive

It is a good idea to write the review in a conversational manner, this lets readers respond and suggest their point of view.

What's more, when you reply back people will find your review more credible and authentic.

You can do the following things to ensure that you are engaging your review readers:

Leave a contact information where they can ask you more questions or share your experience with them
Respond to comments about your review diligently
In case you wrote a completely different review from what one client experienced, you can try to explain your situation or send his/her complaint to the company

Explain the whole process of using the product like telling a story
Describe all the steps you did and the problems you encountered on the way so the readers can follow and comment on specific steps in your process.

#3: Stay neutral

A perfect online review should be neutral as possible.

If you are writing a review after having a bad day at work, this could impact your review and it wouldn't be as accurate as it should be. Therefore, try and put yourself in a neutral mood when starting to write.

On the other hand, when you are writing only good things about the product, it may seem artificial and could be harder for the customers to believe the review. Reviews generally seem more credible when bad or constructive points are included.

Here are some things to keep in mind:

Start with some positive points but definitely include constructive feedback
Try to have an equal number of pros and cons
The negative points, avoid terms like "terrible," "agonizing" or "awful" because they project more your feelings, not like real facts

#4: Proofread

When people read reviews in general, there is a certain level of quality that is expected.

So write carefully and try to read aloud while you are writing to ensure fluidity. The writing can be in a friendly format not academic. You can use personal pronouns and try to write in the active tense instead of passive.

Write clearly and concisely, and always proofread.

We would suggest you first to break up your review into a few parts:

Introduction

In this part you will talk about the product:

What is it?
How to use?
What does it do?
Where did you get it from?
Pros

This part will consist of all the benefits of the product. You may also write in this part that the expectation vs. the result.

Cons

As you would have already understood that the disadvantages are the main focus of the review as well. Try to be honest and impartial. Provide explanations for why you didn't like a feature.

Another method is to explain the pros and cons of each process after explaining the action. For example, while applying the black mask, the advantage is that it takes less time to dry, but the disadvantage is that it gave you a rash.

Your own suggestion

Finally, add a small paragraph where you can give your own suggestion about whether you will buy it again or not. Finish by giving the link from where you bought it. Additionally, give your contact if people have further queries about it.

Tip #5: Details of the product

The details of the product should be accurate and precise. If you are talking about offline services like a home tutor, you can add details of the person, the agency used, the date when started or the schedule followed.

If it is an online product, you should add the shopping website, the date when it was bought, the date it was delivered, and the condition of the product. Also, delivery is a problem in many countries and, therefore, people would be really interested in knowing the time taken for delivery. Consequently, your article will stand apart from your competitor's articles.

Over to you

Providing good online reviews is a huge part of not only online shopping, but also countless apps that help make our lives easier every day such as Uber and Airbnb.

For this reason, it's essential for businesses as well as customers to encourage writing solid online reviews.

CHAPTER 65
FLIP WEBSITES

The stock market and real estate industry have long been populated by day traders and "flippers", those who buy and sell in a short period of time in order to make a quick profit.

In the real estate industry the life of a house flipper can be very appealing. Buy a renovator's dream property at a discounted price, renovate and modernize it and then sell it at a few months later at a profit. This process can then be repeated over and over for a reasonably stable income. You might even get rich.

Flipping Fun

The life of a house flipper is often romanticized, with images of married couples buying old houses, spending a fun-filled six months working renovating and then making a cool $20-$50K profit on the sale and moving on to the next property. Do this three times a year and you have a recipe for a fairly nice lifestyle.

If you plan to renovate yourself then you better have the skills to do it or have the friends or family willing to help out. Alternatively you can hire professionals to perform the labor but you must factor in the cost into your expenses.

There are also many other variables that need to be carefully controlled such as financing fees, real estate agent costs, legal fees, government charges and all the other issues that come with buying and selling property.

Those with a keen eye for a bargain can do exceptionally well but it's just as easy to lose money if you don't do your research and plan. Watching the real estate market, tracking house prices and monitoring economic conditions are all important activities for a successful house flipper. Provided you do your homework and control your variables you stand a fair chance of succeeding.

Trading on the stock market is another area where the educated and diligent researchers can succeed. Knowing market trends, tracking company performance and economic indicators can all provide an extra edge and if you work on it full time you just may come out on top more often than not. Both the stock market and real estate industry have long been considered staple investment opportunities and even full time careers for those that choose to take on the challenge.

There is unique breed of entrepreneur that has taken the concept of flipping to another area; buying and selling businesses. A shrewd entrepreneur will locate an underperforming business, buy it, work their magic to improve performance and then sell it for a nice margin. It is by no means easy and certainly requires a lot of research and due diligence, but the rewards are there and no doubt it's a heap of fun too.

Flipping Websites

Website For SaleBuying and selling businesses is appealing but given the high costs of making the purchase it is quite difficult to start, especially as a young entrepreneur. If you go wrong you may end up loosing a lot of money (just as you can with the stock market and real estate), so you really want to be sure of your skills and ability before investing.

The Internet is very new and the whole online commerce industry is just establishing marketing practices that work. Quite frankly, and this may sound harsh, but most of the people running businesses online have very poor websites. A lot of people running popular sites are not taking advantage of their traffic by monetizing it (this could be by choice or ignorance). Making a profit may be as simple as implementing a smart AdSense campaign on a popular site after buying it from an owner wishing to move on to other things. Perhaps an ecommerce site could use some search engine marketing or some tweaking to an AdWords campaign might do the trick, or better still, monetize, optimize, affiliate and upsell for maximum gain – make use of all the marketing tricks at your disposal.

I'm sure if we did some statistical sampling of the web industry search engine optimization techniques would be understood by a minority of webmasters and implemented well by even fewer. Search engine optimization is becoming mainstream and no doubt as the web continues to mature more and more people will study, test and build better websites, but it's definitely still early days.

What this says to me is "business opportunity". For those with the know-how, the energy to implement and a little bit of funds to buy the sites there are big gains to be made. What makes it even more appealing, especially for young or new entrepreneurs, is the price – we are talking about a lot less funds then it would take to invest in shares, buy property or purchase a bricks and mortar "real world" business. Websites with potential go for as low as a few hundred dollars.

The Advantages of Buying A Website

The big advantage of buying a site is you don't have to establish an audience and wait for the site to be indexed within search engines. Most webmasters, even those that don't know their SEO from their XML, will understand the benefit of link exchanges. Even the most poorly managed sites should have some form of backlink network developed and return a result in the major search engines. It may not be a top ten search result but it will be a result ready for you to optimize and improve.

Taking over a mature site (at least 12 months old) will mean you avoid the Google sandbox, a significant perk of buying established web property. Of course it really depends at what stage you take over a website as to how much of a step-up you gain and will no doubt reflect how much the owner will expect to receive for it (traffic for cash in simpler terms, but there are other variables to consider when selling a website).

Top 7 Website Acquisition Strategies

Before undertaking a search for a website acquisition a smart web entrepreneur will stop and have a good think about what she wants the site to do and how it will fit within her overall web business strategy. Here is a list of the top 7 strategies to consider when buying a new website:

Buy a site that has targeted traffic for a product or service you already produce or sell. You can direct traffic from the new site to your products/services through advertising, email lists or sales pages. This is a great way to establish a customer base very quickly but you have to be confident that the traffic is quality, targeted traffic. Don't fall into the trap of buying a high traffic site that consumes lots of bandwidth but doesn't have the type of user you can leverage for revenue, otherwise you might be buying a liability, not an asset.

Buy a site to generate advertising revenue. In this instance you might not change the site other than by working to increase the amount of traffic and improve the performance of advertisements on the site. Sites with lots of good content but are poorly optimized are perfect for this strategy. Once you own the rights to the content you can then further leverage it by repacking and republishing the content in other ways Ã¢â‚¬â€œ perhaps information products, article marketing or as free give away enticements to join an email list.

Buy a site specifically to flip it quickly. This is perhaps the most risky venture (day-trading!) because you need to find sites that are clearly underperforming with the potential for a big upside result after you complete your renovation. Ideally you should locate e-commerce sites selling a product that has an established market that is only just starting to take off online AND the current owners are not good at search engine optimization or online marketing and are willing to sell.

The theory is that you can quickly implement your changes, tweaking a few percentage point increases in multiple areas, resulting in a good double figure increase in sales in a short period of time. If you can complete your work just before the general marketplace catches up you can make a mint by selling the site at a premium before the Internet becomes saturated and your early mover advantage is eroded or the market slows.

The web is one of the fastest industries in terms of competitive action due to the very low barriers to entry. To execute day-trading style website buying and selling requires an entrepreneur with their finger on the pulse of the web. They must be in tune with what's new and willing to gamble on what's going to be new tomorrow in order to have success.

Purchase a community driven site. A site with a massive forum filled with a nice target niche audience can be a gold mine to a entrepreneur. Often these sites were built by hobbyist fans, not aimed to profit in any way. Their website might have ballooned in growth to the point where the bandwidth is costing them a lot each month and since they are not skilled in website monetization they will be willing to sell the site at a bargain price. This can be a great strategy to make advertising revenue but be very careful with audience selection. Some forum communities are very difficult to make money from and may end up costing you more in ongoing hosting fees. Ideally choose a community demographic that has established high keyword prices in AdSense/high value to advertisers (electronic gadgets for example), has a good selection of affiliate products you could market or suits some products or services you already sell yourself.

Look for a site operating in a highly popular keyword niche or one you expect will become popular in the near future. Keywords drive search engine traffic and if you can pick the trends before they become trends you may own some valuable property. Consider if you could guess what tomorrow's Ã¢,¬Å"blogÃ¢,¬Â or Ã¢,¬Å"podcastÃ¢,¬Â will be and buy the sites with established keyword rich content before they become mainstream topics and overpriced.

Remove the competition or merge with the competition. In this case you buy competing websites or negotiate a merger to combine with them to create one large enterprise. Depending on the industry you operate in this can be a very smart strategy to create market dominance. One of the best examples is website hosting. Often smaller hosts are bought up by larger hosting businesses with the result increased stability and professionalism.

Purchase a site strictly for the domain name. Obviously in this case you don't care too much about what is already developed in terms of website content, you just want the street address (URL). Imagine a few years ago if you purchased mp3.com or blog.com. In this case the address itself is of significant value regardless of the website, or if you are good at picking trends, you might see the future value in a domain name before the market realizes it.

There are many other options available for how to use a new website acquisition and of course what you do with a new website and what type of website you search for will depend on your skills, the industry you operate in and your cash to spend. Remember to take some time listing a few goals you want your new website to achieve and strategize exactly what you will do with the new website before you buy it.

Investing Time And Energy Into Your New Website

Make sure you have the time to manage your new investment in web property. Remember just the transfer process and daily maintenance of your site will take time and energy and if you don't have it available now then maybe you should hold off making the purchase. It would be a shame if your good intentions to improve a website result in you instead killing it because you don't have the time to maintain the status quo. Remember a new website comes with new responsibilities, for example support emails and phone, server maintenance, SPAM control and the usual day-to-day activities of a webmaster. Don't get caught up in the excitement of the purchase making you blind to the reality of how much additional work will be added to your daily activities.

Where To Locate Websites For Sale

I could point you in the direction of a few good website trading sites but you will be very lucky if you find a bargain there. To find good sites you have to search deep into the web. Use the main search engines to find websites operating in an industry you feel confident buying into. Don't look for the big sites, the sites on the first few pages of search results unless they show clear potential – perhaps in industries with low competition so "bad" sites show up in the first page of search results. Professional or popular keyword sites are usually too expensive, well managed (they wouldn't appear in the first few pages of the search results if they weren't) and the owner likely won't be interested in making the sale or will be looking for six figures if they are.

You must look deep in the search results. Find the solo-webmasters that perhaps don't take their site too seriously but have been diligent over the years adding content consistently, if not in large quantities. You need to find the good sites with potential, not great sites already optimized or poor sites going nowhere. The more research you do during the search phase the smarter buy you will make. No matter how much time you put into the search it's going to be gamble when you do decide to buy. There are just too many variables to consider and control, but by being smart and patient you reduce the risk.

Buying The Website

Once you find a good site that meets your criteria start monitoring and researching it. Check backlinks, investigate it's history (try the Wayback Machine) and if the site has a community (forums, chatrooms, comment system, helpdesk, etc) see what goes on there. Check the site design, the structure of the links, headings, titles and keyword density. Check the site statistics if they are available (look for those little webstat icons or try Alexa rankings).

Once you get a good feel for the site and you are interested in buying it's time to contact the owner. You should be able to find an email address for the website owner somewhere on the site, if you can't do a domain name lookup in the WhoIs database where you will find the email address for the person that registered the domain. Remember some websites will simply be hobbies for the owner which will make the purchasing process that much easier, while others will be fully fledged businesses making the transfer process just that little bit longer.

Start casually by introducing yourself to the owner, state you like the site and then slowly gauge how much interest the owner has in their web property. Eventually you are going to have to express your interest in making a purchase and you can spend as much time as you like communicating with the owner to negotiate a deal. Like with buying anything, the negotiation process can be laborious as you gather the information you need to calculate a price. This process can be swift and easy or slow and painful depending on your attitudes and the willingness of the owner to make the sale and release private information about their website. You will need to know details like website statistics, revenues, and costs, all information that the current owner may be hesitant to give out (see How Much Is Your Website Worth? for a discussion of important website metrics when determining the value of a site). Demonstrating your sincerity at this point will go a long way in helping you to divulge as much information as you can order to properly evaluate the website.

If you are lucky the owner of the site may simply be so excited that their website will make them some money that a few hundred dollars will seal the deal, others, the more savvy owners will realise the value of their asset and you might have more difficulty negotiating and will pay a higher price. Remember you are never under any obligation to buy so don't force yourself to offer too much because there are plenty, literally millions, of other sites out there.

Don't Forget The Little Details

When you finally agree on a price don't forget to look after the little technical details as you manage the transfer of ownership. Here is a list of some important factors:

Transfer of the domain name registration details, the business name, incorporation information, hosting ownership and any third party software or subscriptions to your name. Check that everything, absolutely everything, has your name on it by the time the deal is done.

Get a contract made up outlining the deal and have all parties sign and date it. Also consider creating a clause stopping the previous owner starting up a competing site immediately after the sale.

Download the email lists. Download the email lists. Download the email lists. There is nothing more important in a web business then the mailing lists so make sure you have these safely in hand with backups.

Outline how much support, if any, will be provided by the ex-owner for a transition period. Having the owner available for questions for a few months after the sale can make the transfer less stressful.
Buying A Website Is A Very Effective Entry Strategy

Given the time it takes to get a new website off the ground because of issues like the Google Sandbox and the amount of work and effort it takes to create a site, produce content and build backlinks, the prospect of buying a ready established domain and website is very appealing. If you have a sound understanding of search engine optimization and the industry you work in online, you should have no problem finding under optimized websites, or perhaps fully fledged web e-commerce businesses to buy. By adding content, fixing title tags, linking structure and all the other good search engine marketing practices you can very quickly start reaping rewards. Sites with quality traffic but no monetization strategy are huge opportunities ready for you to step in, stick some advertisements up, use your AdSense optimization skills and boom, start profiting immediately. Alternatively you might look for sites that augment your existing web enterprises and purchase the targeted traffic to effectively "buy customers". No matter what your strategy, the web is ripe with opportunities for smart investors and you don't have to have a wallet the size of Rupert Murdoch's to start buying and profiting.

CHAPTER 66
CD'S

Certificates of deposit (CDs) make financial sense for people of all ages who want a low-risk investment to park cash they don't plan to use immediately. Maybe you want to use your cash to buy a car or make a down payment on a house pretty soon.

If you won't need your cash reserve the day after tomorrow or next week, you'll likely want that money to earn a better rate of return than your checking account offers—without taking on too much risk. This is when a CD is useful.

Two factors to consider when deciding whether a CD is right for you:

- Your time horizon. When will you need part or all of your cash? Do you have other cash resources to access in a pinch? If you have a sum of money and don't expect you'll need to use it for six months or longer, a CD may be ideal.

- Interest rates. The anticipated direction of interest rates will help you determine how long to tie up your money. If rates are rising (usually when inflation is on the rise), a short-term CD may be best. If rates are falling (usually when the economy is on a downswing), a longer-term CD may earn you more money, since you'll lock in a higher rate.

How to Invest

Before you shop for a CD, there are two numbers you need to know:

- APR —The annual percentage rate, or the interest rate a bank is offering on the CD.
- APY —The annual percentage yield, which tells you what you'll earn over the multiyear life of the CD as your money compounds.

What's compounding? Put simply, it's how your investment grows over time. Let's say you invest $10,000 in a three-year CD earning 5% annually. In the first year, your $10,000 investment will earn $500. In the second year, 5% of the new total ($10,500) will be $525. In the third year, 5% of $11,025 will be about $551. The total amount of money grows each year, so the amount representing 5% of your investment also grows. That's compounding.

You've decided a CD is an ideal investment for your cash. Here's what to do next:

I. Choose your term. Determine how long you want to tie up your money. This will depend on when you need the money or whether you have other cash assets to tide you over until the CD matures.

2. Pick your type. Decide which kind of CD suits you best. For example, if you want to invest for two years and don't want the risk of being stuck with a low rate, then a bump-up CD may be ideal. Afraid you'll need part of your deposit for an emergency? Consider a liquid CD. (Look here for an explanation of the basic types of CDs.)

3. Review the rates. Once you've selected the duration and type of CD you want, find out what rates are available at different banks.

Consider a ladder

One way to reduce a CD's drawbacks is to use a technique called "laddering." This strategy gives you regular access to part of your cash and protects you against rising interest rates.

Laddering is simple. Instead of investing one big chunk of cash in one CD, you divide your lump sum into equal parts and invest each in CDs of varying durations.

Here's how it works: Let's say you want to invest $15,000. By laddering, you would invest $5,000 in a one-year CD, $5,000 in a two-year CD and $5,000 in a three-year CD. Then, each time one of the three CDs matures, you would either take the cash or re-invest it in another three-year CD to keep your ladder in place.

Laddering provides three benefits:
- Penalty-free access to cash each time a CD matures.
- More favorable interest rates, since you're always investing in a longer-term CD.
- A shot at better returns if interest rates are higher when you re-invest.

CHAPTER 67
SUGAR DADDY/SUGAR MOMMA

I assume that since you are at this site looking for tips on where to find a sugar daddy, sugar momma, or sugar baby then you already know what they are. But in case you aren't totally sure, here are links to some pages with the basic definitions for you...

1) Sugar Daddy
2) Sugar Momma
3) Sugar Baby

Yes, sugar daddies and mamas do exist for all you baby girls/boys out there seeking an arrangement, and you can get one if you do it right. The main keys to finding a sugar daddy or suga mama are knowing where to look. It's also very important that you know how to be a good sugar baby.

By far, the quickest and easiest way to find sugar daddies, mommies, and/or sugar babies, and skip the whole process of doing it on your own is to join some of the sugar daddy dating websites. There are a few really good sugar daddy sites that can instantly hook you up with many potential partners and will likely be much easier and safer than going about it on your own.

However, if you like the challenge of doing the "old-fashioned way" of finding a sugar daddy or sugar baby, and would prefer to get out there and take the bull by the horns, then here is some information you may find useful...

– You should always look your best, smell good, take care of yourself, and work on keeping a hot body. It's important to have confidence and these things help.

– Look in the right places. You are far more likely to meet a sugar daddy or mommy at upper class places in your area. Hang out where the wealthy people go.

– Be a good listener. I know you probably think being hot is enough, but it isn't. There's plenty of hotties out there for them to choose from, so once you think you have found a sugar daddy, you need to really listen to him (or her). Often times they just want someone to talk with. Understand that companionship doesn't always have to mean sex. It can mean conversation or just hanging out.

– Make time for your sugar daddie / momma. Clearly, if he or she is doing something for you, they want to spend quality time with you. If you don't spend time with him you will certainly be cutoff. And absolutely be sure to focus only on your sugar daddy (or momma) when you go out to places. If you don't give him the attention he needs then you will be replaced with someone who will.

– Set your boundaries. Only do what you are okay with doing. You may be asked to do more than you bargained for so you need to know your limits. Most sugar daddy's and/or mama's will be looking for you to engage in a sexual relationship at some point. Not all of them, but most will, so be prepared. You don't have to do anything you don't want to do.

And that is pretty much sugar daddy dating in a nutshell. Of course, each one will be different, so use everything here as a general guideline rather than an absolute fact. Now you know where to find a sugar daddy, how to get them, and what might be expected of you when you meet one. This information also applies to sugar momma's and sugar baby's, although you may need to adjust it accordingly depending on the situation. The rest is up to you. Have fun!

CHAPTER 68
MERCH BY AMAZON

It is an on-demand t-shirt printing service. It allows sellers to create and list t-shirt designs on Amazon for free. There are no upfront costs and you get paid on a per shirt basis. You upload your design, choose colours and set a price—Amazon will take care of the rest.

Many experienced sellers are predicting Merch by Amazon will become huge and now is the time to get involved if you haven't already.

How can l join?

Here's the landing page where you can apply.

You fill out a short form then wait to be approved. This can take somewhere between three weeks and three months so if you're interested, it's best to get your application in soon. Once you're approved, Amazon will ask for some basic information, then you can get started.

The Merch dashboard is where you can upload designs, promote your t-shirt and analyse sales. To begin with, you're limited to 25 designs, but once you sell 25 shirts, you'll be upgraded to Tier 2 where you can have up to 100 designs.

The more designs you have, the more opportunity there is to make money. The tiered system helps reward those who create quality designs and prevents spammers from flooding the program with loads of designs.

Creating your first t-shirt design

You can use any graphic design software that you are comfortable with. Photoshop is the most popular but there are alternatives out there such as Pixlr and GIMP.

You create a high-quality image in the space provided. Your design shouldn't be stretched or pixelated and it's worth checking the Merch by Amazon best practices for further tips on designs.

Another option if you don't want to design something yourself is to buy ready-made designs from companies like MerchReadyDesigns. You can download these and upload them to your Merch account straight away.

Print on Demand process

The Merch on Amazon process can be simplified into five easy steps.

- Upload your design as per Amazon's design specifications.
- Set a price.
- Amazon will create a product listing for you.
- People see the listing and buy your shirt.
- Amazon will print it, pack it and ship it for you.

Amazon Merch Tips

- Research is the key to success. Use the free MerchResearch tool to search your phrase with the Amazon Merch category.
- Avoid copyright infringement. Check relevant websites if you're unsure. If you use a copywritten term/image/quote then you risk having your entire account being shut down without warning.
- Use bullet points and well-written descriptions in your listings. This resulted in a 40% increase in sales for FBA seller Jason Wilkey.
- Find a niche market and come up with new ideas.
- Partner up with a local business.
- Buy Dividend paying whole life insurance policy

- Use Google Trends to see what keywords are trending on the web. Plus, keep an eye on any major events happening.
- Promote your t-shirt designs by creating Facebook and Twitter posts in the portal promotions section within Merch by Amazon.
- Analyse your sales.
- Look into the Teespring T2 program.

CHAPTER 69
BUY DIVIDEND PAYING WHOLE LIFE INSURANCE POLICY

Whole life insurance is a type of permanent or "cash value" life insurance that provides benefits for the "whole" of your life (versus term insurance that only lasts for a specific period of time).

Some companies offer dividend paying whole life insurance policies which means the policies pay dividends. These policies are also known as participating whole life insurance, because the policy owners participate in the profits generated by the company.

Dividends are not guaranteed, however some companies have paid them every single year for over 160 years, including during the Great Depression. You can use your dividends in a variety of ways – you can take them in cash, leave them to accumulate interest, or use them to purchase "paid-up additional insurance," which will increase your policy's face amount or death benefit.

Whole life policies have a guaranteed, pre-set annual cash value increase. The guaranteed increases are based on a "worst-case" financial results scenario projected by the insurance company. In a participating policy, at the end of the year, the company does an accounting of the death claims paid, their earnings, and the expense of running the company and the premiums it collected. If they did better than their worst-case projection, they pay the policy owners a dividend.

A level premium guaranteed never to increase, thus giving you some protection from inflation
A guaranteed death benefit for your beneficiaries
Tax-deferred cash value accumulation
The ability to borrow against your cash value, allowing you to become your own source of financing and bypass banks, credit card and finance companies
The ability to have a guaranteed, predictable income in retirement, without the risk or volatility of stocks, real estate and other investments

CHAPTER 70
COMPARISON SITE

You could make big savings on insurance by using price comparison websites, so it's worth putting in a bit of time to get the best out of them. Remember they're just showing you prices, not choosing the best product – you don't have to pick the top result.

- The golden rules for using comparison sites
- How to use comparison sites
- The golden rules for using comparison sites
- Always check more than one site

Different insurance companies appear on different comparison sites.

No one website can get you quotes from every single insurance company, and some big insurers, such as Direct Line, don't appear on comparison sites at all.

Know how they make their money

Comparison websites do not sell products themselves, they show you details and prices from insurers and make their money in a number of ways:

They get paid from advertising which appears on their site.

From 'click-throughs' where the site earns commission when a customer clicks through to the insurer's website and buys a product.

Some sites earn money from sponsored listings, where companies pay to have their products appear at the top of the search results.

Cheapest isn't always best

Be wise to the fact that comparison sites will try to hook you in by showing you lots of low prices.

Remember that the cheapest insurance policies might not be such great value.

They might have a high excess or not the right cover for what you want.

If you do select a product from a price comparison website you'll normally click through to an insurance provider's website to complete the purchase.

At this point certain insurance providers will look to sell you additional products (add-ons).

Before you purchase additional products you should consider whether you need them and the price (as there will be alternatives).

First isn't always best either...

Comparison sites do not give 'regulated advice'.

That means they provide you with product information but not whether a policy has the type and level of cover suitable for your needs.

So, don't assume the first result is the best.

They're not usually suitable for complex insurance

Many of the insurance policies featured on comparison sites are 'standard products' and won't necessarily take your personal circumstances and needs into account.

Because they don't give advice, you might have questions about unusual home, property or belongings to insure that comparison websites can't answer.

For more complex insurance such as income protection, critical illness or private medical insurance it's also a good idea to discuss the different types of insurance available so you can be sure you choose a policy best suited to your needs.

If this is the case, you can speak directly to the insurance company or an independent financial adviser or broker who will be able to advise you.

How to use comparison sites

Step 1 – Work out what policy and cover you need

Use comparison sites to get quotes, not to judge the quality of a policy.

Once you know the kind of insurance policy and level of cover you're looking for, you'll be able to use comparison sites to help you get a good deal.

Step 2 – Pay attention to which answers are pre-filled

Insurance is complex and relies on many details that are specific to you, but comparison sites often make assumptions so they can make the process simpler for you.

They sometimes use pre-filled answers to give you a standard set of results.

The policies they suggest might not be suitable if you have any non-standard requirements.

For example, if your house has a thatched roof or you're over or under a certain age.

So check all the questions have been answered correctly.

You must make sure the details are right or you might not be covered if you need to make a claim.

Step 3 – Use more than one comparison site

Comparison websites cover different providers and products – remember not all providers appear on comparison sites.

The Money Saving Expert website has done some research on which sites to use and in what order:

How to compare home insurance, by
MoneySavingExpert.com
How to compare car insurance, by
MoneySavingExpert.com
How to compare pet insurance, by
MoneySavingExpert.com

Step 4 – Don't get spammed

It's up to you to opt out of email and other marketing by making sure you tick or un-tick the relevant boxes.

If you don't you could get both marketing emails and phone calls, so read everything carefully.

Step 5 – Always check before you buy

When you're transferred from the comparison site to the insurer's site it is essential that you check all the information is correct.

If you don't do this and incorrect information has been given to the insurer you might end up paying for invalid insurance.

Finally, always read the documentation before you buy a policy.

If the documents aren't available on the comparison site, click through to the insurance company's own website to find and read the documents.

If you can't find them, don't buy the policy. You need to make sure it'll actually cover you if you need to claim.

CHAPTER 71
GUIDE WEBSITES

Whether you're considering building a brand new website or want to redo your current website, you're faced with some basic, but important, decisions.

In this guide, we are going to help you with these decisions by showing your choices and explaining how specific options will fit your unique needs. We'll cover everything from understanding what type of website you need and choosing a domain name, to the finishing touches that will help you launch your website successfully, no matter what your goals are.

Also, we'll show you how to use specific tools or systems to create your site. As an example, we'll explain how you can make a website step-by-step with one of the most popular content management system (CMS) WordPress.org.

The essential steps to launch a website:

- Understand what type of site you need
- Pick a domain name and hosting provider

- Install and setup WordPress CMS
- Design your site and make it look great
- Write and prepare your content
- Test before and after launch

We hope that you are excited at the prospect of having your website. Now, let's look at what are the steps you need to take to get it right.

Understand what type of site you need

There are different types of websites. The type, or combination types, you choose, will depend on what you want to achieve with your site and the functionality you'll need to accomplish this.

Following are the main types of websites:

- Blog or website with a blog. A blog can be an extra feature for any website, or it can be a separate kind of site on its own. Blogs are usually arranged in chronological order, with the most recent entry at the top of the main page and older entries toward the bottom.
- Business card site. For some small businesses, a simple one-page website with the name, description, contact info and maybe a logo may be all that's needed. You can also include some product information, but the basic concept is a one-page website that represents your company or yourself.

- Portfolio site. A portfolio site is similar to a business card website, except you'll have a section on the web page where you showcase your work and give people options for contacting you. Photography studios commonly use this type of website, so do design firms and other creative endeavors.
- Product brochure site. This kind of website is an extension of your company's sales and marketing efforts. You'll be able to include goods and services your business offers for visitors to browse through. This website may include some pricing guidelines but doesn't enable customers to make purchases online.
- E-commerce site. With an e-commerce site, you'll be able to showcase your products or services and allow visitors to buy them online. At first, the setup process for an eCommerce site may seem daunting, but there are many simplified methods and tools on the internet today that will enable you to sell online.

Select the right tool to build a website

Man with tools
With so many options available today, it can be difficult to choose the best instruments for the job. Choosing the best platform upon which you build your site will be one of the most important decisions you make. This choice is critical because you'll be tied to that platform for some time and it's never easy

(or possible) to move your website from one platform to another.

For most websites, the first goal when choosing a domain name is to get the .com top-level domain whenever possible.

Web hosting provider

After choosing a domain name, selecting reliable hosting services will be one of the most important decisions you make. To a large degree, the functionality and performance of your website will depend on your hosting provider. The host makes sure your site is available to potential readers 24/7, and it's where your files are stored online.

The wrong web host can cause many problems with your website. Just imagine choosing a mobile company that has no reception. Your web host is a major piece of the puzzle to maintaining a successful internet site. Therefore, it's crucial that you choose a reliable provider.

We highly recommend Bluehost, which powers over 2 million websites worldwide. And for our visitors only, they offer an exclusive deal that includes a FREE DOMAIN NAME and a 30-day money-back guarantee.

There are two ways to install WordPress: one-click install (recommended) and manual install (advanced)

Bluehost web hosting company is recommended by WordPress.org as one "of the best and brightest of the hosting world".

One-click install

This section provides detailed information to help you signup for the Bluehost web hosting account. We also included screenshots of the pages that you need to go through.

Step One
get the special deal from Bluehost.

Step Two
You should start by selecting your plan. If this is your very first one, you should go with the basic one – at least until you explore your options. The one called basic should be able to cover all your needs once you get your website going, and you should consider the prime version once your popularity skyrockets.

Step Three
Your domain name has an important say when it comes to the future success of your website, so you should take your time to come up with something new. Just type in a desired domain in this "new domain" box and BlueHost will show you whether it's available or not. If not, it will provide you with a list of similar names for you to choose from.

Step Four

After you pick out your domain name, BlueHost will take you to the registration page where it will be required from you to fill in your personal info including the billing data. A couple of minutes is all you need.

Step Five

Pay additional attention to your hosting options. Obviously, the 12-month package has the lowest price, but the other two are great when you want to make a long-term investment. You can feel free to uncheck the rest of the boxes – you can always get them later when you find them necessary.

Step Six

After you enter your payment information, you're ready to set your password which will be used for account verification purposes.

Step Seven

After successfully creating your new password you will be able to login to your account.

Step Eight

When you enter your new account, you will be given the option to choose a WordPress theme which can make your website look better. If you don't like any of the themes provided by Bluehost, simply go to the WordPress.org repository and find one that you like.

Step Nine
Once you've chosen a theme, everything will be ready to create your website. Do this by logging in to your WordPress dashboard.

Step Ten
When you log in, you will be greeted by a "Welcome" message and offered help with creating your site by Bluehost. You can accept the offered help or continue alone, the choice is yours.

Step Eleven
In the upper left corner, you can find the Bluehost button. When you click on it, you will be given many tools that you can use to create your website. Once you are done with the customization and changes, simply click on the "Launch" button to get your site online.

But before your site is up and running, you will be asked to give a title to your website and name it, as well as include a description about it so that your potential visitors might see what it's about.

As simply as that, your new website will now be live and you can start working on it immediately!

CHAPTER 72
INVENTOR

Becoming a full-time inventor takes commitment. Most ideas-even great ones-just aren't brought to market that quickly. Any inventor will tell you that it can sometimes feel as though you're waiting and waiting.

But I think it's worth it. After all these years, I still think of product development as having an element of magic. The joy I feel when an idea I dreamt up is actually brought to life is unparalleled. Thankfully, between the advent of new avenues to market like crowdfunding and the expansion of open innovation, becoming a full-time inventor is easier than it ever has been.

Living the licensing lifestyle has been incredibly rewarding. If you want it to be yours, follow these steps.

1. Don't quit your day job just yet. First, you need to understand that product development happens relatively slowly. The fastest I have ever seen a product brought to market from initial conception is six months. Two years is a more realistic time frame.

So the question becomes, how are going to support yourself during that time?

Chuck Lamprey quit his job in computer science to begin inventing full-time five years ago and has since brought five ideas to market. He cautions others against following his lead though, because he says he underestimated how long it would take him to start earning royalties.

"Ultimately, I was successful, but the runway was much longer than I anticipated," Lamprey explained. "It took me a while to familiarize myself with the industry and to get to know people."

The way Keith Mullin-an inventor who has brought dozens of SKUs to market via licensing-sees it, becoming a full-time inventor requires a willingness to make sacrifices.

"When I had a regular job," he said, "I would invent on nights, weekends, and holidays." That kind of dedication doesn't leave much time for relationships or hobbies.

2. Find a mentor. There are a lot of resources available for inventors and entrepreneurs. You can find an inventors group. You can read books. (I've written a few!) But if you want to progress quickly, the best thing you can do is learn from someone who has

been there. Having someone to run your questions by and help keep you focused is invaluable.

3. Consider joining a startup (particularly if you're young). I learned more about business during the two years I worked at Worlds of Wonder in the mid '80s than I have doing anything else. Because we were always short-staffed, I got to take part in projects I never would have been able to otherwise. It was like I was getting paid to learn.

4. Stick to one or two industries in particular. For the most part, the full-time inventors I know focus on depth rather breadth, which makes a lot of sense. Honing in on a few industries allows you to develop expertise and familiarity. The more you know about an industry, the more easily you will be able to identify opportunities for innovation. And if you keep submitting ideas to the same companies, they will begin to know you and respect you as a professional.

For example, all of the ideas Lamprey has licensed are for the pet industry. As a result, he's developed a rapport with several companies. He thinks potential licensees look at submissions from inventors whose names they recognize more seriously.

"If a company doesn't like my idea, I ask, 'Can you think of another company that might?'" Lamprey said. "More often than not, the company provides me with a few names and even contact information." Befriending other inventors who share his same interests has also been beneficial to him.

One way or another, successful inventors capitalize on the power of their relationships-and relationships take time.

5. Understand and embrace that licensing is a numbers game. Before he set out to become a full-timer, Mullin studied the professional inventors he knew and quickly observed that they all had multiple deals going on.

"There seemed to be a magic number, and that was six. Professional inventors seemed to have at least six royalty-producing licenses at any given time," Mullin explained. "Sure, you hear stories about fantastic one-hit wonders-but those are rare." He knew then that he was going to need to have many ideas.

6. Develop thick skin. You're going to be told no. In fact, your ideas are going to be rejected over and over again. I like to joke that I could paper the walls of my home many times over with all of the rejection letters I have received. All of which is to say: You must learn not to take it personally. If you're committed to becoming a professional, it's more important than ever that you find a way to hold on to your creativity and love of wonder in the face of adversity.

7. Be persistent. As Lamprey put it, "Fail early and fail often." If you want to become a professional, you must be able to abandon an idea that isn't working out and quickly head back to the drawing board. Your goal is to test your ideas quickly, not let them linger for years.

"You can't spend too much time or money on one idea," he said. "If no one is interested, you need to move on. And that can be really hard, because our ideas become our babies. You don't want to throw away your baby. But you have to be brutally honest with yourself."

Mullin agreed that the challenge is having the staying power to break through the walls of resistance in doing something new.

I also want to add that you must do these things yourself. Be wary of any middleman who promises you success.

Do you have what it takes?

CHAPTER 73
PLAY VIDEO GAMES AND STREAM IT

Video game streaming is something many enthusiast and casual players want to partake in, but getting a stream up and running on your preferred gaming platform can be a chore. Streaming gameplay involves sharing the games you play and your reactions in real time with a remote audience. It's like bringing the entire internet into your game room while you're trying to beat that last boss.

Currently, the most popular streaming platform in the world is Twitch, but there's competition in the form of YouTube Gaming on mobile devices and Mixer, a Microsoft-owned streaming service used for Xbox and Windows.

Here's how to stream your gameplay from any device you might be playing on, whether it's a PC, the Xbox One, a PlayStation 4, a Nintendo Switch, or even Android or iOS. The only thing I won't be able to teach you is how to get better at video games and / or be entertaining. That requires practice.

Before we dive into the specific setups for each platform, here are the most basic prerequisites for starting a stream, no matter what you're gaming on: a gaming device, an external microphone or gaming headset, a webcam, a fast internet connection (both upload and download), Twitch / YouTube Gaming / Mixer accounts, and, obviously, at least one game title.

WINDOWS PC

If you're trying to reach a large audience (or be discovered and find the love of your life), your best bet is Twitch. Be prepared: if you want to broadcast your video game sessions to the biggest game streaming service in the world, you're going to have to install a couple apps.

First, you have to sign up for a Twitch account and copy your stream key, a unique code that's used to link and stream to your profile from the free broadcasting apps Twitch recommends. (Be sure not to share it.)

Now, decide whether or not you want a "basic" stream, which consists of a live video capture of whatever you're playing, in-game audio, and your webcam and microphone. In that case, you can download a simple broadcasting app like Open Broadcast Software (OBS). It's a powerful app, despite not having the prettiest user interface. Once installed, you'll be prompted to enter your stream key so that OBS can communicate with your Twitch channel and actually, you know, stream something.

From there, you can select your source if you want OBS to stream from a specific window, your whole desktop, or whenever it detects a full-screen app (a game). Other options like audio levels, stream quality, and the like are available from the sub-menus.

If you want a more "professional Twitch partner" aesthetic, I'd recommend downloading Streamlabs' version of OBS instead. It's also open-source software, but it has a much more user-friendly interface for beginners and overlay templates for donations, branding, Twitch emotes, and even transition animations.

Streamlabs OBS options

The setup wizard is simpler than the bare-bones OBS app, but you'll still have access to relevant information, like desired stream quality, video, and audio sources. Once you've gone through the setup process, you can hit the "stream" button and go live with all of your customizations ready for every broadcast.

It's a great app that requires some experimenting, but the results are worth it. After all, you want to become the next Ninja, don't you?

Streaming with Mixer

Mixer running on Destiny 2

Streaming on a Windows gaming PC with Microsoft's built-in interactive streaming app Mixer, which streams to its website and Android or iOS apps, is a more straightforward process than using Twitch, but your potential audience isn't as large. You can start off by signing up for a Mixer account via its website or the Windows Game Bar, which can help guide you through the process for your first time. You can access the Game Bar by hitting the Windows key + G in-game while waiting on your friends to get in the multiplayer lobby.

From there, click on the Broadcast button that's right next to the red record button, select your capture source (from the game itself or from your desktop) and other details like camera placement, microphone or camera permissions, and video quality (which is a shortcut that takes you to the Windows Settings app).

Once that's all set up from the Game Bar, you can click the "Start broadcast" button within the same window and start streaming. Just make sure you have a powerful enough PC since streaming is an additional workload that can take a toll on your FPS.

XBOX ONE

Due to Microsoft's acquisition and integration of the video game streaming service Mixer, it's included as the default streaming option for both Xbox One and Windows 10 PCs. On the Xbox One, Mixer has a clear advantage over Twitch because it's more tightly integrated into the Xbox OS and supports third-party USB microphones and cameras. Twitch does not.

If you don't yet have a Mixer account, I'd suggest getting on a PC or Mac and signing up via the website instead. It's a far less painful experience than using the Xbox's on-screen keyboard.

Once your account is set up, start streaming with Mixer by starting a game, holding down the Xbox button, moving right to the Broadcast tab, and clicking "Start broadcast." The app wizard will provide options if you want a second player to join you, adjusting broadcast quality, having your mic / camera on or off, and so on. From there, you can hit the "B" button and begin your game session.

To get Twitch working on the Xbox One, there are a few more steps. First, you'll have to stop by the Twitch Store and download the Twitch app. Once that's taken care of, open the app, and you'll be greeted by a unique code that needs to be entered on the desktop via your Twitch admin account.

Now's the time to sign up for Twitch via the website on a PC or Mac, if you haven't already. After that, you can head back the Xbox One to opt to stream with Twitch from the app, instead of Mixer. Keep in mind: you won't be able to use a camera over USB other than a Kinect (which has been discontinued). It's far from ideal, but it's doable.

PLAYSTATION 4

Streaming with Twitch

Perhaps the PlayStation 4 is the easiest way to start streaming because the DualShock controller includes a dedicated "Share" button.

To start streaming for the first time, press the "Share" button on your controller, followed by "Broadcast gameplay," select Twitch (the service offered), and then link your Twitch account information on the website using a PC or Mac. To capture your reactions while playing, you'll need Sony's PlayStation Eye camera. The video settings menu lets you customize the image box that overlays your gameplay.

Once that's done, you'll have to repeat a few of the steps again: press the "Share" button, then "Broadcast gameplay," select your preferred service, title the broadcast, decide if you want comments enabled, in-game commentary (open-mic), set a video quality, and finally select "Start broadcasting." To end the stream, hit the "Share" button again.

Streaming with YouTube

To stream your gameplay to YouTube, hit the "Share" button on your DualShock controller, select YouTube, and enter your login details. Also mirroring the Twitch method, if you want to add a face reaction camera to your YouTube stream, you'll still need to buy a PlayStation Eye camera.

Once you've signed-in, tweak your broadcast settings like quality, stream title, and comments before you hit the "Start Broadcasting" button to kick off the stream.

NINTENDO SWITCH

So you want to stream from your Nintendo Switch right out of the box? Too bad, there's no official support for streaming to third-party services like Twitch and YouTube Gaming. It is possible to set up a stream. But to pull it off, you'll need to buy an external HD capture card, which will have to be connected to a PC, your TV, and your Switch dock.

Furthermore, you can only stream when in docked mode, so take that into account as well.

A capture card I'd recommend is Elgato's HD60 ($179), which you can also use with a PS4 or Xbox One. From there, you'll need to install broadcasting software on your PC that supports the capture card you bought, like OBS or XSplit.

From within either broadcasting app, you'll have to select your source (the capture card with your Switch docked in), add your stream key (if you've decided to go with Twitch), set broadcast details like video quality and a title, and hit the broadcast button to start streaming.

Of the current-generation gaming consoles, Nintendo has made the Switch the hardest to stream and reach an audience with by far.

The YouTube Gaming route

It's surprisingly easy to start streaming mobile games from your Android phone to YouTube. First, download the YouTube Gaming app from the Play Store, select the broadcast button, and select your preferred stream quality (720p HD or 480p). From there, the app will ask you if you want to locally record your gameplay or stream it live to YouTube.

Once you've gone through the initial setup, choose the game you're streaming (or scroll to the bottom and expand the list to just filter apps you have installed). Give your stream a title, description, and copy the share link to send out over your preferred social media.

Now, you can return to the game of your choice, where you'll notice an overlay that includes shortcuts to settings, muting your microphone, turning your front-facing camera on / off, comments, and, of course, the centered stream button.

(An important note: anything you do on-screen will be broadcast to your viewers, including texts, passwords, and any personal information that you'd rather keep private. In this case, I'd recommend using your Android phone's "Do Not Disturb" mode to avoid interrupting your stream and spilling your beans.)

The Twitch route

As with the Nintendo Switch, it's difficult to stream gameplay from an Android phone onto Twitch. First, sign up for a Twitch account from a computer. Next, you'll need to pay the Settings app a visit, go to "About Phone," tap your build number 10 times so you can unlock Developer Options, and from within the dev options list, turn on USB debugging.

Next, while you may not have to spend money on an external HD capture card, you will have to find a decent app for displaying your phone screen in a window on your computer. Vysor is an app that's free to download and try out, but the quality is subpar. Instead, get the $10 annual subscription, which gives you control over bitrate and resolution, then thank me later.

Now that you've got USB debugging enabled, an app to display your phone screen on your PC, and a Twitch account (with stream key), you'll have one more thing to do: download OBS for your desktop. From the OBS app, you can link your Twitch account, webcam, microphone, and a video source (the Vysor desktop app). Finally, you'll be able to hit "broadcast" and stream to Twitch from your Android phone.

The Mixer route

Mixer Create broadcast settings

If you want to stream gameplay to the most interactive of the streaming services, then you can start by downloading the Mixer Creator app from the Play Store. Next, in order to access the app, you'll need to link your Mixer account with a Microsoft account. Start by creating a Mixer account via the website, going into Account Settings, and clicking a grey "Link your Microsoft account" button on the top right. Enter your Microsoft login and you'll be able to access the Mixer Creator app.

Now to actually start streaming, tap the pink broadcast icon at the bottom of the screen. You'll be taken to a preview screen where you can switch between camera streaming or on-screen streaming of what you're playing.

The Mobcrush (YouTube, Twitch, Facebook etc.) route

If you want to stream Fortnite from your iPhone, for example, you'll need to go into Settings and enable Screen Recording (which is available for iOS 11+ devices). Next, download the Mobcrush app from the App Store, which allows you to reroute your screen recording to the app and then to Twitch.

While I dislike that Mocbrush requires you to create an account to use the app, you can sign on with your Google, Twitter, or Facebook accounts. Keep in mind: if you're using your Facebook account to sign in, Mocbrush can automatically link to Facebook's game streaming (if you want to go that route). Whichever sign-in method you use to log into Mocbrush, you'll have to separately link a streaming service, like your Twitch account (with your stream key).

However, we're trying to stream Fortnite on iOS to Twitch, so head to the Control Center and hold down the screen recording icon, which will give you the option to choose a supported app on your phone. Select Mocbrush, enable your iPhone's "Do Not Disturb" mode, set your stream title, and hit the button to broadcast.

To stream your iOS gameplay to YouTube, you can mirror the setup process outlined for Twitch but instead, log-in with you Google account, select YouTube as your preferred streaming service, set a broadcast title, save your changes, and you'll be set.

The Mixer Route

Start by downloading the Mixer Creator app from the App Store. Next, you'll need to link your Mixer account with a Microsoft account in order to access it. Start by creating a Mixer account via the website, then going into your Account Settings, and clicking the grey "Link your Microsoft account" button on the top right. Enter your Microsoft detail and you'll be set.

Now to start your stream, tap the pink broadcast icon at the bottom of the screen. You'll be taken to a preview screen where you can switch between streaming from your cameras or an on-screen broadcast of what you're seeing.

The ReplayKit route

Apple's ReplayKit solution allows you to live stream supported iOS apps and games, but it has stricter requirements. Every app that uses ReplayKit to stream has slightly different steps to get the ball rolling, but they all involve a dedicated share or capture button that you can look for that links to a streaming service.

For example, if you want to use ReplayKit to live stream to YouTube, you need at least 100 subscribers and the latest version of the app. If you'd like to stream to Twitch, you'll still need an app or game that supports it, like Asphalt 8: Airborne.

Also, don't forget to enable "Do Not Disturb" mode. You don't want notification banners to get in the way of kicking off your mobile gaming career.

CHAPTER 74
GET PAID FOR BROWSING THE WEB

Getting paid to surf the web sounds like a dream, right?

Well, surprisingly, there are a quite a few companies that will pay you for doing this sort of work online!

These work-at-home opportunities range from beginner (payouts in gift cards and sweepstake entries) to intermediate, and full-time gigs. Some jobs require only basic web skills like being able to click and answer simple questions. Others require more in-depth experience, research skills, and tech-savviness.

Most of us spend a lot of time on the computer: reading, checking email, and sharing pics on social media; you may as well get paid for your time; right?

Here Are Some Ways You Can Get Paid to Surf the Web:

1. Swagbucks

Swagbucks is a popular site where you can earn points called SB for performing basic tasks like playing games, taking surveys, or watching videos. Your SB can be redeemed for rewards like Amazon, Starbucks, and PayPal gift cards (in $5 increments). In addition to earning money by doing tasks, you can earn by registering Swagbucks as your primary search engine. Every time you search using the Swagbucks search bar you earn more SB. Users report they can earn between $50-100 a month, but some users earn even more.

2. Microsoft Rewards

Microsoft users can register their account to earn points for surfing the web simply by signing in. Users can also earn points for buying Windows and Microsoft products and using their preferred search engine, Bing. Microsoft rewards points can be redeemed for gift cards for movies, apps, games and retail stores. Depending on your level of use, you can earn points for completing 10-50 searches per day. Earn 5,000 points and you can redeem them for a gift card worth about $5. So, while you won't earn a huge income off Microsoft Rewards, you certainly earn a little money for something you'd probably be doing anyway.

3. Nielson Digital Voice

Nielson has been performing market research to analyze the preferences of television viewers for years. Nowadays, with Nielson Digital Voice, you can share your opinions by downloading an app to your phone. Watching videos, playing games, and posting on social media is counted as demographic research, so you can earn points for nearly everything you do online. The points are then redeemed for sweepstakes entries into $10,000 monthly giveaways, plus several chances to win $1,000 every month. You can also be invited to take other surveys for chances to win even more sweepstakes entries and extra prizes.

4. InboxDollars

InboxDollars is also a popular program in which you can engage with other players in friendly competitions to earn cash prizes. You can earn points for using your phone's GPS to check in at partner stores and also earn discounts and coupons. InboxDollars pays you to watch your favorite TV networks and shop online, where you can also earn members-only discounts and free samples. Offers and deals result in earn-outs of 10 cents per completed item up to $6. Higher paying rewards often require an additional purchase. Oh, and did I mention new users get a $5 bonus just for signing up?!

5. Qmee

Qmee runs in conjunction with search engines like Google or Bing. When you search for sites, Qmee shows relevant results in a sidebar on your screen. If you click on those results, you can earn points to be traded in for cash or gift cards. You can receive additional points for more engagement with brands and you can also receive money saving offers. You can take surveys and earn rewards for each survey you complete. Payouts are available through PayPal or you can exchange points for gift cards (and there's no minimum point requirement).

6. Leapforce

If you're internet-savvy and you have a background or familiarity with research, you can get paid an hourly rate to perform searches and tasks to help improve the quality of Internet search engine results. This position offers Independent Home Agents a chance to conduct Internet research and provide evaluations for companies on how well they're meeting the needs of customers and their performance results. To be a Leapforce agent, you must be 18 years of age or older and own a computer with high-speed internet and anti-virus software. Agents must complete a qualification exam before they start. According to Glassdoor, Leapforce Agents earn an average of $13.88 per hour.

11 Ways to Get Paid to Surf the WebSave

7. Appen

Appen is also a web search evaluation company. Agents complete projects to gauge how well search engines and websites are performing. Appen also offers opportunities to become a Social Media Evaluator. Researchers should have a computer that's less than three years old, high-speed internet, and a strong understanding of technology, social media, and search engines. There are an initial screening process and a qualification exam. Appen Agents can expect an average workload of four hours a day, plus there are bilingual work opportunities. According to Glassdoor, Appen pays between $12.90 and $13.72 per hour.

8. UserTesting

User-testers evaluate websites and give their opinions via a recording. Testers' voices and screens are recorded as they complete a given task and evaluate their experience out loud. Each test takes between 10-20 minutes and user-testers earn $10 per video or task. One great thing about UserTesting is that you can set your own hours and complete them on your own timeframe. The number of opportunities varies based on factors like your demographics, skills, and quality rating. The money you earn is transferred through PayPal within one week of completing tests.

9. Ask Wonder

If you're good at Internet research and you enjoy learning about a variety of subjects, Ask Wonder might be a great opportunity for you. Active Researchers can make up to $2,000 per month by answering questions with credible, researched answers and providing references. Questions are proposed on a central dashboard and researchers can pick and choose which ones to answer. Qualified Researchers must demonstrate that they are able to research a topic thoroughly and provide succinct, well-researched answers.

10. Clickworker

Clickworkers create texts and documents; they proofread and make corrections, take surveys or categorize data. The work is research-driven and you set your own schedule. Many of the tasks can be completed from a laptop or mobile phone, and your earning potential can grow based on the size and difficulty of the task. The average worker earns around $9/hour. There's an initial screening process, which includes an evaluation of language and writing skills. Clickworker is based in Germany, but many projects are in English.

11. CrowdFlower

CrowdFlower offers research positions where tasks are geared toward technology, search relevance, and user experience. CrowdFlower offers micro-tasking opportunities with a flexible schedule, so it's perfect for workers who can only complete tasks in small pockets of time. Researchers are given more tasks and higher-level tasks as they successfully complete projects. Pay also varies by task with higher-level research and projects offering more compensation.

Working online and performing Internet research can be great ways to earn money from home, especially if you're looking for work that's fun and offers a flexible schedule. Try some of these great ways to get paid today!

CHAPTER 75
GET MONEY BACK ON PURCHASES
(EARNY)

How does Earny know what I bought?

When you shop online or in certain stores, merchants email you an electronic receipt.

Earny only recognizes the receipts that were sent to you by these specific merchants. He then analyzes the information to understand what you bought and starts searching for a better price.

When you first sign up with Earny, you give him permission to collect these specific receipts from the mailbox you signed up with.

Don't forget to allow Earny to help you out with your Amazon shopping as well. You would be surprised by how many price drops he finds there every day.

How much does it cost?

Earny doesn't take any money until he gets you back money. He keeps 25% of the money he gets you back. In other words, Earny is happy when you are!

How do I know if I got a refund and where does it go?

Earny will send you a notification and / or an email to let you know when a refund has been approved.
Your Earny feed will also update to reflect this refund.

At any point you can go to your Earny feed and see the status of each item.

"Tracking" means that Earny is searching high and low for a better price. Please be patient, stores take time to drop prices - just know that Earny will be there when they do!

"Claiming" means that Earny found a price drop, and has submitted a claim on your behalf to the relevant retailer or credit card issuer. This process can take a few days to a few weeks, depending on the specific retailer or credit card issuer.

Please note, the claim is not always approved. It is the final decision of the retailer or credit card issuer to approve or refuse a claim based on their policy. Earny is doing the hard work for you!

"Refunded" means that Earny successfully got you a refund! That's great news!

Earny makes sure that the money you earned automatically gets refunded back to your original payment method in which you made the purchase.

Please note that some retailers may refund you in the form of store credit, depending on their policy.

Also, some credit card issuers may send you a check in the mail. This can take up to 10 business days to arrive once approved.

"Returned" means that your item has been cancelled or returned.

*When getting a refund through Earny, please remember that the refund is returned to you from the retailer or credit card issuer. Look for a credit on your statement from them, not from Earny.

I don't see the refund Earny told me about on my statement. How come?

This could happen because the card you are looking at for the refund is not the same card you used to purchase the item you received the refund on. Let's say you bought something at Macy's with your Macy's card and received a refund from Macy's through Earny, you should be looking at your Macy's card statement. Retailers and credit card providers take a bit to process a transaction. Please check your statement again in 3-7 business days from the moment you received the notification to make sure your refund is there.

If you did not receive the refund, please contact the Earny team contact@earny.co.

If I get a price adjustment and the price falls more, can I still get more money back?

Retailers will only refund you once for any given item, but Earny will make sure that it is the maximum amount he can get for you.

What retailers does Earny currently cover?

Earny will track items bought from Amazon, Best Buy, Bloomingdale's, Costco, the Gap Group including Gap, Banana Republic, Old Navy, Athleta, and the factory stores. Also, JCrew, Jet, Kohl's, Macy's, Newegg, Nike, Nordstrom, Overstock, Sears, Target, Walmart and Zappos.

CHAPTER 76
ENTER SWEEPSTAKES & CONTESTS

Yesou may already be a winner! Or so the junk-mail and email come-ons tell you. But is it too good to be true? Well, yes and no. The odds of your winning any single sweepstakes are tiny. But "sweepers," those who enter hundreds of giveaways a week, do win: vacations, jewelry, cars and cash. Whether entering pays off depends on how much time and energy you're willing to devote, and it won't be worth it unless you...

1. Do your research.

The more you enter, the better your chances, so start digging up contests by using free listings such as www.online-sweepstakes.com or the "Promotions" app on Facebook. Some sweepers spend as many hours researching sweepstakes as entering them, but sweeps newsletters, which cost about $60 a year and cull giveaways from all over, can save you time.

2. Go mobile.

If you have a smartphone or tablet, enter extra contests while you're on the bus or waiting for your kids at the dentist. You can also try texting sweepstakes, which tend to receive fewer entries than those online, says Patti Osterheld of the newsletter SweepSheet.com. "But be sure to have a generous texting plan—it can get costly if you pay per text," she warns.

3. Enter as many sweepstakes as you can— and enter often.

Enter as often as contest rules allow (which may be daily)! To have a chance at winning, experts advise filling out entry forms for at least 30 minutes, three times a week. Repeat winners, like Osterheld, spend about three hours a week. Go to Roboform.com for a free app, which can fill out forms for you in seconds. Carol McLaughlin, publisher of This 'n' That Sweepstakes Club Newsletter, wins about one of every 200 to 300 sweepstakes she enters.

4. Work the odds.

Spend more time entering multi-prize sweeps rather than those with a single payoff, advises Gwen Beauchamp of the newsletter SweepsU.com. Focus on local and regional contests, which get fewer entries than national ones. Osterheld enters around 10 per month—and wins about 50 precent of the time!

5. Play by the rules.

Pros say 20% of all entries are disqualified for being done incorrectly, so for everything you enter, read the instructions carefully!

6. Know your newsletters.

Some online favorites of pros include: This 'n' That Sweepstakes Club, SweepSheet.com and SweepsU.com.

7. Watch out for scams.

No legitimate sweepstakes will ask for information like a credit card or bank account number. Also, ignore emails with bad grammar or poor spelling, or that promote contests from other countries.

8. Track your winnings.

Even noncash prizes are taxable income. Sponsors will send 1099 forms for winnings over $600. Start a spreadsheet for the rest, and pay up on April 15.

CHAPTER 77
RENT CAR FOR AD SPACE

You can make your car into a rolling billboard and get paid to drive. Instead of maintaining their own fleet of cars, companies now pay drivers to use their personal cars as advertising space. This presents a unique opportunity for you to sell advertising space on your car to make money.

Part 1 Finding Opportunities

1 Meet the key criteria. The most straightforward way to sell advertising space on your car is to sign up with one of the specialist companies that act as go-betweens for businesses and drivers. To do this, you will first need to ensure that you meet the essential criteria required by the company. The conditions may vary somewhat, but in general you should:

- Have a clean driving license.
- Own your own car.
- Have full and active auto insurance.
- Be an active driver who makes frequent journeys.

Note that companies often prefer drivers who are in high-traffic urban areas.

2. Find specialist companies. If you are confident that you meet the eligibility criteria, it's time to look for some companies that can help you get paid for advertising on your car. Start by searching online for car wrap advertising and advertising on your car. There are a number of national companies, which will provide you with more information about what they do on their websites

3.Know what you can earn. Before you sign up, it's sensible to research the going rates for vehicle advertising. The rates you are offered will not necessarily be negotiable, but it's a good idea to have a clear picture of what you can expect before you progress too far with the application.

The rates will depend on your location and the visibility of the ads, but you can expect about $300 to $600 per month.

The amount you get will depend on the size of the wrap.

A truck or trailer can bring in much more money in advertising revenue.

The company that wants to advertise on your car may require you to install a GPS system on your vehicle to make sure they are getting the expected exposure.

4.Sign up online. Once you have found one or more companies, you can simply sign up through their website. You need to provide some personal details, and information about your car and your driving habits. After you have completed the form, you should will be contacted by the company who will tell you whether or not they are interested in advertising on your car.

It is free to sign up for most of these companies, but make sure you understand the terms and conditions.

There are potential scams out there, so pay close attention to the website and be confident before you sign up for anything. Some companies will charge you to become a member of their scheme.

Look at forums and online reviews to check the companies.

Part 2 Getting on the Road

1. Get selected. When you have signed up, it is a matter of waiting until you are selected or made an offer to apply an advertising wrap or decal to your car. Signing up to more than one company may

shorten the amount of time you have to wait before you get an offer.

2. Sign a contract or advertising agreement. Once you are selected, you will be presented with a formal contract. The document should provide the details of the arrangement, including the distance you will drive daily or monthly, and where you will park the car. Make sure you know what kind of ad you will be obligated to put on your car before you sign

Car ads can be anything from a window sticker to a full-car wrap. The rates you earn will vary, but you should ask to see some pictures before you agree.

If you think you will not be comfortable having your entire car covered in a wrap, speak up before it is installed.

3. Take your car in to be wrapped. In most instances the company will install the wrap on your car themselves. You will take your car to a designated space, where the advert will be stuck onto your car. How long this takes will depend on how large the advert is.

If you opt for a small ad, such as an ad that only goes over the back window, you may be required to install this yourself.

If this is the case you will be given full instructions on how to do it

4. Drive as normal. Now the wrap has been applied, your job is just to drive as normal and as per the agreement you have made with the company. You will likely have a GPS installed to monitor your driving to ensure that you are driving the required amount and in the required areas. As long as you were honest in your application, this shouldn't be a problem.

Fulfill your obligations and after a month, or however long your contract is for, return the car and have the advert removed.

If you have an accident, or the advert gets damaged in any way, contact the company immediately so they can replace it if necessary.

CHAPTER 78
BUY AN EXISTING ONLINE BUSINESS

As an online entrepreneur, you can start from scratch and build an online business from the ground up. Figure out your niche. Set up a website. Build an email list and market to it. Write blog posts and other content. Create products or promote affiliate products — or use the drop shipping model.

But it does take time before your new online business will actually start making money and become profitable.

The alternative is to buy an existing already established online business for sale.

What to Look for When Buying an Online Business

To be clear, you're not just buying a website. You're buying a complete business with products and customers, proven marketing methods to generate leads and make sales, a social media presence, ongoing ad campaigns, an email list, even employees and/or virtual assistants.

This is a turnkey opportunity that you take over. After you buy it you can let it run as it was before or attempt to increase profits by making changes — perhaps you recognize something the current owner is not doing that could boost sales. Once you buy, it's your business.

The online business should have a track record of sales and profits you can see before you buy the business — always check out the financials. Don't rely solely on what the seller tells you. One thing to keep in mind is that you shouldn't buy an online business for sale solely because it is a big moneymaker. That's important, of course. But you should have an interest in the niche too.

A great thing is that you don't have to figure out the business for yourself once you buy — you might have been worried about that. Often, the seller will include training for you to make sure you know how everything runs.

Buying an online business is kind of like buying an offline business; such as a popular pet store in a community, complete with shelves full of products, relationships with vendors, a lease on the space, and more. Setting up your own pet store would mean finding a storefront to lease and negotiating the rent, researching the best location, renovating the interior as needed, putting up signage, advertising in local publications, sourcing products... You get the idea.

By buying a business, whether it's an online business for sale or a bricks and mortar store, you'll shortcut around many of the time-consuming and sometimes expensive tasks required to build a thriving venture.

Of course, you will have to pay to buy the site. So you have to measure if paying that price is worth not having to build a complete e-commerce business yourself. Also keep in mind that really successful sites will be quite pricey, with prices in the tens to hundreds of thousands of dollars. But you can find full-fledged online businesses for a few hundred or a few thousand dollars too.

A good rule of thumb is multiply the annual profits of the business by 2 or 3 times to get a fair for sales price. Factors like assets, a good domain name, a recognizable brand, a large amount of quality website traffic, a good social media presence, and a large email list of responsive names might also influence the purchase price.

Here are some other things to keep in mind that should influence your decision. You want to make sure the business you want to buy:

Is growing

Has multiple streams of income and doesn't really on just one product

Gets traffic from a variety of sources

Has revenues that are consistent from month to month

Has systems in place for marketing

Where to Find an Online Business for Sale

Great news — there are plenty of e-commerce sites for sale out there. And there are plenty of places to buy them too. Here are four great options. Something to always have top of mind no matter where you buy the business is to do your due diligence. Just because a site is listed for sale on a reputable platform doesn't mean it's completely legit. The seller may have inflated his numbers as far as traffic or sales. Just because something is on the listing doesn't mean it's true. Do your research.

Online marketplaces feature list of online businesses for sale, usually organized by market niche with statistics like revenue and profit, web traffic, email subscribers included. You can quickly scan dozens if not hundreds of sites for sale. If you see one or several you like, first check it out online, then just send a message to the owner through the marketplace's messaging system.

When you correspond with the owner ask any question you like about their business model, their marketing methods, where they get their products...

if they're wanting to sell, they'll do their best to answer your questions.

For example, the massively popular e-commerce platform Shopify has a marketplace where you might find the ideal online business for sale for you. And the cool thing that Shopify gives its own valuation for how much they believe a web business is worth and a look at its revenues in easy to read chart form.

Sometimes you'll encounter brokers running the sale on behalf of the owner. As you correspond with the seller, you can also start bargaining. Send them a lower price offer — oftentimes sellers are flexible, especially if a website has been on sale for a while.

Here are some online marketplaces to check out:

https://flippa.com
https://exchange.shopify.com
https://www.bizbuysell.com/internet-companies-for-sale/
https://www.websitebroker.com
https://www.freemarket.com/sites/
How to Buy an Online Business at an Auction Site
You can get a bargain on an online business by going on an auction site. Like a regular online marketplace, you'll find long lists of ecommerce sites for sale. But instead of paying the list price or contacting the seller and negotiating, you bid using the auction process.

Just like any auction site for consumer goods or collectibles, you enter in what you'd be willing to pay for the online business. Other potential buyers might put in a higher bid... and you decide whether to increase your bid. Auctions are run for a limited time and whoever is at the top wins — and gets to buy the site.

There is a learning curve with putting in bids in an auction is a skill all on its own. In particular, look for "shill" bidders who are acting on behalf of the website for sale trying to drive up the price.

Ebay offers a platform putting up ecommerce businesses up for auction:
https://www.ebay.com/sch/Websites-Businesses-for-Sale/

You could also check out this auction sites:

https://flippa.com/buy/categories/internet/auctions

Buying an Online Business Through a Broker

Website brokers facilitate the buying and selling of ecommerce businesses. Perhaps the seller doesn't the time or inclination to deal with potential buyers. So he hires a broker to put the site up on the online marketing places or auction sites and handle any inquiries. There is a bit of security here in that because, more often than not, the broker has vetted the site before agreeing to try and sell it. He doesn't want his reputation ruined if his client scams somebody.

At the same time, they'll have lots of questions for you to make sure you are a serious buyer — with the money to buy the site.

Another advantage to using a broker is that they are experienced. They know how to conduct this transaction and the exchange of money. And they can handle any problems that pop up. Brokers only get paid once the sale is final, so it's in their best interest to make sure everything runs smoothly from beginning to end.

One broker website worth checking out is: https://feinternational.com. You can also network with online business owners on forums to get the names of other recommended brokers.

Buying an Online Business Directly From the Website Owner

This last technique is a bit bold. But basically you make a list of e-commerce businesses in niches you are interested in. You might just know them because you are a customer or you've seen their ads online. Or you can even check out Facebook pages and forums related to your niche to see what sites pop up in the comments.

Using available tools like Alexa.com, you'll figure out these sites' website traffic. Sign up for its email lists and follow its Facebook pages, so you can see its marketing in action. A simple Google search might yield all sorts of information — including some hints of how it's doing financially.

Now you contact the website owner, which might be listed on the site itself or yielded through looking them up on Whois.com. Then you contact them and tell them you are interested in buying their website. Be polite and show you are serious. But no need to make an offer at this point. They might get back in touch with you or maybe not.

Next Steps for Buying the Perfect Online Business You

Now you're ready to find your new online business. Why not try all of the methods above to see which one fits you best. Start scanning the sites that are available. See what the asking prices are. Just doing that will teach you a lot that will help you make your own deal.

And remember that before you put in offers and certainly before you buy something, make sure you do your due diligence and run the numbers to make sure the financials, traffic, and other important features of the business are accurate.

Buying an established business can certainly be a great way to buy into a success venture and start making right away... you could even make back the money you invested in the purchase fairly quickly.

CHAPTER 79
SELL INSURANCE

Selling health insurance over the phone sounds easy enough, right? Most insurance agents think so...until they pick up the phone for the first time.

There are unique challenges in trying to sell anything over the phone, but insurance is a distinctly personal product that can impact the consumer's life in profound ways. The right insurance coverage can affect the health and financial well-being of the consumer and their loved ones.

With the gravity of the need to buy insurance weighing on your prospect, your ability to get them to trust you, your expertise, and your empathy over the phone is vital to your success as an insurance broker.

If the idea of accomplishing all of this is intimidating, you're not alone. Trying to make a connection with a stranger over the phone can be difficult. You can't predict what type of distractions you may encounter on your end or your prospect's, and without body language and facial expressions, your words, tone, and volume become your only tools to convey the benefits of your products and services.

Building confidence in your over-the-phone sales skills can make an impact on your long-term success, especially If you are just starting out as an insurance agent or trying to expand your business and increase sales. The benefits of selling health insurance over the phone, including the time and flexibility it affords you and your clients, are worth the effort you make to hone your skills.

Try some of these invaluable tips for selling insurance over the phone:

1. Set up your office thoughtfully – before you make your first call.

Many insurance brokers work from home successfully. Having a home office certainly cuts overhead costs, but there are downsides. If you have a family or pets, you will need to designate a specific room as your office – one that is far from any noise and distractions – and your family will have to honor your work hours.

Have all the tools at your fingertips that you will need to be successful when before you start your call. Aside form basic office supplies, and marketing materials ready to mail, you will need to have an updated computer already equipped with the programs and applications necessary to help your clients research insurance plans and enroll.

Many brokers find that customer relationship management (CRM) software with real-time quoting engines and auto-response technology works extremely well in conjunction with their current online tools, and can be customized to reflect your agency's specific brand and vision.

This might feel funny at first, but consider keeping a mirror near your desk. It can be helpful to watch yourself while you speak on the phone to help you identify potential areas of improvement in speech or facial expressions. It will also remind you to smile, which can naturally change the tone of your speech without realizing it and make you even more likely to engage and connect with a prospective client.

2. Be organized.

If you feel flustered, your clients will sense it in your voice. Keeping an organized office space can help you stay calm, collected, and focused. Keep a fluid calendar on hand to keep your appointments and scheduled calls on time, and make sure online tools are installed with your own needs and preferences in mind.

You should have easy access to any information you will need during a sales call – you don't want a prospect to have to wait while you shuffle papers to find something.

3. Prepare for objections.

Choosing insurance can be stressful – and your client may have valid concerns. Other people just hesitate to make important decisions and may offer excuses as to why they aren't ready to commit. Overcoming objections is just part of selling insurance – be prepared to listen, show compassion, and use your knowledge to help a client get past their reservations.

4. Ask questions.

Don't make assumptions. Instead, ask guided questions that will help you determine your client's needs. Understanding what is important to your client will help you narrow down the types of insurance products and services they would be interested in. Asking questions is also a great way to make a connection with someone. Developing a good rapport with a client is vital to a productive and lasting relationship – one that will hopefully result in continued sales and referrals.

5. Listen.

Listening skills are not as easy to master as you may think. Most of us listen in order to respond, instead of listening to learn. As an insurance agent, your job is to learn what products and services your prospect will value. It can be challenging to sift through a prospect's concerns and hesitations to figure out exactly what they need, but listening effectively can help you close the sale.

6. Evaluate your success – and failure – frequently.

Once you've been making sales calls for a few hours, they can become routine. Take a moment to periodically review your successes and failures. It's better to recognize a weakness in your sales tactics and make adjustments.

Review recorded calls to evaluate them as objectively as you can. Continue to use the sales techniques that work, and make changes when necessary.

7. Be sincere.

Try to avoid sounding like you have a scripted sales pitch prepared when you speak to a client over the phone. Sincerity comes across in your voice, inflection, and tone – and it is invaluable in establishing the trust that is necessary to insurance sales success. The insurance market is flooded with brokers competing for business. Stand out among your competitors by expressing your genuine interest in helping your clients access quality, affordable healthcare coverage.

8. Customize your conversation.

Use your client's name throughout your conversation, and if you've spoken before, review your notes from your last conversation before you pick up the phone. When appropriate, mention what you talked about and follow up on any concerns or questions they had mentioned previously. No one wants to feel as if they are just another sale. Make your clients feel as important as they are. Each client can help you build your reputation and increase sales – let them know how much you value their business by customizing your conversation.

9. Choose your words carefully.

Words matter. Avoid slang, acronyms, and language that could be construed as unprofessional. While it is important to build a friendly rapport with your clients, maintain a level of respectfulness during all your conversations.

Recognize words and key phrases used by your client in order to assure them that you are indeed understanding and responding to their particular concerns.

10. Exude confidence.

There is a fine line between confidence and arrogance, but as an insurance sales agent, you will have to manage your speech and behavior in order to demonstrate your expertise while remaining humble. Allow your genuine desire to serve your client shine through in every conversation, but don't hesitate to explain why they should choose to work with you.

11. Create an opening and closing.

Practice makes perfect – so, create a sales call opening and closing that you are comfortable using.

Some calls will require a variation of it, but if you have a general sense of how you'd like to introduce yourself, practice it until it sounds natural, confident, and sincere. You need a prospect to stay on the phone in order to make the sale, so try your opening with someone you trust to give you honest feedback. Once you are making calls, evaluate the success of certain approaches and determine which ones work best for you and appeal to your clientele.

You want to seamlessly transition to your closing during your conversation. Whether your client is ready to choose a plan and enroll, or needs a follow up meeting, make sure you have an idea of what you want to say in order to move your conversation to the next step in the sales process.

12. Automate follow up.

Once you make a sales call, you need to cultivate your relationship. The timeliness of the follow-up is crucial, but we all know how busy and hectic a day in the life of an insurance agent can be. Follow-up emails to clients can certainly get lost in the shuffle unless you have a system in place that allows you to communicate with your clients in an appropriate time frame while you are still working other leads.

CRM tools that include auto-response technology are game-changers for insurance brokers who want to maximize their time and streamline sales efforts. Insurance software programs like Quotit give insurance agents the ability to customize communications, build their business, and provide the level of customer service that will keep clients and encourage referrals.

Selling health insurance over the phone can be a lucrative and successful way to build your business, but don't let your discomfort or inexperience stop you from tapping into this very profitable market. Practice your sales techniques to sell insurance until you feel ready, and take time to evaluate your progress every so often. With tips for selling health insurance over the phone at your fingertips, you will be able to maximize the potential sales opportunities and expand your business.

CHAPTER 80
RANK AND RENT

The Rank and Rent method simplified is building a website that ranks on the first page of Google and other search engines for keywords that real customers are searching for on a daily basis. Start generating calls and enquiries from the website and then rent the website to a business who is looking for more leads. It really is that simple.

Generally, Rank and Rent websites target cities and a niche eg: Plumber London or Sydney Lawyer but that is not to say you can not pick a keyword and target that traffic.

If you Google Rank & Rent in Google, you will get a variety of websites all offering their techniques and how they build and monetise their websites.

Some notable Rank and Rent tutorials:
Glen Allsop (Gaps.com, Detailed.com, Viperchill.com)

Daryl Rosser (Lionzeal.com)

Chase Reiner (Chasereiner.com)

All three of these SEO legends offer different guides to building websites to rent to business, my guide is a combination of all three techniques.

What are the benefits of Rank and Rent?

The Rank and Rent method has been around for a number of years and even though the technique is quite popular and I feel it is not being utilised 100% which leave the market open to you and me.

The benefits of building Rank & Rent websites is you own the asset which is completely different to client SEO where you are hired to optimise their website and you can be "fired" at any time.

By owning the website, the moment the client (business renting the website) decided to stop paying you, you can go and find a new business to rent your website and supply them with leads.

By working on your own websites, you never have to deal with "bad clients", you only deal with a business once you have ranked your website on Google.

The best way to think of your R&R website is like a house. You own the house and someone pays you to stay there. When they leave, you get someone new to stay in your house. You become a website landlord online!

Rank and Rent mistakes

A very common problem I see with people doing Rank and Rent is targetting keywords/cities that are too competitive.

Everyone wants to go to the big cities and niches where the competition would be paying SEO companies to rank their own websites in the search engines.

When starting out, it is always advised to pick a smaller city with lower competition and when you get better at ranking and renting your websites then you can target the bigger cities.

Remember a plumber in a smaller town still wants more leads!

website for rent
Choosing your City
As stated above, when choosing your city, always start with a smaller city/town with lower competition. By doing this you will be able to rank your website faster and the faster it is ranking the faster it will be for you to start earning a passive income.

When choosing a city, aim for a population between 100k and 300k people.

Remember less population, less competition.

Choosing your Niche

Deciding on your niche can be tricky but when you find the right niche for you, it will pay off massively.

Personally, when choosing a niche I look at two aspects:

Businesses who have a big price tag and want fewer jobs
Businesses who have lower price tags and want many jobs
Big price tag ideas
Lawyers
Dentists
Landscapers
Driveway contractors
Pool Installation
Builders
Plumbers
Electricians
Lower price tag ideas
Hairdressers
Beauty Salons
Printing Shops
Handyman Services
Dog Walkers

When selecting your niche, you have to think of the value they will be receiving per job. If you choose a niche with a low price tag, you will not be able to rent that website for a high price per month.

Do your research on every niche in the city you have chosen until you have found the perfect combination for your rank and rent website {Niche + City}.

Rank and Rent website design
Rank and Rent setup
This is one of the most important parts of having a successful Rank and Rent passive income lifestyle.

The website you build has to look and feel like a real website, it has to give the "customers" a sense of trust. Basically, it needs to look like a real business in order for you to start generating leads (calls and emails).

Choosing a website domain

Whenever you are building a rank and rent website, always choose a TLD for that country. It gives the sense of a local business. What do I mean:

Australia R&R site: .com.au
United Kingdom R&R site: .co.uk
South Africa R&R site: .co.za
There are 3 options when it comes to choosing a domain for your rank & rent website:

EMD: exact match domain
PMD: partially match domain
Branded: branded domains
Personally, I tend to go for a PMD or Branded domain for all my rank and rent websites. The reason, I feel it gives a sense of trust to the end user.

After all, I am trying to build an authentic website that will build trust and get enquires from the internet.

Building your rank and rent website
There are many ways to build a website. Personally, I only use WordPress as it is the CMS that I know and love. Many Rank and Rent tutorials also mention WordPress but do not discount:

Weebly
Wix
Joomla
and many more...
However you build your website, it needs to be easy for you because the moment you don't enjoy it, the project will stop. I can assure you of it. For the rest of this post, I will be using WordPress as the CMS.

The reasons why I prefer WordPress for building websites is because you have so much control of the website. There are elements that you will need to customise to improve your rankings in Google (On-

Site SEO) and WordPress (and added plugins) will give you that control.

Here is a mega On-Site SEO guide by Brian Dean.

The On Page SEO of your website is one of the biggest ranking factors of Google and other search engines. It is very important that you get this right to ensure your new rank and rent website appears for the keywords you desire.

Website Content

Personally, the content on your website and how you design your Rank and Rent website is something that does not get the attention it should as it is so very important.

You are designing a website that should look and feel like a real business. Before you start creating pages and writing content, go and search for your {Niche + City} and look at the websites that are appearing on pages 1 and 2.

Make a note of what pages they have on their website, these are the pages that real websites have and so should your R&R website!

Common pages to have on your Rank and Rent website

I recently launched a plumbing website and these are the pages that I created. It depends on the niche as to what pages you will need. Remember more content is better than less content on your website:

Home
About
Services
– Emergency Plumber
– General Plumbing Services
– Drain Cleaning
– Booster Pump Installations
– Geyser Installations & Repairs
– Leak Detection
Plumbing {City}
Contact

All the pages, except the contact page) has a minimum of 500 words and the home page and Plumbing {City} page have over 1000 words totally over 6000 words. #ContentIsKing

These are the pages that visitors see in the menu of the website and the website is designed with a plumber look. All the images are optimised, pages are optimised, pages are linking to each other.

The website looks, feels and operates just like a real plumber website in the city I have chosen.

website optimisation

Now that you have built your new Rank and Rent website, designed your website and written killer content. It is time to make sure your On-Page SEO is great to ensure your website ranks in Google.

Website Optimisation

I mentioned above a great On-Site SEO guide by Brian Dean. This is one of the best places to start and I am going to share a few more resources for you to read so you can get a better idea of what you need to do to your website before you start.

Moz.com

SEOmark.co.uk

NeilPatel.com

All of the guides above will go through how to optimise your website to get better rankings in Google.

On-Page SEO is a technique and by following the guides provided and also by doing your own research you will find your way of optimising websites.

Here is a very powerful video showing you 9 tactics to use to optimise your website. Watch it, learn it, implement it!

Now your website is ready!!!

It is time to get it ranking in Google. These are the steps I take after building a brand new website and getting it found by the search engines and ranking of your desired keywords.

Submitting your website to Google
There are two elements you need to prepare before you submit your website to Google Webmasters.

Sitemap
Robots.txt
There are a number of XML Sitemap Plugins and even some SEO plugins offer the XML Sitemap feature. Depending on how you have setup your website will determine how you edit and create both elements.

Once you have these two ready, it is time to add your website to Google Webmaster. Here is a great Youtube guide on how to add your website to Google Search Console.

Now your website is added to Google Webmasters, your website will soon be crawled by Google and soon other search engines.

Your website is optimised and submitted to Google and other search engines. It is time to start doing Off Page SEO on your website. Time to get ranked!!!

Off Page SEO
Ranking your Rank and Rent website
Generally, after I personally have submitted a website to Google Webmasters, I leave it for 7 days.

the reason for this is to allow Google to crawl the website.

Remember, you are building a "Real Website" and normally a website would not be built and then 100's of links built to the site. That is unnatural.

To rank a local website in the search engines, these are the elements that you will need to do. Personally, I do not skip any of them and the reason why... When your website reaches #1 on Google for your keywords, your website will remain there! The process works.

To rank your website (Step 1 – 6):

- Google My Business
- Press Release
- Social Profiles & Signals
- Web 2.0 supporting websites (Keyword diversity)
- Website Content
- PBN Links

I am going to break each section down and explain the reasons for doing all of these steps.

Google My Business

Google has their own local directory for business and it is called Google My Business. I am 100% positive that you have come across GMB listings when doing searches online for your {Niche + City}.

GMB Listings on Google

GMB listings are one of the best forms of marketing for local businesses and by having one for your Rank & Rent website will increase calls and website visits.

It is imperative that you create a GMB listing!

The benefits of a GMB listing:

It is 100% free
The 3 pack sits above organic websites in the search results
They build trust in your business by allowing customers to leave reviews
Build local relevancy for searches online.
Click to call off mobiles
Customers can message directly from their phones and more
To verify your GMB listing, a postcard is sent to an address in the city you have chosen.

If you do not live in the city you are building your R&R website. Try and find a friend/family who you can send the postcard too. If that fails, go to Craigslist, Gumtree etc and put an add asking to "get a business verified" and you pay them $20 – $40 for the verification code. It is money well spent.

The postcard can take anywhere from 3 days to 30 days. Depending on which country you are in.

This is a must for any Rank and Rent website campaign.

Press Release

A press release is a great way to launch a website and there are some great agencies who specialise in writing and publishing your press release.

A press release will be distributed to +450 news and media outlets that all link back to your website.

It is always best to outsource your press release. Here are some great agencies to order:

Web20Ranker
SEO Outsource
Your press release will take between 5-10 days to be published and because of the time frame, I suggest doing this as soon as you launch your website and it has been submitted to Google.

Remember, your press release is not meant to be read by the public, it is purely an SEO tool so do not worry if the information written by the agencies above is not completely correct.

Social Signals

Social Signals
There is a great debate about social media and SEO. Some SEO experts believe that social shares can boost a website in Google and others believe that they don't.

My theory is when a company builds a new website, they share it on their social media accounts and from that people will visit their website. This is a traffic signal.

I do believe it benefits a website as proof of the links that you build to your website.

Again, this is a service that you outsource. Here are some great agencies who will generate social signals for your website:

Real Social Signals
Signals Ninja
SEO Butler
Depending on the package you buy, your signals will come between 10 – 60 days. This is something you can run every month as they are priced perfectly.

Web 2.0 Supporting Websites

Web 2.0 Supporting Websites

Link building has changed over the years. You CAN NOT build inbound links to your website using your target keywords only. It is a big No No!

Think about it link this... if a website is talking about a company or a service, they very seldom will they only use the contextual text of the exact match keyword that that company offers. They will use various combinations of keywords:

http://domain.com
Domain.com
Company Name
Click here
More information
Visit website
and the list goes on...
We know that exact match anchor is more powerful but by using your main keywords only, you will be shouting to Google that you are over optimising your website and it will be flagged for a penalty.

Web 2.0 websites are a great way to "Share the Love" of your keyword anchor text.

How I use Web 2.0, I personally build out 10 – 20 each week and each of those Web 2.0 sites will use a generic anchor text back to my money website. I will never use my main keywords.

You can find 100's of vendors who will build Web 2.0 sites for you on:

Legit.com
UpWork.com
When you order a campaign they will ask you for your niche, anchor text and also your website link. It is very simple and easy to order.

ABOUT THE AUTHOR

Sir Patrick is a dynamic Investment banker, Fund Manager, and JUDGE for the International Court of Justice and International Criminal Courts, he is also a published Author.Sir Patrick's journey into content writing has allowed him to become an exceptionally motivated and enthusiastic author and professional communicator. Experienced in both proactive campaign-driven and responsive communications.

He lives and writes from the United Kingdom and is the author of several books in finance and fiction.